CLIMAX AT BUENA VISTA

GREAT BATTLES OF HISTORY

HANSON W. BALDWIN

General Editor

CLIMAX AT BUENA VISTA

THE AMERICAN CAMPAIGNS IN NORTHEASTERN MEXICO 1846–47

DAVID LAVENDER

J. B. LIPPINCOTT COMPANY
Philadelphia & New York

Maps drawn by John Carnes

For that most unwarlike of people,
my mother,
EDITH G. LAVENDER

CONTENTS

MAPS

CLIMAX AT BUENA VISTA

1

FORESHADOWINGS

IN NOVEMBER 1821 Lieutenant Colonel Zachary Taylor moved four companies of the Seventh Infantry Regiment of the United States Army across the Red River of the South into the frontier regions of Louisiana. His assignment was the building of a post to help guard his country's new boundary with Mexico, a nation that had achieved independence only three months before.[1] *

The area he entered had been a trouble spot ever since the arrival of French traders at Natchitoches in the early 1700s, an incursion that had stirred Mexico's Spanish overlords to retort by stringing six missions and their defending presidios across the lower reaches of Texas. The most advanced of those missions, remote Nacogdoches, was only a hundred miles west of French Natchitoches—called "Nakitosh" by Taylor's non-linguistic troopers.

When Napoleon sold Louisiana Territory to the United States in 1803, the two similarly named, picayune-sized outposts of empire took on fresh significance. To whom, exactly, did the ground on which they stood belong? The United States in 1803 and for years thereafter insisted on the Rio Grande as its boundary. Spain replied that the Red was the limit of American territory.[2]

* Superior figures refer to the Notes starting on p. 231.

During the quarrel Spanish and American patrols feinted grimly at each other out of the two posts. Aaron Burr, disgraced former Vice-President of the United States, started down the Mississippi to fish in the murky waters. To prevent an irreparable explosion, General James Wilkinson of the American Army (he may or may not have been involved with Burr) and the Spanish commander at Nacogdoches signed, on November 6, 1806, a truce that established a strip of neutral territory between Arroyo Hondo, roughly Natchitoches, and the Sabine River, fifty miles to the west.[3] (Today the Sabine forms the western boundary of Louisiana.) This neutral ground was, by agreement between the commanders, to endure until diplomats of the rival nations settled on a permanent frontier.

Decision was thirteen years arriving. Meantime, in 1812, an embroilment erupted in the area that was indicative of the future. Several forces were at work. Mexican rebels wanted independence from Spain. American settlers hoped to obtain fertile farm lands in Texas. Adventurers of many stripes schemed to use turmoil as a mask for plunder.

The man who knit the disparate elements briefly together was Bernardo Gutiérrez de Lara, a blacksmith from a village on the Rio Grande known today as Cuidad Guerrero. After bootless appeals in Washington City for help, Gutiérrez appeared in Natchitoches. There, partly by promising land grants to Americans who would join him, he added 450 filibusterers to his motley collection of Mexicans and Indians. Incredibly, this heterogeneous, totally undisciplined force captured first Nacogdoches, then the stone fort of La Bahía (later Goliad) on the lower San Antonio River, and finally San Antonio itself, capital of the province of Texas.

In San Antonio, where the victors wantonly slit the throats of several captured Spanish officers, the rebellion fell apart. Gutiérrez, declaring Texan independent, showed bluntly that

Americans were to be subordinate in the new government. Conspirators thereupon deposed him and put José Álvarez Toledo y Dubois in his place.

Meanwhile—it was now the summer of 1813—a thousand Spanish regulars under General Joaquín de Arredondo were marching north to quell the uprising. Among the minor officers on Arredondo's staff was a lean, handsome, hard-eyed lieutenant, only nineteen years old, named Antonio López de Santa Anna. Young Santa Anna, who eventually would become master of Mexico and Zachary Taylor's great antagonist, had been born on February 21, 1794, in Jalapa, capital of Veracruz province. His father was a prosperous businessman, but commerce held no appeal for the mercurial boy. For a time he attended a military academy at Veracruz City, apparently gaining little from his books but learning well how to gamble, conspire, and wear gaudy uniforms with such dash that just the looks of them lent him authority.

Almost surely this Texas experience made an indelible and unfortunate impression on his alert, unscrupulous mind.[4] The insurgent general, Toledo, divided his bickering rebels into two groups: *norteamericano* filibusterers in one section, Mexicans and Indians in the other. Taking advantage of the split, Arredondo lured the disorganized rabble into a crude ambush near the Medina River. He annihilated a thousand of them, slaughtering many after they had surrendered, and drove the rest in stricken flight back to the neutral ground.

The cruelty continued as the victors marched into San Antonio, across the river from the remains of one of the old missions established originally as a riposte to the French at Natchitoches, a place colloquially called the Alamo. Within sight of the Alamo's stained old adobe walls, which Santa Anna no doubt glanced at without presentiment, the victors shot down or imprisoned in dreadful compounds anyone suspected of having been linked with the rebels—men, women, even chil-

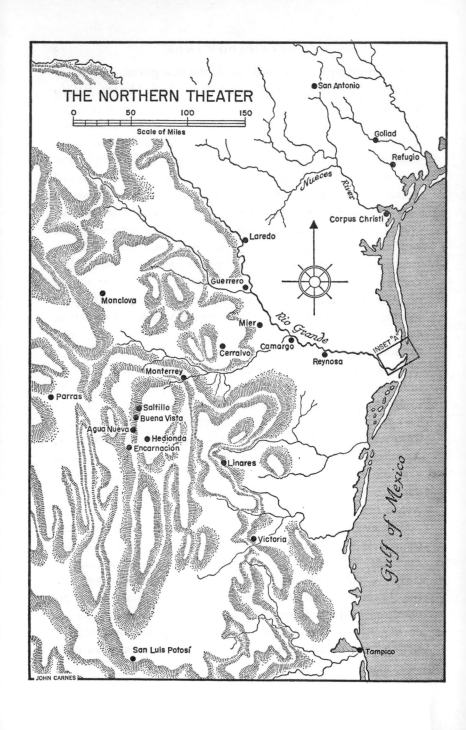

THE NORTHERN THEATER

0   50   100   150
Scale of Miles

San Antonio

Goliad

Refugio

Nueces River

Corpus Christi

Laredo

Guerrero

Monclova

Mier

Rio Grande

Cerralvo

Camargo

Reynosa

INSET "A"

Monterrey

Parras

Saltillo

Buena Vista

Agua Nueva

Hedionda

Encarnación

Linares

Victoria

Gulf of Mexico

San Luis Potosí

Tampico

JOHN CARNES

dren. What Santa Anna actually thought of this vicious crushing of Texas's first effort at independence—a crushing that he
in time would endeavor to duplicate—remains unknown. But
to a youth of his tendencies, the triumph may well have suggested the usefulness of trickery and cruelty in wartime. Probably, too, this first Texan episode was the seed of his contempt
for Americans. The ambushed filibusterers had been totally incompetent on the battlefield, and the survivors had run away
as fast as anyone else. Surely such people were nothing to worry
about—or so he thought for years.

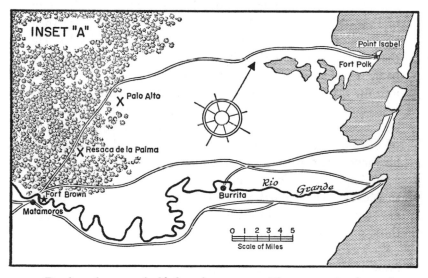

During the next half decade or more Texas remained a sad,
torn land. Finally, in 1819, when the United States purchased
the Floridas from Spain for $5,000,000, the neutral strip was
eliminated. As part of the bargain the American diplomats
abandoned their claims on the Rio Grande and accepted the
Sabine, the western side of the neutral area, as their country's
southwestern boundary. Land-hungry pioneers in the Mississippi Valley protested angrily against this "surrender" of

Texas, but for the time being their outcries produced no results.

Unsettled conditions in Spain prevented ratification of the Florida treaty until February 1821. That same month Mexican insurgents, led this time by Colonel Augustín de Iturbide, again revolted against Spain. One of the opposing Loyalists leaders in Veracruz province, made a captain in 1817, at the age of twenty-three, for his efficient work in hunting down rebels, was Antonio López de Santa Anna. After promoting Santa Anna to lieutenant colonel to ensure his loyalty, the government sent him into the mountains above Jalapa to quell a small group of Iturbide's supporters. When the rebels offered Santa Anna a colonelcy for his allegiance, he promptly changed sides. He then marched against the city of Veracruz and after a long, badly managed siege forced the Spanish defenders to retire into the massive fortress of San Juan de Ulúa, built on a coral reef at the entrance to the harbor. As a reward for this limited success, the opportunistic young rebel was made governor of the Port of Veracruz. At once he began plotting against his immediate superior, a man named J. A. Echevarría.

In August 1821 Spain capitulated and granted independence to Mexico. The United States quickly recognized the proud new nation and reaffirmed the Sabine as the boundary. Under those provisions Mexico stretched northward to embrace not only Texas but also areas that currently make up the states of New Mexico, Arizona, California, Nevada, Utah, and much of Colorado.

The onetime neutral ground was now the clear responsibility of the United States. It was a chaotic place still. Illegal traders smuggled arms and openly dealt in stolen horses that raiding Indians brought in dusty herds out of Texas. In 1819 a semi-out-law, James Long, had raised another army of filibusterers, crossed the Sabine, and declared the Second Republic of Texas. Mexican troops eventually captured Long, but similar invasions would inevitably continue unless a check of some sort was imposed. To that end the War Department sent Zachary Taylor across the Red River onto the erstwhile neutral strip, there to build a fort symbolic of the new order.

Taylor, who was ten years older than Santa Anna, had been born in Virginia on November 27, 1784, the third of nine children. His father, Richard Taylor, had just finished five and a half years' service in the Revolution and as a reward had been granted bonus lands in Kentucky. Crossing the Alleghenies before Zachary was a year old, Taylor settled his family near modern-day Louisville. Those were bloody times, and he met them with cool efficiency; one Kentucky governor reputedly declared that if he had to storm the gates of hell he would want Dick Taylor at the head of his column.[5] Between Indian fights Taylor proceeded to carve a substantial farm out of the woods. Soon he was a leader in his district: justice of the peace, delegate to the convention that framed Kentucky's first state constitution, prosperous slaveowner.

Young Zachary grew up knowing the alternate terrors of Indian raids and the monotony of a frontier farm, toilsome even where slaves performed the heaviest drudgery. His father and mother, both well cultured for the time and place, oversaw much of the education given him and his eight brothers and sisters. Otherwise there was little schooling.

In 1808, during the troubles with England that preceded the War of 1812, President Jefferson called for volunteers to expand the regular Army of the United States. On the strength of his father's Revolutionary War record and through the political influence of an uncle, Zachary, then twenty-three years old, won an appointment as a first lieutenant. His first service was in the South, where his enemies were mosquitoes, boredom, and sickness. In November 1810 he was made a captain. That same year he married Margaret Smith, daughter of a prominent planter.

In 1812 he moved to Fort Harrison on the Wabash River in Indiana. On the night of September 4, while he was ill with fever, Indian allies of the British attacked, setting fires to the stockade and to one of the blockhouses. Wind spread the flames along the building's roof. The fifty-man garrison, and the nine wives and the children who were with them, fell into a panic.

Taylor dragged himself from bed and rallied enough men to tear the roof off the building. Other squads wet down its standing end and threw up a breastwork between the salvaged wall and the unburned part of the stockade. Four hundred or more Indians howled outside, firing a storm of lead balls and arrows, but the men held. Afterward the acting governor of Indiana, applauding Capt. Taylor's promotion to the brevet rank of major, called the defense "the one bright ray amid the gloom of incompetency which has been shown in so many places."[6] In time Taylor's men would find a nickname for their commander, to epitomize his cool improvisations during the hottest actions. "Old Rough and Ready" they would call him, repeating the sobriquet until he was a minor army legend and the sight of him on the battlefield was, of itself, enough to bring inspiration.

The rest of Taylor's campaigns during the war of 1812 were lusterless, though he continued to draw praise from his superiors for his zeal. The columns he accompanied marched through Illinois without encountering the enemy. He spent several months doing recruiting and mustering service. In August 1814 he was sent up the Mississippi to destroy a village of British-allied Sauk and Fox Indians at the mouth of Rock River but was driven back by the unexpected appearance of a handful of Canadians with a small cannon.

After the peace, when the ranks of the Army thinned and Taylor failed to obtain a permanent appointment as major, he resigned. A year later he was offered the rank and accepted, to enter on a series of plodding duties at various isolated frontier forts. At them he developed a carelessness toward military spit and polish that in time became notorious. There too he first showed signs of the jealousies that would trouble his later career. He bristled when others advanced more rapidly than he—and with some reason. His future rival, Winfield Scott, who had entered the Army in 1808, the same year Taylor had, was already a brigadier general.

Zachary was by no means a glamorous figure. He was short-legged and stocky. Shaggy black hair topped his leathery, deeply creased face. He thought and moved with heavy deliberation. Sometimes, when his temper slipped, he would "wool" a trooper—shake the man by the ears—but generally he was lenient in matters of discipline, though insistent on drill. According to Winfield Scott, who met him once during those postwar days in Louisville, he was "a dear lover of money."[7] What else could he be on a salary of $50 a month, meager ration allowances, and a growing family to support, most of them daughters? Yet he stayed bluntly honest always, incurring heavy personal expenses to stand behind sureties he had injudiciously signed.

In 1819 he was finally appointed lieutenant colonel and sent south to complete a link in a military road being pushed through the Choctaw Indian nation from Baton Rouge to Nashville. He found his predecessor's accounts tangled, supplies short, morale low. Reorganizing the project, he won the loyalty of the men and finished ahead of schedule. His next major assignment was the building of the fort near the new border with Mexico.

At Shields Spring, a pretty spot twenty-five miles southwest of Natchitoches on a gently rolling, pine-covered ridge, he had his men clear a broad opening in the trees and begin sawing the logs into boards from which to build a rectangle of barracks, mess halls, storerooms, and a deep-porched headquarters building. In due time the whole would be painted a gleaming white and named Cantonment Jesup in honor of Taylor's friend,

Thomas Sidney Jesup, recently appointed Quartermaster General of the United States Army.

As the builders worked, a trickle of American settlers flowed past them, bound for a new colony in Texas, brain child of a transplanted Yankee named Moses Austin. Born in Connecticut, Austin had started his career in Virginia. In 1798 he had emigrated with his family—his son Stephen was five that year—into what was then Spanish Missouri and had become a Spanish citizen. In 1803 the Louisiana Purchase Americanized him again. Later, ruined by the depression of 1819, he drifted southwest to San Antonio, hoping to find fresh lands he could exploit.

The governor in San Antonio listed favorably. Wracked by ten years of revolution, Texas' population, never extensive, had melted away until scarcely four thousand people remained. Ignorance, poverty, and fear of Indians, who raided unchecked to the very gates of the Alamo, all but paralyzed these unhappy handfuls. If the province was to amount to anything, help had to come from somewhere, yet conditions were so unstable that new setttlers could not be lured northward from the mother country.

Inviting in sinewy Americans from the southern frontier regions of the United States might be an answer. It was dangerous. Spain had long realized that the advancing Americans were highly absorptive. Still, or so the desperate governor of Texas reasoned, if the immigrants adopted the Roman Catholic faith and swore fealty to the King of Spain, perhaps they could then be controlled by the steady hands of Moses Austin, a onetime Spanish citizen. Accordingly the governor authorized the planting of a colony on 200,000 acres of cotton land to be located somewhere along the lower reaches of either the Colorado or the Brazos River.

Shortly thereafter, on June 10, 1821, Moses Austin died. The work of colonization fell upon his son Stephen, who placed his initial settlement on the banks of the Brazos. Just as the first log-cabin homes were taking shape, disturbing news arrived. Agustín de Iturbide had ousted the Spanish viceroy, and Mexico was free.

How would the new government regard this grant? Hoping to guide the decision, Stephen Austin, in March 1822, joined two other travelers and started south on his twelve-hundred-mile horseback ride to Mexico City. Zachary Taylor, meantime, was just starting work on Cantonment Jesup.

The three Mexico-bound travelers rode south through sandy Laredo, crossed the Rio Grande, and jogged on into Monterrey. There one of the riders halted. The other two continued west and then south through bleak, sharp-peaked mountains to Saltillo. Capital of Coahuila province, Saltillo was a cool, white, well-watered town—the name means "Little Falls"—perched five thousand feet above sea level on a slope that dropped northwest to a plain dotted with orchards and grain fields.

Austin's last companion halted in this "high land of many waters," as the Mexicans called it. One tale has it that Stephen Austin thereupon disguised himself as a ragged peon so as not to attract the attention of bandits and rode boldly south into a valley that broke through the mountains ahead of him.

After traveling five miles up this valley he passed a typical Mexican livestock ranch called Buena Vista. Like most *estancias* in northern Mexico, it was a self-contained little community. About one hundred souls had gathered there in a walled settlement for protection against Comanche raids.[8] A little street ran between their handful of adobe buildings—humble *jacales*, or huts, for the workers, a somewhat more pretentious sprawl for the master, storehouses, stables, corrals, and the ever-present chapel. Inside the rectangular barricade more walls separated the household yards and lined the single street, both as a protection against wandering donkeys and as breastworks in case of Indian attacks. The place was very old. It had been founded late in the 1500s as a ranch for raising horses and mules to sell to the silver mines of northern Mexico. Its name, Buena Vista, came from the spectacular view it commanded of the mountains.

Just south of Buena Vista a ravine-wrinkled benchland pushed out from the foot of the valley's steep eastern wall. In skirting the toes of this bench, Austin jogged close to a precipitous gully, perhaps twenty feet deep, which formed the bed of the valley's small, north-flowing stream. Across the stream to the west was a clay lacework of tributary gullies that carried water from a spring called Chupadero. In Austin's time the short, tight throat of road running between the bluffs on the east and the tangle of gullies to the west was also called Chupadero.[9] Later, following the battle that raged nearby, the stretch would be known as La Angostura, or The Narrows, and Mexican historians, with that as a lead, would label the conflict as the Battle of Angostura Pass. Americans, however, have always referred to it as the Battle of Buena Vista.

As completely unaware, inevitably, of these impending events as was Zachary Taylor, busy with his fort building at the far end of the same road, Austin jogged on through the strategic narrows, on across the grim deserts to San Luis Potosí, on to Mexico City. He arrived in the capital April 29, 1822.[10] It had been his intention to stay there no more than a fortnight. As matters developed, however, he was tied up for 355 days, begging audiences with influential people whenever he could, studying Spanish to pass the time, and even pawning his watch to keep himself in funds.

Rebel leader Agustín de Iturbide had other things than Texas land grants to think about. On May 19, 1822, three weeks after Austin's arrival, he had himself crowned Emperor Agustín I. New revolutions straightway began shaking his throne. One of the leaders was that same handsome, opportunistic colonel who had recently helped boost Iturbide to power, Antonio López de Santa Anna.

Ever since his appointment as governor of the Port of Veracruz, Santa Anna had been plotting against his superior, J. A. Echevarría. Forced to choose between them, Iturbide removed Santa Anna from office. Fleeing for safety to his home town of Jalapa, the angry young officer galloped into the plaza and raised a shout for a republic. Cynics say that he did not know what a republic was but used the word only because he had seen how it excited people who were opposed to Iturbide's monarchial pretensions.

Other persons dissatisfied with Iturbide's short but autocratic and wildly extravagant regime raised similar cries throughout the nation. Troops began to march. Iturbide, meanwhile, tried to pretend that nothing serious was happening. On February 18, 1823, while revolutionists ringed his capital, he reaffirmed, as a routine gesture, Stephen Austin's land grant. Wisely Austin did not lean heavily on the royal edict. Within a month Iturbide had fallen. Guadalupe Victoria, a long-time rebel, first against Spain and then against the self-crowned Emperor, became Mexico's first president. In recognition of Santa Anna's services on behalf of the new republic, Victoria proclaimed his young supporter (Santa Anna had recently turned twenty-nine) a full general.

The new Mexican Congress might well have repudiated the Emperor's authorization of Austin's colony, as it did many of Iturbide's other acts. But evidently the legislators felt, as the governor in San Antonio had, that immigration even by Americans was needed to stabilize Texas. On April 14, 1823, the lawmakers nodded their own approval of the settlement and Stephen Austin returned home. There is no indication that Gen. Santa Anna heeded these developments. What was a handful of *norteamericano* agriculturists to him, absorbed as he was in his new glories?

It is not likely that Lt. Col. Taylor, thirty-nine that same year, thought much more than Santa Anna did about the settlers whose wagons had gone creaking past Cantonment Jesup.

By April 1823 he had finished his work on the post and had moved on to other uninspiring chores and other monotonous forts along the edges of the expanding American frontier.

In time he would return to Texas, however. So would Santa Anna, both of them with armies. Stephen Austin's successful ride through Buena Vista and back had, in the inscrutable ways of history, all but guaranteed that.

2

ANTAGONISMS

WHEN MEXICO reorganized herself politically after liberation from Spain, Texas was attached for administrative purposes
not to Tamaulipas province, on the south, but to Coahuila,
which lies west of Texas' southern snout. Capital of this gi-
gantic new department, Coahuila y Texas, was little Saltillo in
the high land of many waters, four hundred or more weary
horseback miles from San Antonio.

Under the terms of Mexico's first liberal Constitution of
1824, the legislature that sat in that distant capital controlled
all foreign immigration into Texas. At first the lawmakers were
fairly generous. During the years 1824–1830 they issued fifteen
huge land grants to various *empresarios,* as the promoters of
colonies were called. In return the *empresarios,* most of them
natives of the United States, agreed to bring 5,400 families into
Texas. Stephen Austin, whose father had set the pattern, held
two of these grants in addition to the one confirmed earlier in
Mexico City.

Not all of the *empresarios* were as successful or as honest as
Austin, and not all of the Americans who emigrated to Texas
came as members of a colony. By and large, however, the program was the main instrument in luring some twenty thousand
people from the United States into Texas. Partly because of
the protection these newcomers offered, emigration out of Mex-

ico proper also increased, though on a much slower scale. By 1830 there were about thirty thousand persons in the once-stagnant province.

Although the settlers from the United States went through the requisite motions of adopting Mexican citizenship and the Roman Catholic faith, the conversions were superficial. Most of them stayed Protestant American liberals at heart. Highly individualistic, aggressive, and impatient, they scorned the Mexicans as an ignorant, indolent, supine people, most of them pure Indians or else mongrelized by heavy admixtures of Indian blood. Because the majority of the onetime Americans hailed from the border areas of Kentucky, Tennessee, and Arkansas or from the backwoods communities of the deep South, they were either slaveholders or were sympathetic toward slavery. They were outraged, accordingly, when first the legislature of Coahuila y Texas and later the central government in Mexico City took steps, 1827–29, to outlaw the institution throughout the nation, save for certain placatory exceptions in Texas itself —exceptions that did not satisfy the Texans. These conflicts over slavery intensified the immigrants' bitter resentment at being allowed only one (a little later two) representative in the governing body that ruled them from distant Saltillo.

The Mexicans returned the antipathies in full measure. To them the Americans were crude, benighted, and barbaric, ruled by materialistic greed. In support of these opinions they pointed to the actions of the United States government itself. Having had second thoughts about the relinquishment of Texas, President John Quincy Adams instructed his minister to Mexico, Joel Poinsett, to offer $1,000,000 for the province. The Mexicans declined. When Andrew Jackson followed Adams as President he raised the offer to $5,000,000 and instructed emissary Anthony Butler to further the deal as best he could. Butler's efforts to bribe the acquiescence of certain Mexican officials were so blatant that eventually he had to be recalled.

Like most new nations, Mexico was very touchy. Furthermore, Santa Anna had just given his countrymen still another
reason for holding their heads high. Spain, hoping to reconquer
the nation, foolishly chose the yellow-fever season of 1829 as
the time to land a small army on a long sandspit near sultry
Tampico. When Santa Anna brought the invaders to bay beside the Pánuco River, they were so emaciated with disease
that they surrendered with scarcely a fight. The Mexicans
exulted. Bells pealed throughout the land, monuments were ordered built to the hero, and Santa Anna was given the official
title "Victor of Tampico." Partly as a result of this enthusiasm,
he felt strong enough to lead still another revolt and seize the
presidency of Mexico for himself. He was intensely ambitious.
According to legend, he once openly said that even if he were
to become God he still would not be satisfied.[1]

At first the Americans in Texas applauded his success, hoping that he would repeal certain restrictive laws, including a
prohibition against immigration from the United States, that
had been passed not long before. Instead, the new President
proved more oppressive than any of his predecessors. He finally
capped his growing autocracy by abolishing the federal Constitution of 1824, disbanding both the national Congress and
the provincial legislatures, and establishing himself as dictator.
From that point on, tensions between federalism and centralism
became a principal storm breeder in Mexican politics and led
both Texas and the United States to continued mistakes in
military strategy. Move after move was planned in the hope
that the northern provinces, strongly federal in their tendencies, would help the campaigns by rising in rebellion against the
central government. They never did, hating invasion from the
outside even more than autocracy inside.

Discontent in Texas soon erupted into open conflict with
the government forces stationed there. To punish the insurgents, Santa Anna himself marched north to San Antonio with

heavy reinforcements. Late in February 1836 he surrounded the walled grounds of the old mission of the Alamo, where William Travis was encamped with a garrison of 187 men, including Davy Crockett and redoubtable Jim Bowie, inventor of the heavy-bladed dueling knife that bore his name. A bit later, on March 2, a convention of delegates meeting 160 miles from San Antonio at the village of Washington declared Texas to be independent and appointed Sam Houston commander in chief of their ill-equipped army.

Houston lacked time enough to reach the beleaguered garrison at the Alamo. On March 6, after several days of bombardment, Santa Anna threw wave after wave of men against the adobe walls. The deadly rifle fire of the defenders mowed down 1,600 men, according to the Mexican officer in charge of burial details. Santa Anna himself announced losses of 70 killed and 300 wounded.[2] Whatever the cost, it was a Mexican victory. Every defender inside the Alamo perished, and San Antonio, the principal city of Texas, was again in the government's hands.

Triumphs for the attackers continued to mount. They all but wiped out two small, badly led parties of Texan guerrillas that had started south to raid Matamoros, near the mouth of the Rio Grande. Near Goliad, another 330 or so Texas volunteers surrendered to General José Urrea under his promise of clemency. Santa Anna countermanded the pledge and ordered the prisoners executed in cold blood.[3]

Fearful of a general pogrom, the American settlers in Texas began a frantic flight toward the Louisiana border. Sam Houston's little army of fewer than eight hundred men drifted eastward with them. Santa Anna closed in with 1,360 men and trapped the fleeing Texan soldiers against the curls of water where the San Jacinto River flowed among groves of magnolias and rhododendrons on its way to Galveston Bay. Overconfident and careless, the Mexican force on the afternoon of April

21, 1836, settled comfortably down to rest for the coming triumph. Houston caught them completely by surprise and in
eighteen minutes, at the battle of San Jacinto, annihilated the
enemy—630 men killed, 730 captured, 200 of them wounded.
Among the prisoners was Antonio López de Santa Anna.

Most of the Texans wanted to hang the Mexican general
forthwith. Aware of their hatred, Santa Anna proved very
cooperative about signing two treaties with his captors. One,
published immediately, called for an end to hostilities and Santa
Anna's safe return to his homeland. The other, kept secret until
he could start furthering its designs in Mexico City, pledged
Santa Anna to help secure independence for Texas.[4]

Neither treaty achieved anything. The government in Mexico City disavowed Santa Anna's suspension of hostilities and
declared that a state of war still existed with Texas. Santa Anna,
safely home in his own country, repudiated his secret pledges
on the ground that they had been won by duress. He then
dramatically resigned his presidency but planned to return to
power as soon as popular odium aroused by his defeats had
been forgotten.

The Texas electorate, meanwhile, voted overwhelmingly in
favor of entering the United States. To their angry surprise
the offer was declined by the American government. Mere
sympathy for the Texans in their struggle for freedom—it had
been warm and lively in most sections of the country—was not
strong enough to dim the dangers of actual annexation. Political
strategists feared that the introduction of new congressmen
from so vast a territory would upset party balances. Abolition-
ists feared the spread of slavery. Business interests, pinched
by the acute depression of 1837, pointed to an 1832 treaty of
amity between Mexico and the United States and warned
against bringing on a war that the New England states might
not support. Sobered by these considerations, Congress did
nothing more of an official nature than extend its recognition

to the new nation, a step that was duplicated in the ensuing years by only four more governments, France, England, the Netherlands, and Belgium.

Forced back on her own resources, Texas found independence a very rocky road indeed. Indians hammered at the outlying settlements; the little army was dissatisfied; the treasury was empty. But at least Mexico made no effort to carry out her threats of reconquest. She was almost as prostrate as Texas. Paralyzing infighting between centralists and federalists had followed Santa Anna's retirement. The treasury, like Texas', was bankrupt, and during this period of wretchedness a series of disputes came to a head with nations to whose citizens Mexico owed money.

Most serious of these wrangles was the one with France. Finally that country dispatched four frigates, nine brigs, two corvettes, and their supply vessels across the Atlantic to blockade Veracruz and thus bring Mexico to terms. The Mexicans scorned the gesture. Veracruz was guarded by the huge, quadrangular stone fortress of San Juan de Ulúa, built on a coral reef one-half mile outside the city's docks. Difficult to approach because of the shoals surrounding the reef, San Juan de Ulúa mounted 207 pieces of artillery. With those as their shield and buckler, the Mexicans peremptorily refused the written demands of the French admiral.

An artillery duel began at 2:30 P.M. on November 27, 1838. The Mexican powder was so faulty that very few of their projectiles came near the mark. The guns of the French ships were more accurate. At 4:00 P.M. a magazine on one of the fort's bastions exploded. Except for this the attack did little damage to the heavy stone walls. Casualties, however, were heavy: 64 dead and 147 wounded. When the early darkness of winter ended visibility, the firing ceased.

Deciding that the emergency offered a chance to regain popularity, Santa Anna hurried from his nearby country es-

tate to Veracruz and offered his services to the general in command of the city. He was ordered to inspect the damage to the
fortress. Just as he arrived, the garrison sent word to the French
that they were ready to surrender.

The outraged government placed the surrendering generals
under court-martial and turned the defense of Veracruz over
to Santa Anna. The French tried to capture him on December
5 by landing a force of marines under cover of a predawn fog.
Warned in time, Santa Anna slipped away, half-clad, through
the darkness. The marines, however, seized another general.
Feeling they had made their point, they spiked the cannons
guarding the port and began to withdraw. As they were board-
ing their small craft, Santa Anna fell on them with such forces
as he had been able to rally. He succeeded in killing a handful
of the invaders but was soon driven back and in the confused
fighting was himself seriously wounded in one leg.[5]

The injured limb had to be amputated just below the knee.
From his hospital bed, Santa Anna uttered what purported to
be a dying testament: Let his countrymen forgive his political
mistakes and grant him the only title he desired to bequeath to
his children, that of "a good Mexican." The effect on his mercurial people was exhilarating. The goat of San Jacinto became
the hero of Veracruz. When President Bustamante marched off
to quell still another revolt, Santa Anna, who had never been
in danger of dying from the amputation, was placed in charge
of home affairs, an honor that under the constitution should
have gone to the president of the council. The only step remaining for him to take with his new peg leg was the resump-
tion of supreme authority.

Continuing revolts provided the occasion. Yucatán broke
away from the Mexican union in the south. Insurgents in the
north, joined by unauthorized filibusterers from Texas, loudly
announced the Republic of the Rio Grande. Though the northern rebels were soon defeated, the episode left observers in

the United States more convinced than ever that, in the event of a serious clash between the two countries, the North Americans could count on active support from disaffected federalists south of the Rio Grande.

By 1841 the strife-battered Mexican government was prostrate. Aided by General Mariano Paredes, who manipulated the army, Santa Anna was reinstated on October 6 as the only possible savior of the tottering country. One of his first acts was to disinter his amputated leg, which he had preserved with remarkable foresight on his Veracruz estate, Magna de Clavo. Declaring the defunct limb to be a martyr to its homeland, he placed it in a stone urn, brought it to Mexico City, and called for a state funeral. Squadrons of cavalry, a battalion of artillery, two regiments of infantry, and several bands provided the escort. While Santa Anna listened complacently, orators delivered eulogies, guns fired, and the leg was hoisted to its resting place atop a flag-draped, gilt-painted column in one of the city's central plazas.[6] Behind all this lurked more than mere vanity; Santa Anna knew how to play on the emotions of the Mexican crowds, though not how to hold them.

Texas, meanwhile, was producing a ridiculous gesture of her own. Because the constitution forbade successive terms by the same man, Sam Houston had been succeeded as president by Mirabeau Bonaparte Lamar. Distraught by bankruptcy and hoping to give his countrymen something fresh to think about, Lamar in 1840 had sent an emissary, William Dryden, to New Mexico, there to investigate the possibilities of Texas merchants cutting in on the Santa Fe trade. If conditions seemed propitious (the federalist delusion again), Texas might even annex the neighboring province.

Dryden reported favorably. All the American traders in Santa Fe, he said, two-thirds of the Mexicans, and the bulk of the Pueblo Indians would welcome union with Texas. Lamar accordingly printed half a million dollars of paper money to

finance what purported to be a commercial expedition of fifty
or so traders owning twenty-four wagons, the whole escorted
by 270 volunteer soldiers equipped with a small brass cannon.
Off they marched to pluck the New Mexican plum.

Nothing went as planned. The group became lost and hungry. Indians nipped at stragglers. A prairie fire destroyed some
of the wagons; other vehicles broke down and were abandoned.
No help came from the supposed friends in Santa Fe and Taos.
Thirst clouding their wits, the command split into two sections.
General Manuel Armijo, the gaudy governor of New Mexico,
captured the ragged fragments without firing a shot, shackled
the men together, and placed them under a brutal officer, Captain Domasio Salazar, for the long march to prison in Mexico.[7]

By the time word of the disaster trickled back to San Antonio, early in 1842, Sam Houston had replaced Lamar as president of the Republic of Texas. Though Houston tried to calm
the revengeful congressmen, they passed over his veto a bill
annexing to their republic all of northern Mexico, including
California. Sole effect of this sweeping bombast was to prod
Santa Anna into resuming the war against Texas, which for
six years had lain quiescent.

The Mexican general could not give the northerners his
full attention, however. Continuing troubles in Yucatán absorbed most of the new taxes and army recruits he mustered,
and insofar as Texas was concerned he had to content himself
with unleashing a series of raids against Goliad, Refugio, and
San Antonio. In September 1842 a follow-up attack was made
on San Antonio by an army of 1,200 men under General Adrian
Woll. Although Woll fought off a hastily raised force of Texas
militia, he was satisfied merely to plunder the town, seize fifty-
three prisoners, and withdraw without inflicting any permanent damage.

Now it was Texas' turn to raid. Houston called for volunteers. As he anticipated, several Texas Rangers were among the

men who responded. These Rangers as a whole formed a most anomalous body, born of Texas' stern need for economy. Unpaid, they had no formal organization or discipline. They were not part of the regular army, or of the militia, or of the police. They were simply on call for fighting off Indians or raiding Mexicans. Their campaigns were improvised on the spot by their own leaders. Because of the extraordinary personalities of those early Ranger captains, this apparently impossible setup actually worked.

One commander was taciturn Ben McCulloch, native of Tennessee. When he was nineteen, McCulloch had planned to emigrate to Texas with an older neighbor, Davy Crockett; but Crockett, brooding over his failure to be re-elected to Congress, had gone on before Ben and his brother Henry could make ready. Fortunately for them, they did not quite catch up and so missed being at the Alamo by days. Partly for the sake of revenge, Ben McCulloch joined Houston's retreating army and at San Jacinto helped work one of the Texans' two small cannons. After that he ranched near Gonzales. He never married. He had a broad, unreadable face, a straight nose, high forehead, and glass-clear, light blue eyes.

Another Ranger leader was black-haired, dark-eyed John Coffee Hays, also a Tennessean and a boyhood friend of the McCulloch brothers. He followed them to Texas a year or so after San Jacinto. A man of legendary boldness and dash, he became the Rangers' first captain.

And finally there was Samuel H. Walker. His looks were deceptive. He was short and slender, with mild blue eyes and sandy hair. He reached Texas early in 1842, long after the other Ranger leaders had earned their reputations, yet by the end of the year, when Houston authorized the strike against Mexico in retaliation for Woll's raid on San Antonio, Sam Walker, despite his gentle eyes and slight frame, was already recognized as the sort of man the Rangers would be glad to have along.

A physical and mental capacity to keep hanging on past ordinary limits was one asset that made the Rangers formidable. Another was the new weapon that many of them carried, a revolving pistol that could be fired five or six times without reloading. The matter was vital in the new environment of Texas. The famous Kentucky long rifle, which the original settlers had brought to the Southwest, had been designed for hunting and fighting on foot in forest areas, where a man had time to reload and cover to protect him while he did it.

Conditions were different in Texas: open prairies and mounted enemies, Indians and Mexicans, who were among the best horsemen in the world. Here a rifleman was at a disadvantage. Once he had fired his weapon and the brace of single-shot dueling pistols he generally carried, he was helpless until he could measure and pour more powder, ram the ball down the rifle barrel, prime the firing mechanism, and then adjust the cap or flint. All this was difficult on the back of a skittish horse and even under optimum conditions required close to a full minute. During that same sixty seconds a mounted Mexican could do considerable damage with his lance or lasso, and a Comanche could discharge, while riding at headlong gallop, up to twenty arrows. Some effective counter had to be devised.

The solution came from a teen-age sailor who had never seen the plains, Samuel Colt of Boston. During a monotonous sea trip around the Cape of Good Hope in the early 1830s, young Colt whittled a model revolving pistol out of a block of wood. Later he released his patents to a New Jersey company that in 1838 or so began turning out a few multiple-shot .34-caliber hand guns. Some of these weapons soon reached Texas. The Rangers seized on them and used them with stunning effect against the Comanches. But the gun still was not quite right. For horsemen it needed greater facility in loading, a trigger guard, and enough weight so that the empty pistol could be used as a club in hand-to-hand combat. The Rangers talked endlessly about these problems, none more so than Sam Walker, a firearms tinkerer by nature. But at the time nothing could be done. The Texas government had no money for ordering experimental gun models, especially for so irregular a force as the Rangers. Walker's chance to bring about adaptations would have to wait for war.[8]

The Rangers were hard to discipline. A dragoon who saw some of them lounging around San Antonio four years later described them with what was at the time an almost standard mixture of awe and disapproval.

A more reckless, devil-may-care set, it would be impossible to find this side of the Infernal Regions. Some wore buckskin shirts black with grease and blood, some wore red shirts, their trousers thrust into high boots; all were armed with Revolvers and huge Bowie knives. Take them altogether, with their uncouth costumes, bearded faces, lean and brawny forms, fierce wild eyes, and swaggering manners, they were fit representatives of the outlaws which made up the population of the Lone Star State.[9]

Equally obstreperous were the rest of the 750 volunteers who, late in 1842, started out under General Andrew Somervell to avenge Woll's attack on San Antonio. After plundering Laredo on the south bank of the Rio Grande—to their disgust Somervell made them return the booty—they moved downstream, bickering and quarreling. Two hundred resigned and mached home. The rest brushed aside a few Mexican cavalrymen and captured Guerrero, but when Somervell heard that heavy Mexican forces were in the vicinity he decided to abandon the expedition. Although disgusted with the decision, John Coffee Hays and Ben McCulloch joined the section that returned obediently to San Antonio. Three hundred others, including Rangers Samuel Walker, Ewing Cameron, and Big Foot Wallace, refused. Electing William Fisher as their colonel, they continued downstream another fifty miles or so and then turned inland toward the little stone town of Mier. A considerable force of Mexicans was camped there under command of General Pedro de Ampudia.

At dusk on Christmas Day the Texans attacked recklessly across a waist-deep creek in a cold rain. As they battered ahead by breaking holes through the walls of the adjoining houses, sixteen of them died and thirty or more were wounded. Falling into a panic that was intensified by the pain of a wounded thumb, Fisher suddenly surrendered to the Mexicans.

Swollen with triumph, Gen. Ampudia marched the Mier captives (ever afterward the adventure would be known as the Texian expedition to Mier) under unspeakable conditions downstream to Matamoros. There he exhibited them in triumph like wild animals and then herded them onto the same road Austin had followed—Monterrey, Saltillo, Buena Vista, and into the desert. At a hacienda a hundred miles or so south of Buena Vista, Rangers Walker and Cameron led a surprise attack on the guards. Five Texans were killed and several hurt. Later, during a grueling, futile flight back through the desolate mountains, five more died and three disappeared. Recaptured, the survivors were presented with a small earthen jug containing 176 beans, seventeen of them black. Each prisoner drew a bean. Those who ended with the black ones were lined against a wall and shot. Although Cameron drew a white bean, he too was executed at the request of an influential Mexican officer whose enmity he had excited during the abortive 1840 attempt to establish the Republic of the Rio Grande.

Some of the Mier prisoners who lived were put to work on the streets of Mexico City. Big Foot Wallace, a huge, droll bear of a man, was harnessed to a cart and forced to haul dirt. He amused himself by shying every now and then like a nervous horse, whinnying and running away, scattering pedestrians and bringing forth a clamorous pursuit by his guards. Others of the captives were taken down the road toward Veracruz and incarcerated in the massive, moated fortress of Perote, where several of the men whom Woll had seized at San Antonio were already languishing. Sixteen of the Texans escaped from Perote in classic fashion by burrowing under the walls. Eight eventually reached home, including Daniel Drake Henrie, a onetime midshipman in the United States Navy who had learned fluent Spanish while lounging around the sleepy ports of California.[10] Henrie's later life was to prove equally charmed.

The rest of the San Antonio and Mier prisoners were not freed until Santa Anna, mourning the death of his wife, granted a general amnesty in September 1844. Turned loose almost in destitution, the Texans went home with a terrible bitterness in their hearts. There they found, to their grim joy, that relations between their country, the United States of America, and Mexico were near a breaking point.

3

THE DRIFT TO WAR

T HANKS TO A GENEROUS PROGRAM of land bounties to immigrants, Texas in the ten years of her independence (1836–1846) experienced a fourfold increase in population, from perhaps 35,000 to 142,000. No other governmental program succeeded, however. Expenditures continued to outstrip income, the Indians remained a problem, and virulent political jealousies crippled such remedies as the Texas Congress tried to devise. South of the Rio Grande, meanwhile, the fiery leaders of fifty times that many Mexicans were still vowing to reconquer the rebellious province.

Maneuvering adroitly to shore up his wobbly country, President Sam Houston ceased importuning the United States for annexation and turned instead to Great Britain and France. They responded amiably. Both wanted a strong, independent Texas to serve as a check on the headlong growth of the United States. England envisioned, furthermore, a competitive supply of cotton for her textile mills and markets for her manufactured goods free of U.S. tariff restrictions. Her humanitarians dreamed of a Texas so fully under English influence that they could end slavery in the southwestern republic and thus come one step nearer their ideal of world-wide freedom.

Peace was a first essential. In pursuit of it English and French

39

diplomats arranged an armistice between Texas and Mexico. Reaction in the United States was instantaneous. Slaveholders took alarm; government officials cried out that this was an opening breach in the Monroe Doctrine; jingoists fanned again at the anti-British emotions that had smoldered on the frontier ever since the War of 1812.

Jarring the United States in this fashion may have been Houston's whole intent. In any event, diplomats from the United States quickly met with ministers from Texas and drew up a treaty outlining the terms under which Texas could enter the Union as a full-fledged state. A special emissary, Gilbert L. Thompson, rushed from Washington to Mexico City, hoping to buy Mexico's acquiescence with hard cash. Santa Anna refused and reiterated his determination to reconquer the Texans. In spite of the Mexican protests, however, the treaty of annexation was presented to the United States Senate for ratification on April 22, 1844. There it touched off a long and acrimonious debate.

Fearing that Mexico might launch her attempt at reconquest during this interim of talking, Houston appealed for protection. The administration declined to commit American troops to foreign soil, as Texas then was, but it did send American warships on maneuvers into the Gulf of Mexico and it did order Zachary Taylor, by brevet a brigadier general, to take 1,150 men to Fort Jesup near the border and there act as a "corps of observation."

Twenty-two years had passed since Lt. Col. Taylor had constructed the post's predecessor, old Cantonment Jesup, rebuilt in 1836 as a fort. During those years Taylor had met his assignments in various parts of the South and along the Mississippi frontier with faithfulness but with no particular flair. His fighting experience had been limited to Indian campaigns. The first had been the so-called Black Hawk War, which had not been a conflict so much as a disorderly pursuit of a hopelessly outnum-

bered band of Sauk and Fox Indians. In the course of it, Col.
Taylor had wheeled ponderously hither and yon with a force
composed mostly of obstreperous, short-term militia volunteers from Illinois, among them a young lawyer named Abra-
ham Lincoln. The lack of discipline shown by most of these
men (Lincoln had been elected captain of his company because
he was so easy-going) dismayed Taylor. "The more I see of the
militia," he wrote his commanding general, Henry Atkinson,
"the less confidence I have in their accomplishing anything of
importance; and therefore tremble not only for the safety of
the frontiers, but for the reputations of those who command
them."[1] A fruitless remark; America had traditionally fought
and for some time would continue to fight her wars with hastily
mustered volunteers. Later, at Buena Vista, after he had been
all but stripped of his regulars, Taylor would again have to
stake his reputation on citizen soldiers, this time to the hilt.

Fortunately he would have help, there at Buena Vista, from
a handful of professionals. One of them was with him during
the Black Hawk skirmishes—young (twenty-four in 1832)
Jefferson Davis, a graduate of the United States Military Academy at West Point. After Black Hawk's surrender, Taylor
entrusted the Indian chief to Davis for delivery to the authorities at Jefferson Barracks near St. Louis. Three years afterward, in 1835, Davis married one of his colonel's daughters,
Sarah Knox Taylor, and resigned his commission to turn to
cotton planting in Mississippi. Sarah died three months after
the wedding. Ten years later, in 1845—the same year that he
began his first term in Congress—Davis remarried. The change
would in no way diminish the warmth of Taylor's greeting the
next summer, 1846, when Davis rejoined his former father-in-
law on the Rio Grande at the head of a regiment of Mississippi
volunteers.

Two more of Taylor's daughters brought him military sons-
in-law. Ann, the eldest, had wed in 1829, when she was seven-

teen, the assistant surgeon at Fort Snelling in Minnesota, Robert C. Wood. Wood became a favorite of the old gentleman's and during the Mexican campaign Taylor passed on his suspicions and frustrations to the doctor in a long series of rough-hewn letters written from the scenes of the fighting.[2] After the war the youngest daughter, Mary Elizabeth, chose William W. S. Bliss, called Perfect Bliss by his classmates at West Point. During the conflict Bliss served ably as adjutant to his future father-in-law and wrote Taylor's reports with a literary flourish that helped create a favorable Taylor image in the mind of the public.

More Indian troubles followed the Black Hawk campaign. During the 1830s the United States undertook to remove the so-called Five Civilized Tribes—Cherokees, Chickasaws, Choctaws, Creeks, and Seminoles—from their homes in the South to new lands in what was designed to be a "permanent" Indian country, roughly today's Oklahoma. The Seminoles resisted. Late in 1835 they withdrew deep into the Florida swamps and launched a long hit-and-run war that was to last until 1841, cost the United States 1,500 men and $20,000,000, and devour the reputations of several American generals.

One unfortunate commander (though he fared better than some) was General Thomas Sidney Jesup, for whom Taylor had named Cantonment Jesup. Most of Jesup's service since the War of 1812 had been spent as Quartermaster General of the Army. In spite of his lack of experience in the field, he was called from his desk to take charge of the floundering attempt to bring the Seminoles to terms. Unable to pin the Indians down in battle, he requested, in October 1837, that Chief Osceola and seventy-five of his principal warriors meet with him under a flag of truce. As soon as the Indians had gathered, Jesup ordered them seized. (Three months later Osceola died in prison.) Investigations followed that exonerated Jesup. During them Taylor "sustained" his general—the word is Jesup's[3]—

but later, in the Mexican War, the long friendship would end in recriminations about the handling of supplies.

After Jesup's recall from Florida, Col. Taylor took his place. The new commander began vigorously, marching 600 men around the north side of Lake Okeechobee and on through prairie swamps of tall saw grass to the Seminole camp near Lake Kissimmee. After a stubborn battle—the Americans lost 26 killed and 112 wounded[4]—the Indians withdrew. On the strength of that the War Department called Kissimmee a victory and rewarded Taylor with the brevet rank of brigadier general. The Seminoles were far from conquered, however. The skirmishes dragged on and on. Taylor in his turn was transferred. Not until still another general, handsome, impetuous William Jenkins Worth, began a ruthless campaign of methodically burning the Indians' villages and destroying their crops did the Seminoles at last give up.

In 1841 Taylor assumed command of the military department charged with patrolling the borders of what was then the American Southwest. Largely for that reason—his happening to be near the scene at the appropriate time—he was placed in charge of the "corps of observation" that took up position at Fort Jesup in 1844 during the long debate over the proposed treaty to annex Texas.

The Senate eventually rejected the proposal, mostly because Secretary of State Calhoun unwisely urged its passage as a way of protecting slavery from the wiles of the English humanitarians. In spite of the setback, however, many American expansionists continued to clamor not only for union with Texas but also for the acquisition of California (a Mexican province) and the occupation of Oregon. Their demands, soon to be verbalized in the magic slogan "Manifest Destiny," became a strident part of the presidential campaign of 1844. In the hairclose November elections, the Whig party was defeated and James K. Polk, a Democrat from Tennessee, became President.

Choosing to interpret the election as a mandate for annexation, the outgoing President, John Tyler, stole some of Polk's thunder by suggesting that Congress annex Texas not by treaty (which required a two-thirds majority in the Senate for passage) but by a joint resolution of both houses. The document was presented to the House of Representatives late in January 1845. By then sentiment in the country as a whole had shifted enough that the bill passed by a vote of 120 to 98. In the Senate the margin was thinner, 27 to 25. On March 1 President Tyler, as one of his last official acts, affixed his signature to the resolution. If the voters of Texas approved a similar declaration, annexation would at last be a political reality.

Mexico reacted as expected. Some months earlier, in the fall of 1843, her minister to Washington, Juan Almonte, had warned that if the United States dared appropriate a foot of Mexican territory, as Mexico considered Texas to be, his country would declare war. Now appropriation was under way. Characterizing the joint resolution as the most unjust act of aggression in the annals of modern history, Almonte demanded his passport and left for home. On March 28, 1845, all diplomatic relations between the countries came to an end.

No slowdown in the march of events resulted. Special couriers raced with word of the joint resolution to the raw new city of Houston. Drum rolls, cannon shots, and giant bonfires celebrated the news. The Texas Congress approved the step and a special convention was summoned to meet on the suggestive date of July 4, to frame a state constitution for submission to the general electorate, at which time they would also declare for or against the terms of annexation drawn up by their Congress. No observer on the scene seriously doubted what the results would be.[5]

Texas was only part of Polk's ambition. He also wanted California, to some extent for its land—increasing numbers of covered-wagon emigrants were beginning to respond to tales about its golden shores—but mostly for the sake of its fine harbors and the stimulus these would give to trade with the Orient. A natural adjunct to California would be the intervening lands that Mexico also owned: today's New Mexico, western Colorado, Utah, Nevada, Arizona. Although in 1845 these areas were not considered to have any particular value in themselves, they were necessary to complete the geographical continuum of the nation. Polk was willing to pay for the territory, along with California, but first Mexico had to be persuaded to sell.

As the spring of 1845 drew to a close, little straws indicative of the new President's interest began to blow along the western winds. In order to test the problems of moving troops across the western wilderness, five companies of Colonel Stephen Watts Kearney's First Dragoons marched, during the early summer of 1845, along the Oregon Trail to South Pass at the edge of the area under dispute with Great Britain. Having rattled the saber, Kearney then went south to the Arkansas River, at that time the boundary of New Mexico, picked up information about Santa Fe, and returned east along the famous Santa Fe Trail.

Shortly thereafter Captain John C. Frémont led a party of sixty tough topographical engineers, mountain men, and Delaware Indian scouts across Mexican soil to examine the passes into California. If trouble developed while he was in that distant province, he would be able to cooperate with naval forces under Commodore John Sloat, who was told to strike at California's harbors the moment he heard war was declared. And finally, another minuscule party of topographical engineers prowled along the Indian trails threading the plains and canyons that today make up the panhandle sections of Oklahoma and Texas. This, too, was Mexican territory, where detachments of the United States Army had no legal right to be.

These movements, coming in conjunction with the tensions

about Texas, could certainly be interpreted by Mexico as provocative gestures. Retorts in kind might very well precipitate open hostilities. That being so, it was high time, surely, for both countries to take stock of their resources and to initiate vigorous measures for remedying their weaknesses. Incredibly, neither nation did. Each was aware of glaring defects in the other's armor but lost in singular delusions about its own situation. Seldom, if ever, have two nations marched to the brink of war with so little hardheaded objectivity guiding their preparations.

Mexico was still distracted by internal turmoil, initiated this time by General Mariano Paredes. Feeling himself ill-rewarded for his aid in boosting Santa Anna back into the president's chair, the disappointed general decided to install still another president. His cat's-paw on this occasion was pliant José Joaquín Herrera. Texas was one of the issues Paredes used. He charged that if Santa Anna had not squandered money and lives on his Yucatán campaigns of 1842, but instead had supported Gen. Woll's attacks on San Antonio, Texas could have been brought safely back into the Mexican fold. As the possibility of Texas' annexation to the United States grew steadily stronger, Paredes' argument swept through the country on a wave of intense emotionalism. Texas—lost by Santa Anna's folly! At the same time Santa Anna himself stirred the swift passions of his people still higher by marrying, a scant five weeks after the death of his wife, a fifteen-year-old girl.

Manifestoes appeared; orators declaimed. Mobs ripped Santa Anna's defunct limb from its shrine in Mexico City and dragged it through the streets. Thundering defiance, Santa Anna marshaled an army of sorts and marched toward the capital to deal with the insurgents. His courage faded with the miles, however, and he paused for "discussions." His discontented troops melted away. Surrendering, he and his adolescent bride were exiled to Havana in May 1845. There, needless to say, the wily opportunist began plotting how best to return to power—even, as we shall see, with the help of the United States, if he could swing that daring feat.

Herrera, backed by strong-man Paredes, moved uneasily into the presidency. It was an unenviable position, and he could do very little to prepare against the American threat. Federalists and centralists were more interested in gaining control of the Congress than in initiating needed reforms, a situation intensified by intriguing Santanistas, who wove in and out of the angry political clashes as seemed best to suit their schemes of the moment. There was no money—a lack, incidentally, that created fresh rancors in the United States. Because of the void in her treasury, Mexico again defaulted on money owed American citizens under the ruling of an international arbitration committee. This repeated failure to meet legitimate obligations (there had been others) intensified American convictions that Mexico was an irresponsible child in the family of nations and needed chastisement for her own good.

This same lack of money meant, at home, that the troops of the Mexican Army were ill-fed, poorly clothed, and seldom paid on time. Their equipment was faulty. Most of their muskets were secondhand discards from England. Powder charges in the cartridges were invariably too heavy and produced unnecessary recoil. To avoid it the infantrymen often shot from the hip, with the result that most bullets went high of the mark.

Regeneration was next to impossible. Corruption was rife and morale low. Officers, who came from the loftier stratas of Mexican society, filled their own pockets through outrageous commissary contracts. Very few of them had any true interest in the welfare of their men. Naturally they commanded little loyalty. The rank and file were ready, at the sound of each new promise, to swing after whatever demagogue momentarily caught their attention.

The country was backward industrially. Her textile factories, for instance, operated a mere 131,280 cotton spindles as compared to nearly 1,500,000 in the United States. She possessed very few industrial plants capable of producing war material, and her threadbare merchant marine was incapable of importing what she needed. Her population, composed mostly of illiterate Indians, numbered about 7,250,000 and was very nearly static. That of the United States was 20,300,000 and was growing vigorously.[6]

In spite of these discouraging statistics, the Mexicans, a fiercely proud people, really believed that in a war with the *norteamericanos* they would win. The dazzling personal glitter of the officers was accepted as a sign of competence. Long years of revolution had hardened the troops, who again and again had proved their ability to cover amazing distances in swift time afoot, on skimpy rations of parched corn and dried beef. The cavalry was redoubtable. Though the horses were small, they were nimble, and the men were magnificent riders.

Strategists believed that Nature would prove to be a powerful ally in turning back any attempt at invasion. Land attacks from the United States would involve long, vulnerable supply lines across waterless deserts. Coastal landings on the humid coast would face the deadly black vomit, as yellow fever was called.

Outside nations would prove sympathetic, especially Great Britain, currently at loggerheads with the United States over the Oregon question. If Mexican armies marched north, surely (so the strategists argued) the oppressed Negroes and Indians would rise to help them. More importantly, the North Americans were divided fatally among themselves over the issues of slavery and the tariff. The Yankees were moneygrubbers. They would not pay taxes to support an unpopular war. In their yielding to pressures for economy, had they not already cut their army to a pathetic skeleton?

Conditions in the United States furnished some justification

for that sort of reasoning. Clashing economic philosophies and
Northern fears that slavery might spread into any territory
wrested from Mexico were indeed divisive elements. A New
England intellectual, Henry Thoreau, did refuse to pay taxes
that might be used in support of the unpopular war and afterward wrote a pamphlet urging the moral correctness of such
"Civil Disobedience." Even among some of the officers of the
army that would have to do the fighting there were strong
doubts about the justice of the threatening conflict. Ulysses S.
Grant, for one instance, always maintained that the war on
Mexico was an unwarranted and unforgivable act of aggression.

The U.S. Army was, as the Mexicans realized, little more
than a framework. Congressional reactions at the close of the
Seminole War had cut its authorized strength from 12,539 men
to 7,833—scarcely a quarter the nominal size of the Mexican
Army. Actual enrollment slumped even lower, touching a bare
5,300 at times in the critical year of 1845.[7] These troops were
scattered among nearly a hundred small posts, most of them on
the frontier. Because of this dispersal, very few commissioned
officers had ever had an opportunity to maneuver a unit larger
than a company.

The morale of the enlisted men, like that of their Mexican
counterparts, was low. Many were foreign immigrants or even
deserters from the British Army in Canada. Some had enlisted
to escape unexpected economic dislocations in their new land;
others had signed on to find refuge from the furious Native
American riots that had wracked the foreign sections of several cities during the mid-1840s. They bettered themselves very
little. Pay ranged from $8 a month for a private to $17 for a
sergeant major. Punishment was by flogging with a cowhide
whip, more painful, veterans said, than the notorious English
cat-o'-nine-tails.[8] Prospects for advancement were almost non-
existent; American policy demanded that officers be drawn
solely from the Military Academy at West Point—and Con-

gress even then was debating the advisability of abolishing the Academy!

Equipment was mediocre. Although a new Model-1841 percussion Lock rifle, called "the most accurate and dependable spherical bullet rifle ever made," was slowly being introduced, lagging appropriations kept most of the troops saddled with old-style flintlocks. Grant later remarked of them, "At a distance of a few hundred yards a man might fire at you all day without your finding it out." Still, the weapons were more accurate than the small arms of the Mexican Army, and the powder was infinitely superior.[9]

There were other strengths behind the apparent weaknesses. The reduction in army numbers had not been accomplished by eliminating any of the eight regiments of infantry, the four of artillery, or the two of dragoons. Rather the cuts had been made by paring the enrollments of infantry and artillery companies down from a hundred men to forty-six each, dragoons down to fifty. Expansion could be achieved rapidly by adding personnel to units already in existence, without the confusion of creating new organizations. A large pool of trained officers existed to be drawn on: West Point had graduated approximately one thousand men. Although half of these had retired from the Army to civilian life, many would respond to a general call for volunteers by joining the different militia groups.

Although the American cavalry, the dragoons, were outnumbered by their Mexican counterparts, they were not without advantages. As an economy measure, they were trained to fight on foot as well as on horseback. More importantly, they were mounted on heavy animals, selected to withstand the shock of head-on cavalry impact—a decided superiority over the Mexicans with their wiry little mustangs.

The real secret weapon was the artillery. Like the dragoons, artillerymen had been turned by economy into infantry and during the war would often be maneuvered as such. But they clung stubbornly to the red stripes down their trouser seams that marked them as a distinctive branch. And they made the most of the few batteries of fieldpieces each regiment was allowed to retain. Certain ardent West Pointers—James Duncan, Braxton Bragg, and, most fervently, Samuel Ringgold—worked out what they called "flying artillery." A battery of this consisted of four to six guns, generally bronze 6-pounders, each pulled, with its caisson, by four to six highly trained horses. Endless drill produced extraordinary mobility in comparison to the more ponderously handled Mexican fieldpieces, and the devotees of the new-style fluid operations, frustrated by the flitting Indians who seldom called for artillery attack, were eager to show what they could achieve against conventional masses of foot soldiers.

Ordinary prudence suggested the wisdom of long-range planning by the War and Navy Departments, in order to bolster such efficiency as the skeletonized forces could produce. Little of consequence was done, however, even after it became obvious that annexation was going to carry—an act that Mexico had flatly warned would be construed as deliberate hostility. The truth is that neither Polk nor his cabinet really believed the threat. In their opinion, the impoverished, revolution-torn Mexicans could not and would not go to war over either Texas or California, both of which had already slipped beyond the mother country's effective control. In the last extremity, Polk thought, Mexico would turn realistic and yield to the gold she so desperately needed. Accordingly, the American President applied only as much pressure as he felt he had to.

One bit of pressure he could not avoid—a support of Texas' boundary claim against Mexico. The Mexicans insisted that the original state of Coahuila y Texas had ended at the Nueces River, some hundred and fifty miles north of the lower Rio Grande, and that therefore, even if Texas were independent (which Mexico refused to concede) Texas' territory also stopped at the Nueces. The Republic of Texas retorted that her southwestern frontier was the Rio Grande and that Santa Anna himself had admitted as much in the treaties he had signed after the battle of San Jacinto (treaties he had repudiated on his return to Mexico).

If Texas entered the American Union, then of necessity the United States had to assume her claim to reach as far as the Rio Grande. Any crossing of that river in force by the Mexicans would have to be regarded as an invasion of American territory. By the same token, the Mexicans would have to regard an advance by the United States Army over the Nueces as deliberate hostility. Whichever country moved first could expect an answering riposte by the other.

The Americans made the first gesture, but it was a very tentative one. Late in the spring of 1845, the Secretary of War, heavy-browed, snuff-taking William L. Marcy, ordered Zachary Taylor to advance from Fort Jesup, within the United States proper, to a position from which he could repel any aggressive action by the Mexicans in the vicinity of the Rio Grande. The Gulf Squadron under Commodore David Conner was ordered to support the movement by cruising near the Mexican coast, prepared in the event of hostilities to seize the port of Tampico and even, if opportunity allowed, the fortress of San Juan de Ulúa outside Veracruz.[10]

All this sounded more belligerent than it turned out to be. The mouth of the Rio Grande was difficult to navigate. Furthermore, a disembarkation there would be dangerously exposed. Taylor therefore temporized and sought a safer staging area for his operations. The site chosen, largely on the advice of the Texans, was the trading post of Corpus Christi. It lay just south of the mouth of the Nueces but not far enough south, perhaps, to call for a retort from Mexico City.

The movement out of Fort Jesup began in July 1845. The dragoons, most of them from the Second Regiment, and the long train of wagons that Taylor might need in the future for hauling supplies, went overland. The infantry and artillery shifted to New Orleans, its streets all but deserted because of an epidemic of yellow fever. There the troops boarded steamships and sailing vessels and started southwest at widely spaced intervals.

The approach to Corpus Christi was through a shallow passage between two flat, sandy islands. No charts existed. Unable to take his transports into the bay beyond, Taylor landed his first contingent of 1,200 men on one of the islands, St. Joseph, and then rounded up enough fishing smacks to ferry the soldiers and their supplies twenty-five miles on to the head of the bay. Slowly the rest of the command followed, not without accident. One steamboat struggling to negotiate the difficult channels blew up, killing seven or eight troopers and injuring seventeen.

During the next few months half of the entire Army of the United States was concentrated at Corpus Christi—a statement more impressive in sonority than in actuality. The force numbered just over thirty-nine hundred men, including a few companies of Louisiana volunteers and a detachment of mounted Texans under Ranger John Coffee Hays. Another hundred and fifty dragoons were scattered through the interior, maintaining communications with Texas officialdom and with the border posts of the United States.[11]

Corpus Christi was a settlement of about one hundred persons, the domain of Henry L. Kinney, or Kenney, an American who carried on a brisk trade with Mexicans for miles around in slaves, cattle, blankets, guns, and smuggled silver. At first the swarm of soldiers who planted their rows of tents around the head of the bay found life pleasant. Sea breezes kept the weather moderate. Unexpected bonanzas of food came from the fantastic oyster beds that had to be raked out of the channels used by the lighters and from the green turtles that were stranded on the shore by each high wind. Officers with a penchant for hunting found ample deer, ducks, and wild turkeys. Rattlesnakes abounded. Lightning bugs, one private wrote, were six times the size of those in New England.[12]

Camp followers poured in to set up grog shops and brothels. Mexican horse traders from Matamoros on the Rio Grande arrived with big remudas of unbroken animals to sell. They also brought word of Mexican troop concentrations on the Rio Grande—and took home information about the doings of the *norteamericanos*. No effort was made to check the traders. Officially the two nations were still at peace, and anyway the American officers needed horses. Young Captain Ulysses S. Grant—they called him Sam in those days—was the talk of the encampment for a day or two after he paid an outrageous $12 for a fierce stallion, blindfolded it long enough for him to mount, and then rode it into submission. Sam was adept, all right. But Jack Hays and his Texans, who helped train the Americans in horsemanship, were better. They could put three silver dollars in a row on the ground and then pick up the coins from their saddles with their horses at full gallop.

As fall sank toward winter, living conditions deteriorated. Very little wood was available for cooking, let alone for warmth. The tents leaked like sieves under the heavy rains and were icy cold in spite of windbreaks of earth and brush that the occupants heaped up around the outsides. Taylor was completely careless about sanitation. Epidemics flared. At times 20 per cent of the personnel were on the sick list. The unsupervised grog shops bred bickering, and the only effort to counter their attractions was the building of an 800-seat theater. Some of its plays were staged by the officers; a few professional productions were imported from New Orleans.

Idleness nibbled at morale. Hearing false reports that Taylor was about to resign, hotheaded Brevet Brigadier General William Worth, conqueror of the Seminoles, fell into a quarrel over succession with his senior in point of service, unbreveted, white-bearded, red-faced, bull-voiced Colonel David Twiggs. The dispute, which Taylor should have resolved, divided the commissioned officers at Corpus Christi into acrimonious factions and eventually reached President Polk himself. The bitterness arising from this tempest and from the jealousies normal to any isolated, uncomfortable, inactive community cloud an attempt to evaluate Taylor's activities that winter. Most of the senior officers were highly critical of him. Lieutenant Colonel Ethan A. Hitchcock sneered at his superior's failure to drill the men and scout the country between the Nueces and the Rio Grande—and at Taylor's unwillingness to follow Ethan Hitchcock's advice. Gen. Worth wrote acidly, "Whether an idea, strategic or of any other description, has had the rudeness to invade the mind or imagination of our chief is a matter of doubt."[13]

Significantly, perhaps, the junior officers left posterity fewer indictments of Taylor. After studying their letters and reminiscences, one historian has concluded that instead of neglecting drill the commander pushed it vigorously, so that "when he took the field, his force, in organization and efficiency, was for its size probably the best ever seen in the United States."[14] This statement is too sweeping; still, Taylor probably did train his troops as adequately as the abominable weather allowed.

Without question the common soldiers liked their commander. There was nothing awesome about him. He stayed near his tent much of the time, but when he did show himself it was without formality. He sauntered about in old shoes (Worth would have worn glossy military boots) and a floppy palmetto hat, or paused on his famous horse, Old Whitey, to sit sideways in the saddle, both legs dangling, while he chewed tobacco and swapped small talk about farming. He disapproved of flogging and was more forbearing than were most of his officers with the foreign-born enlisted men, many of whom spoke little English.

The usual winds of rumor whistled through the camp. The

Mexicans were massing troops at Matamoros—seven thousand men was one common report—and were ready to take the offensive. Other talks, fastening on evidence of new revolutions, denied the likelihood of war. And, indeed, revolutions were in the making—the main reason why Mexico did not react at once to Taylor's advance to Corpus Christi. The Herrera government had proved as impotent as Santa Anna's in meeting domestic crises while at the same time preparing for war. Although the Mexican Congress on September 21 had authorized the treasury to float a defense loan of $15,000,000, results were meager, and the frustrated administration was showing a timorous willingness to negotiate, just as Polk had hoped it would.

Dissatisfied with Herrera's limpness, the president-maker, Gen. Paredes, now considered seizing the government for himself. His plotting kept the three thousand (not seven thousand) men concentrated at Matamoros facing toward Mexico City rather than north across the Rio Grande. Before the year was over, the outlines of the situation had reached Taylor through reports brought from Matamoros by trader Henry Kinney's Mexican spies. Because of this information, Taylor was all but convinced there would be no fighting.[15]

Polk knew even earlier of the dissensions in Mexico City. On August 16, his secret agent, William S. Parrott, wrote that the Herrera government was ready to listen to suggestion. The American President accordingly hurried John Slidell, a Spanish-speaking member of Louisiana's delegation in the House of Representatives, to Mexico with offers to assume that country's debts to United States citizens in exchange for the Rio Grande as the boundary of Texas and then add $20,000,000 or so more —up to $40,000,000, if absolutely necessary—for what is now the United States Southwest, California included.

Although Slidell supposedly traveled in secret, word leaked and outrage shook the volatile Mexicans. Herrera's opponents cried "Traitor!" and added dark whispers of bribery. Taking fright, the government refused to receive Slidell, who on December 17 wrote Polk of Mexico's "bad faith." Immediately thereafter Paredes struck. The script was tried and true: proclamations pasted on the walls, a mutiny of government troops in Mexico City. Herrera resigned, cathedral bells pealed joyously, and the newest savior rode horseback along the bedecked avenues. Slidell meanwhile lingered in Mexico, hoping to see Paredes, but was again rebuffed. In March 1846 he started home.[16]

Events there were already in motion. On receipt of Slidell's first message (that of December 17), Polk's cabinet had decided to apply a little more pressure to the unexpectedly stubborn Mexicans. Orders dated January 13, 1846, were sent to Taylor to advance to the Rio Grande—but not to consider Mexico an enemy unless he was attacked.

In Mexican eyes this advance constituted an invasion of their territory, even though by then Texas had been formally taken into the Union. Polk's political opponents agreed with the Mexicans. Senator Benton of Missouri, chairman of the Senate's Military Affairs Committee, charged the President with deliberately inviting war.[17]

The indictment is too broad. War with Great Britain over Oregon was still an alarming possibility, and the administration was eager to avoid conflicts on two fronts. Polk was simply running a bluff, based on Mexico's known weakness, hoping to force that country to listen to his offers. Even so, he took extraordinary chances. Hoping not to give his opposition any chance to raise cries of warmongering, he made absolutely no preparations to meet hostilities if they should come. No pressure was put on Congress to strengthen the woefully weak Army. No studies of transport or supply needs were made. No information was collected about Mexican troop dispositions or resources. No one had any sound idea of the means of communication available south of the Rio Grande. There were not even any consultations between the civil administration and General Winfield Scott, the ranking general of the United States Army. Polk not only was not trying to pick a fight but, in truth, was singularly unrealistic about the possibilities that one might develop.[18]

4

COLLISION

THE ORDERS to advance to the Rio Grande reached Taylor on February 3, 1846. The instructions were not rigid about time; he could move at his convenience. This was fortunate, for the winter had been unusually wet, and before undertaking the march he had to send out an experimental column of wagons to test the gummy earth and swollen streams. They reported favorably. With no great haste Taylor then made ready to break camp.

Early in March, Inspector General Sylvester Churchill called for a review. Lt. Col. Hitchcock, ever critical, thought it badly handled. Though individual companies may have been well drilled during the winter, there had been little maneuvering of regiments or brigades, and Hitchcock scorned the fumbling of the other colonels. Only Hitchcock's Third Regiment knew what it was doing, he said. But there was no opportunity for further improvement. On Sunday, March 8, the movement began, led off by 378 dragoons and Major Samuel Ringgold's smoothly trained company of horse artillery, the whole under command of Colonel David Twiggs. The rest of the Army, including a dozen artillery companies of the First and Third Artillery functioning as infantry, was divided into three brigades that left camp a day apart, the men marching two abreast. The 1st Brigade, commanded by Brevet General William

Worth, departed on March 9. The Third and Fourth Infantry Regiments made up its bulk; at the rear, riding proudly beside their gleaming 6- and 12-pounders, came the mounted cannoneers of Captain James Duncan's light battery of Second Artillery. Next, on March 10, went the 2nd Brigade, composed of elements of the Fourth and Fifth Infantry, fortified by a scattering of red-legged artillerymen without cannons. Their immediate commander was Lieutenant Colonel James S. McIntosh, a rough but effective disciplinarian. Colonel William Whistler, alcoholic and incompetent (he would later be removed), followed with the 3rd Brigade, its core the Seventh Infantry, to which Sam Grant had recently been attached, and several companies of the Eighth. At the rear of this last brigade trundled another battery of flying artillery, commanded by First Lieutenant Braxton Bragg, a vain and contentious officer, but efficient. Accompanying each brigade were its supply trains, a total of 307 wagons, eighty of them pulled by oxen, the rest by ill-broken horses and mules. Most of the teamsters were inexperienced volunteers from the ranks.

The ambulatory sick, four ponderous siege guns, and Major John Monroe's field battery, which was the last of Taylor's four companies of flying artillery, traveled by sea transport. All told, no more than thirty-one hundred men were involved in this first push toward the Rio Grande. The remaining eight or nine hundred either were too sick to leave the hospital at once or were detailed to serve as a garrison for the suddenly forlorn-looking camp at Corpus Christi.

Springtime and the exhilaration of moving again after winter's immobility buoyed the spirits of the marchers.[1] The green and undulant countryside was dotted with oaks and was fragrant with blue lupine, flowering acacia, and the waxy white flowers that cluster on tall stalks of Spanish bayonet, or yucca. Such unbelievable herds of mustangs roamed along the route that young Sam Grant was sure the entire state of Rhode Island would not hold them.

All this was entrancing to see, but, added Captain William Henry, "to the feet it is a very different matter." The soil turned sandy. In places Mexican guerrillas had burned the grass, and the marchers stirred clouds of ash. Sun and wind burned their cheeks and blistered their lips. Trees disappeared; the brackish water holes grew farther and farther apart.

They averaged ten miles a day. Thirteen days out of Corpus Christi, Worth's advance column came to a tidal stream called Arroyo Colorado. The banks, their rims shrouded by mesquite and prickly pear, were twenty to thirty feet high. The stream itself was a hundred yards wide and four feet deep. There were Mexican soldiers in the brush on the far side—scouts could not discover how many. Their commander sounded a parley and warned Taylor to come no farther.

Taylor answered by moving four companies to the edge of the arroyo. Ringgold's field battery unlimbered. Powder encased in flannel boiled in oil was pushed home and solid shot rammed on top. Fuses were readied. The gunners blew on their slow matches to light the portfires. Commands rang out. The blue-clad troops slid down the banks and splashed into the stream, muskets held over their heads.

All this while Mexican bugles had been clamoring to left and right beyond the stream. Dust eddied as if large numbers of soldiers were hurrying into position, but when the soaked attackers scrambled up over the lip of the south bank, they saw that the Mexicans, amounting to no more than a patrol, had merely been trying to appear formidable. Now they were flying toward Matamoros, thirty miles away.

Taylor waited to help the wagon train across the arroyo and then marched on. Eighteen miles out of Matamoros he swung with the vehicles and a cavalry escort toward his predesignated rendezvous with the sea convoy, Point Isabel.

Save for the Point, a bluff twenty feet high, the coast was dead flat. The shoal water lapping the mainland was bordered, a few hundred yards out, by barren sandspits. Entrance to

Laguna Madre, as these coastal shallows were called, was by way of Brazos de Santiago, a narrow opening between two of the sandspit islands. A fort of sorts, a customhouse, and several huts atop Point Isabel commanded this opening. Although landing men and cargoes at the Point and transporting them eighteen miles southwest to Matamoros seemed roundabout, the Mexicans long since had learned that the way was easier than bucking the bar and twining channels of the lower Rio Grande. Since Point Isabel lay on land claimed by the United States, Taylor had determined to make it his supply port. From his viewpoint the Mexicans had no right to object.

Timing was perfect. Smoke from Commodore Conner's escorting warships was smudging the horizon beyond Brazos de Santiago when Taylor's wagons hove into sight from landward. Pinched between enemy forces, the Mexican commander set fire to the settlement and withdrew with his garrison of 250 men to Matamoros. Seeing the flames, the American dragoons put spurs to their horses and saved part of the establishment. The convoy came up against the wind through Brazos de Santiago—one ship ran aground and another blew a hole in her boiler—and began unloading. Taylor filled his wagons, arranged for the building of earthen redoubts called Fort Polk for protecting the base, and then led his supply train down the Matamoros road to overtake his waiting army.

It was strange country. Here and there meadows of tall saw grass broke the dense mats of chaparral, described by one diarist as "scraggly, scrubby, crooked, infernally illegitimate and sin-begotten bushy trees loaded with millions of thornpins."[2] Even bushy trees looked tall in that montonous region, and, because those on a slight ridge near the meadow where the army waited were the largest in the vicinity, the area was known as Palo Alto.

Reunited, the force moved out of Palo Alto and on past twisting depressions dotted with shallow lakes and rustling palm trees—an ancient river channel, one section of it known as

Resaca de la Palma, Ravine of the Palm. Late in the morning of March 28 they came in sight of the Rio Grande itself, 200 yards wide, dirty brown, and tepid. A scattering of wretched huts, abandoned by their frightened occupants, lay on the north bank. On the south bank of the curving stream sprawled the city of Matamoros, a winding strip of white houses set in an emerald oasis. The flat roofs were packed with people staring across the river at the first foreign army most of them had ever seen.

A salient of land, most of it plowed for crops, protruded like a blunt arrowhead into one of the river's curves. Taylor parked his wagons in the center of the fields and set up camp around the vehicles. It was an exposed spot. Mexican shells could fly across the river from east, south, and west. Mexican cavalry could cross the river above and below the salient and swing around to cut it off from behind. Movement was restricted by a shallow pond that occupied the salient's north base. Only a single road existed for bringing in supplies from Point Isabel, eighteen miles away. Nevertheless, that is where Taylor chose to stay.

Still protesting to the Mexicans that his intentions were peaceful, he ordered his engineers to lay out a hollow fortress large enough to house two thousand men and their tents, and the horses of the dragoons. Six jutting bastions guarded the earthen walls, which were designed by Captain Joseph F. K. Mansfield to be 15 feet wide at the base and 9 feet tall. A dry moat 8 feet deep and 20 feet wide surrounded the whole, which was named Fort Texas. Powder magazines were walled by sand-filled barrels and were roofed with earth.

The Mexicans meanwhile built on their side of the river six gun emplacements that bore on the American fortress from three directions. In calm defiance Taylor drew his four 18-pounder siege guns, far larger than anything the Mexicans had, into the fortress with ox teams and set them up to cover every part of Matamoros. Throughout this time Mexican cavalry drilled assiduously on narrow prairies beyond the river, in full sight of American foragers out for wood and hay.[3]

Supply trains moved along the single road from Matamoros; patrols rode in and out. Otherwise the scene was scarcely martial. The opposing army bands serenaded each other in the evenings. Young infantrymen from the north shouted across the water at scantily clad, olive-colored girls doing their laundry in the river. Peddlers from Matamoros rowed busily over the river to wander among the American tents selling food and souvenirs.

As soon as the Mexicans finished a gun emplacement, it was blessed by a priest in white vestments sprinkling holy water. Protestant watchers on the American bank called the pageant mummery, but it awoke yearnings among certain Irish and German volunteers. The Mexicans knew of this Catholic element in the American Army. They were aware, also, of the antiforeign Know-Nothing riots that had aroused deep resentment among the immigrants to the United States not many years before; and they set about playing on these feelings by scattering pamphlets in the American camp decrying what they called a godless aggression for the sake of more slave territory. Later propaganda barrages offered 320 acres of land to men who deserted to the Mexicans.

Scores fled across the river, a movement whose emotionalism was intensified when American sentries in full view of many watchers shot some of the swimmers to death in the middle of the stream. Those who escaped were known at first among the Mexicans as the *Voluntarios Irlandesas*, the Irish Volunteers, sometimes called the Red Battalion from the ruddy complexions and red hair of many of their number. Among their leaders was John Riley of Company K, Fifth U.S. Infantry, a deserter from the British Army in Canada and an expert artilleryman. (The Mexicans called him Juan Reyley.) He and his fellows

—many of them French and German as well as Irish—in time formed what became the infamous San Patricio Battalion of the Mexican Army. At Buena Vista they would cause Taylor the sorest kind of trouble.[4]

Meanwhile the newest revolutionary president, Mariano Paredes, had consolidated his position tightly enough so that he at last felt able to spare reinforcements for the Rio Grande. Command whirled through a succession of generals chosen largely as a result of their usefulness to the revolution. Francisco Mejía was replaced by Pedro de Ampudia, conqueror of the Texans at Mier in 1842. Ampudia promptly sent Taylor orders to start pulling back toward the Nueces within twenty-four hours. Taylor retorted by ordering Commodore Conner to blockade the mouth of the Rio Grande, the principal port of entry for Mexican supplies following the fall of Point Isabel to the Americans.

While Ampudia was still sputtering about the blockade as an act of war, he was relegated, on April 22, to second in command behind newly arrived General Mariano Arista, a stately, redheaded officer who once had lived for a time in Cincinnati.[5] Arista bore orders from Paredes to start action at once. To legalize the attack, Paredes by prearrangement appeared before the Mexican Congress on April 23 and declared that a state of defensive war existed against the invading troops from the United States. (Formal declaration by the Mexican Congress did not come until June, however.)

Even before this there had been guerrilla activity by Mexican irregulars. They had surprised and slain Taylor's quartermaster, Colonel Trueman Cross, and had killed a lieutenant and one man of an American patrol. To check them Taylor mustered in guerrillas of his own—Samuel H. Walker and seventy-five Texas Rangers—and sent them off into the chaparral.

Apprised by these Rangers of major troop movements beyond the river, Taylor increased his patrols. One group of sixty-three men under Captain Seth Thornton moved sixteen miles up the river. Thornton looked frail and skinny but was wildly reckless, as if in compensation. This day, April 25, he was too reckless. Seeking information and tricked perhaps by his guide, he led his entire force inside a high, tight fence of chaparral surrounding a large rancho. Outside, screened by the brush, was part of sixteen hundred Mexican cavalry commanded by General Anastasio Torrejón, the upriver arm of a developing pincer movement designed by Arista to cut off the American salient. A detachment of these riders—blue uniforms, red stripes on their trouser legs, red pennants fluttering on their lances—slammed the rancho gate shut on the patrol. Thornton tried to fight clear. After sixteen men had been killed and several wounded, the rest surrendered.[6]

The next day, April 26, couriers raced out of Taylor's camp with dispatches for Polk and for the governors of Texas and Louisiana. The message to Polk announced, "Hostilities may now be considered as commenced." Those to the two governors asked for 5,000 three-month volunteers. Until Congress passed new laws, three months was the maximum term allowed. The short span had been designed years before as a means of rallying militia for quick campaigns against hit-and-run Indians, and there had been no changes in anticipation of longer wars.

Work on Fort Texas intensified. Realizing belatedly that he needed more supplies to withstand a possible siege and worried about the situation at Point Isabel, Taylor decided to open the way to the coast, evaluate matters there, and bring back a train of 250 loaded wagons. He prepared to leave on May 3, but Mexican activity hurried the schedule. Enemy patrols killed or captured some of Walker's Rangers, whom they surprised in bivouac without a sentry.[7] A little later Walker himself arrived with word that a major crossing of the river was about to start.

Taylor decided he would have to move fast. He put Major

Jacob Brown in charge of five hundred men, including the sick, to garrison Fort Texas. With two thousand he began, at 2:00 P.M. on May 1, a forced march to the coast. He was luckier than he knew. Arista had planned to be astride the road by then, but a shortage of boats delayed the Mexican crossing, and when the enemy general at last moved up through the chaparral he found that the Americans had gone by.

Rumors of him abounded, nevertheless, and Taylor's rank and file were jittery. One lieutenant tried to console his men by telling them that in battle scarcely a shot in a thousand found its mark.[8] More effective in distracting them was the pace the commanders set through the high grass and over the rough and often muddy ground. Darkness fell; they kept on slogging. The Dipper wheeled around the North Star; still they slogged —or else halted for galling waits while the frantic officers coordinated the hasty drive. A little after midnight they were allowed to drop in their tracks. At dawn they were moving again, fortified only faintly by a cold breakfast without coffee. At noon they reached Point Isabel, where Conner had just landed five hundred marines as reinforcements for Fort Polk.[9]

Working industriously, the soldiers and hired Mexican laborers began transferring clothing, ammunition, food, and guns from ships to wagons. On the morning of May 3 they heard from the direction of Matamoros, twelve air-line miles away, the grumble of artillery. That night Sam Walker and four of his Rangers slipped back past the Mexican patrols to learn what was happening. At dawn Walker left his men hidden in the brush, wriggled alone into the moat surrounding Fort Texas, and whistled for a ladder. He stayed inside the walls most of the day and learned by experience that the Mexican bombardment was not doing very much harm.

The round shells that the enemy lobbed across the river exploded on landing, funneling most of their force upward. The soldiers avoided the blasts by falling flat whenever they heard a warning sputter overhead. As a protection against direct hits, they were building shelters of earth-filled barrels, timber, and sandbags stitched up out of the canvas of their tents. Casualties had been negligible, even among the horses. Meanwhile the American 18-pounders had silenced two of the Mexican cannon. Maj. Brown told Walker he was confident he could hold out, though to conserve ammunition against a possible assault he had all but ceased replying to the Mexican fire.[10]

This news Walker took to Taylor on another daring ride through the Mexican patrols. On May 7, reinforced by 200 undrilled soldiers who had recently landed at the Point, the column started back with its loaded wagons and two more clumsy 18-pound siege guns, a battle burden that aroused criticism among some of his officers, although supplies were the reason for the march. Along the way they heard the deep boom of Fort Texas' 18-pounders and guessed that pressure on the bastion was increasing. Later they would learn that Maj. Brown's leg had been blown off (after he died the post's name was changed to Fort Brown, precursor of today's Brownsville) and that under cover of an intensified shelling the Mexicans were deploying for a possible assault. The 18-pounders were calling for help. But in between them and the relief column was the main part of General Mariano Arista's army. It numbered somewhere between 3,270 and 6,000 men—accounts vary.[11] In any event it was bigger than Taylor's force of 2,200.

That night, May 7, the advancing Americans slept on their arms in the field. At sunrise they marched again, the distant thumping of the 18-pounders urging them to haste. Arista, who had been waiting at a water hole called Las Tanques de Ramireño, moved forward to meet them. A little after noon, at the edge of a mile-wide meadow of tall grass interspersed with ponds, the Mexicans caught their first glimpse of the Americans —dragoons riding in the van of the foot soldiers. Promptly Arista spread his men across the full width of the meadow in two thin lines. He anchored his right against a slight rise covered with knotted trees. The left, where Torrejón's lancers took position, reached beyond the road to mingled swamp and chaparral. Scattered at intervals among the Mexican infantry regiments were twelve small guns, the largest of them two 8-pounders. In the ammunition wagons were 650 cannonballs, solid brass or iron—no shells. Brass bands tootled mightily. Arista, glittering with braid, rode out front to deliver a ringing speech.

At sight of the Mexicans, the American column halted. It was a hot day. Soon the rush of feet through the dust-powdered grass would make the afternoon still more stifling. Taylor ordered a platoon of each company to stack its arms and fill the canteens for its unit. While the work was being done he sat slouched on Old Whitey, chewing tobacco and passing remarks to the men. Tension slacked off. And now the troops began to realize where they were. This was the same Palo Alto prairie on which they had waited for Taylor when he had made his detour by way of Point Isabel during their southwestern march six weeks before. Somehow the familiarity was reassuring.

When deployment began the troops moved eagerly. The wagons stayed at the rear, guarded by Captain Charles May's Second Dragoons. The two big ox-drawn 18-pounders moved up the road a way and unlimbered between the Third Infantry on their right and the Fourth on their left. Ringgold's battery swung in beyond the Third; Duncan's took position to the left of the Fourth, which was moving ahead in conjunction with an artillery battalion serving as infantry. The Fifth and Eighth Infantry Regiments formed the right and left flanks respectively.

Slowly the line advanced. For a time the rattling of the stiff saw grass, shoulder tall in places, was the only sound. Nervous, the Mexican artillery began firing at 700 yards, farther than the

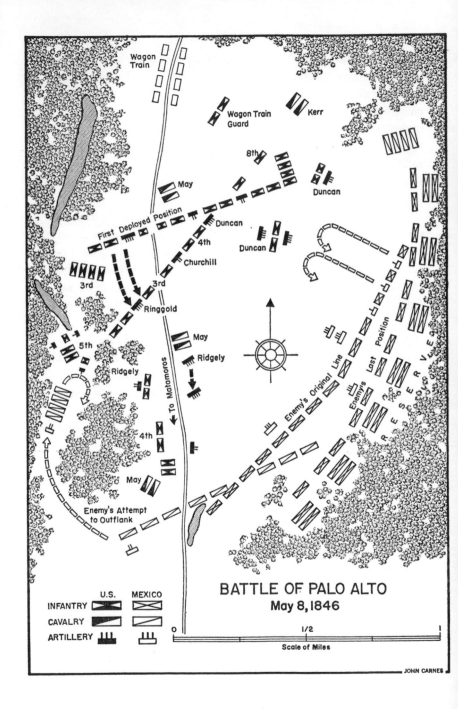

BATTLE OF PALO ALTO
May 8, 1846

Wagon Train

Wagon Train Guard

Kerr

8th

May

Duncan

First Deployed Position

Duncan

4th

Duncan

Churchill

3rd

3rd

Ringgold

5th

May

Ridgely

Ridgely

To Matamoros

4th

May

Enemy's Attempt to Outflank

Enemy's Original Line

Enemy's Last Position

RESERVE

U.S.   MEXICO
INFANTRY
CAVALRY
ARTILLERY

0   1/2   1
Scale of Miles

JOHN CARNES

guns were effective. The balls plopped onto the ground and rustled through the dry grass so slowly the Americans simply sidestepped them. It was about 2:30 P.M.

When the American 6-pounders had reached range, Ringgold and Duncan cut loose. Their dwarf guns threw balls that were smaller than the shotputs with which neophyte high school athletes begin their practice today, but their accuracy was a shock to the Mexicans. Men began to drop, and the 18-pounders added to the impact. The line held, however, and gave Torrejón a chance to thrust one thousand cavalry, infantry, and two fieldpieces, graced by a brass band, ahead through the dense chaparral, hoping to outflank the Americans and reach the wagons.

Twiggs's Fifth Infantry formed into a square and moved obliquely ahead to meet the threat. They poured musket fire on the Mexicans in column as the enemy wallowed out of the swampy brush. Torrejón fell back, regrouped, and tried again. By this time two 6-pounders from Ringgold's battery had dashed up in support. Their canister drove Torrejón back a second time. Taking advantage of the confusion, Taylor sent some of his dragoons against the Mexican left.

Off on the American left the infantry had not yet engaged. Duncan's battery was doing all the fighting, pumping out seven or eight shells a minute. Smoldering powder wads set the tall grass afire. A stiff sea breeze blowing slantwise between the lines carried the smoke away from the Americans and into the faces of the Mexicans.[12]

Fighting now stopped for nearly an hour. The Americans used the pause to remove their wounded and replenish their caissons. Among the casualties was the developer of the "flying artillery," Samuel Ringgold, mortally wounded while on horseback by a cannon shot that mangled both his legs just below the crotch.

Arista, whose left flank had yielded ground to the dragoons, used the smoke as a cover to bring his cavalry around to the right, hoping that a charge there would relieve the pressure on his left. As the smoke lightened, he ordered part of his infantry ahead in support of the lancers. Duncan, standing in his stirrups to peer across the waving grass, spotted the movement as it was forming and gained permission to limber up and intercept. His grape withered the Mexican maneuver before it could gather momentum.

Again Arista rallied his lines. Originally they had extended across the meadow from east to west, but the yielding on the left and the aborted thrust to the right had pivoted them around so that now they extended raggedly northeast to southwest. This brought the evening sun into the faces of the weary Mexicans. When they tried a last charge against the Americans, their bands still playing spiritedly, they could scarcely see the enemy batteries. But they felt plainly enough what those swiftly maneuverable little guns were doing. Great gaps opened in the ranks. The charge faltered, turned back on itself in confusion. Then darkness came and halted the action. The Mexicans had lost somewhere between 229 men dead and wounded, as reported by Arista, and 500, as estimated by Taylor. The American total is also inexact but far smaller, between 46 and 53.[13]

Both armies camped in the field in full moonlight, listening to the cries of each other's wounded as surgeons groped about with smoky torches. The Americans expected a renewal of the fighting in the morning and were astonished, at sunrise, to see the tail end of the Mexican column disappearing toward Matamoros.

Was this a retreat or a withdrawal to safer ground, where the American batteries could not be used with such devastating effect? While the dead were being buried and a last search was made through the high grass for the wounded, Taylor called his principal officers into conference. Against the advice of the majority he decided to pursue the Mexicans. Leaving the wagons and unmaneuverable 18-pounders behind under a guard of five hundred men, he started the rest of his army—seventeen hundred riders and footmen—along the narrow road toward Matamoros. After advancing about three miles, the advance party of dragoons and Texans rangers came within cannon range of the enemy and learned abruptly where the Mexicans had faced around.

It was a formidable position—Resaca de la Palma, an ancient river bed about two hundred feet wide bordered by perpendicular banks three to four feet high. The bottom was cluttered with brush, stagnant ponds, and runted palm trees. Mexican infantry, heavily dressed as usual in spite of the oppressive heat of the afternoon sun, crouched behind the banks and in the matted chaparral through which the road sliced. One Mexican battery was planted directly in the road. Two other batteries, standing on the south side of the ravine, could also drop shells onto segments of the highway. Because of the banks of the resaca and the heavy brush, neither the guns nor the Mexican cavalry could be maneuvered easily. By the same token, however, the effectiveness of the American battery would also be reduced. Furthermore, Arista had drawn fresh troops from Matamoros and from the battalions that had been camped ouside Fort Texas for the assault that the general in charge, Francisco Mejía, had never quite dared launch.

Lulled to confidence by the geography sheltering his five thousand men and thinking that Taylor had been more severely hurt the day before than was the case, Arista retired after lunch to his sumptuous marquee beyond the river bed to write letters. When a courier brought word the Americans were coming, he scarcely glanced up from his desk. It must be skirmishers. Taylor could not possibly be planning to attack this powerful entrenchment so soon after yesterday.

Taylor meanwhile was bulling straight ahead, unaware of

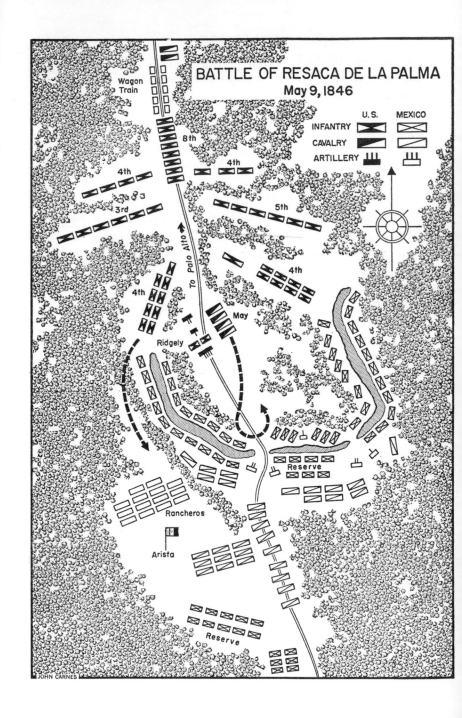

BATTLE OF RESACA DE LA PALMA
May 9, 1846

Wagon Train

8th

4th

4th

4th

3rd

5th

4th

4th

Ridgely

May

Reserve

Rancheros

Arista

Reserve

To Palo Alto

U.S.   MEXICO

INFANTRY

CAVALRY

ARTILLERY

JOHN CARNES

just what he did face. It was plain enough, though, that only one of his batteries could be used on the road for dueling with the Mexican guns that blocked the way. He gave the assignment to Lieutenant Randolph Ridgely, who had taken Ringgold's place. The mounted cannoneers galloped with their little 6-pounders along the road between walls of brush to within four hundred yards of the north rim of the resaca. Maneuvering was tight. When the teams could not complete the swings in harness, the guns had to be wrestled into battery by hand. Gasping in the windless heat, the artillerymen stripped to the waist. Infantry support hacked ahead through the thickets on either side. Taylor sat calmly on Old Whitey just behind the grunting gunners.

Mexican lancers charged while the guns were being manhandled into place but were driven off. Ridgely began throwing shot at such targets as he could bring under his sights in the brush and on the far bank of the resaca. Grape from the enemy battery in the road ahead whistled around him—and around Taylor too, who stayed right where he was. Cramped by the narrow space between the thickets, the Americans were not able to silence the Mexican guns, although the sweating artillerymen did their best to haul their weapons into better position by hand. Losing patience, Taylor ordered the guns to open a space between their wheels so that Captain Charles A. May's dragoons could charge the enemy battery.

May was a colorful figure, thirty years old, with wavy black hair and a lustrous black beard that reached to his waist. He put his riders into columns of four, waited until Ridgely's firing drew an answering blast from the enemy, and then, while the Mexican gunners were reloading, went down the road hell for leather, sabers swinging.

Anticlimax. The horses ran away. The Mexican gunners jumped aside into the brush and returned to their pieces after the charge had bolted by. The dragoons thundered almost into the resaca before they could halt, turn, and charge back. Rifles on either side cut them down mercilessly—nine men killed, ten wounded, eighteen horses dead, and several injured. But they came back with a Mexican general, R. D. de la Vega, in tow. Perhaps May captured him, or perhaps the dragoons swept him away from an infantry sergeant who really deserved the honor. Anyway, a correspondent made such a story out of the charge that afterward May was jumped ahead two brevets in rank, to the jealous disgust of some of his fellow officers.

Meantime, Lieutenant Colonel William G. Belknap succeeded where May had failed and led an infantry assault that took the guns and cleared the road. By this time, savage little hand-to-hand conflicts were swirling off through the thickets on either side. During the hot, choking thrusts and counterthrusts, Captain Philip Barbour and a small party from the Third Infantry found an unwatched footpath that took them around behind the front line of the Mexicans in the resaca. More and more men fell in behind them.

Too late Arista threw Torrejón's cavalry against the surprise encirclement. Other Americans were pressing down the road and appearing here and there along the lip of the ravine. Panic shivered through the Mexican Army. Turning, they fled wildly to the river, crowded the ferry until it sank, then dove fully clad into the brown water. No one knows how many drowned. Total Mexican casualties for battle and flight probably neared 1,500. American losses lay somewhere between 29 and 39 killed, 71 and 89 wounded.[14]

The triumph so impressed young Sam Grant that he wrote his sweetheart, "I think you will find that history will count the victory just achieved one of the greatest on record." Later in his memoirs he would smile at his enthusiasm,[15] but at the time the Army felt well content with what it had achieved in its first encounters with foreign troops since the War of 1812.

Too content, perhaps. Almost at once critics began asking

why Taylor did not pursue the shattered Mexican Army and finish it off completely. He answered that he could not. His men were exhausted by the march from Point Isabel and by two days of hard fighting in the stickiest sort of heat. Even so, he said, he might have tried to cross the Rio Grande if the War Department had sent him the materials for a pontoon bridge that he had requested from Corpus Christi the previous August 1845.[16] Defenders of the War Department snapped back that at the time no advance to the river had been ordered, and when finally the march was authorized in January 1846 Taylor had said nothing more about bridges. Presumably he had decided against them . . . and the debate bogged down into bootless recriminations.

There was plenty to do even without pursuing Arista. Mexican and American corpses had to be taken away from the buzzards and coyotes and hauled by wagonloads to the burying grounds. The supply train that had triggered the fighting had to be brought to Fort Texas (renamed Fort Brown) and unloaded. After sending medical supplies to Arista, licking his sores in Matamoros, Taylor himself went to Point Isabel to hurry up mortars for an assault on the city as soon as he could arrange a crossing. First the Americans took the village of Burrita (sometimes Barita), fifteen miles below Matamoros. Daring volunteers then swam the river to steal small boats— any craft was welcome—and take them two or three miles upstream, out of range of the Mexican guns, for ferrying the troops when the time came.

Seeing the preparations to squeeze him from both sides, Arista sent over an officer, General Requeña, under a white flag to ask for an armistice. Taylor refused and threatened to start shelling the town from Fort Brown unless the Mexican Army withdrew, leaving all public property. Persuaded in part by the agitated citizens, Arista spiked the cannon he could not carry, threw his ammunition into the river, and under cover of darkness started for Linares, 160 miles across the parched deserts to the southwest. Behind him he left, almost unattended in the overcrowded hospitals, 300 wounded.

Although rumor said the enemy had flown, Taylor moved his 18-pounders up to the river ford to cover his crossing. Walker and ten Rangers swam their horses across to reconnoiter. Ridgely's guns had been dismantled for loading and the First Infantry had been ferried to the south bank when out from town came a delegation dressed in white, under white flags, riding white horses. Surrendering their city with fulsome phrases, they asked that the rights of the inhabitants be respected. Taylor agreed. May's dragoons galloped ahead to raise American flags over the Mexican forts. The bank struck up "Yankee Doodle," and the troops marched into the main plaza with a lift to their spirits. In the eyes of young Barna Upton, even nature brightened; the air felt lighter, the sky seemed higher and more dazzling.[17]

They set up their rows of tents in the suburbs and for a few days busied themselves making inventories of captured booty, storing it, and bringing supplies across the river. A steamboat twisted up from the Gulf wtih a load of soldiers—the first such craft to reach Matamoros since one had made an unrepeated trial run in 1832—and the citizens poured to the banks in wide-eyed excitement to see the marvel.

The Americans found a few minor wonders of their own to gape at: the contiguous brick houses with their heavily barred windows, the ornate front of the cathedral, the lofty market place, the exotic groves of bananas, oranges, dates, and pomegranates. And the girls—dark-skinned to American eyes, but "their bosoms were not compressed in stays, or mantled in cashmeres, but heaved freely under the healthful influence of the genial sun and balmy air."[18]

Dragoons under Lieutenant Colonel John Garland took Arista's trail to harry stragglers. Everywhere they saw evidence of the horrors of the flight—discarded equipment, abandoned corpses, wounded pleading for mercy. For three days Arista's army had dragged through fierce heat without water, then into rain and sucking mud. Men collapsed of sunstroke and exhaustion; some went mad and committed suicide. Less than half of the force that had gathered originally in Matamoros to face Taylor limped finally into Linares. While they settled miserably down to recuperate, Arista and his staff were ordered to come under court-martial to Mexico City, there to face an investigation of the disaster.

Garland, halted by lack of water, returned to Matamoros with twenty-two prisoners and a report that in the face of the coming summer heat the American Army could not safely travel the route Arista had taken into Mexico's interior. Taylor, dressed in a linen roundabout and seated in front of his tent beside a table made of two wooden chests, added this information to other considerations he had been marshaling, and then wrote the Secretary of War a letter. What next? He thought he should advance at least as far as Monterrey, but he wanted Washington's views in case other plans were in the making.[19]

5

WISHFUL PLANNING

N EWS TRAVELED SLOWLY from the Rio Grande to Washington. On May 9, 1846 (the date of Resaca de la Palma), President Polk knew nothing of the outbreak of hostilities, and yet, by curious coincidence, he was that day preparing a message to Congress urging a declaration of war. John Slidell, the emissary whom Polk had sent to Mexico to try to buy the Southwest, had just returned from his final rebuff by Paredes. Nothing could be done with the Mexicans, the envoy reported, until they had been "chastised." Polk accordingly summoned his cabinet. All its members except Secretary of Navy George Bancroft agreed that he should urge Congress to declare war, and he set to work drafting his recommendation. His reasoning: Mexico persisted in defaulting on her debts to American citizens; she was insolent about the Texas (now U.S.) boundary; she had insulted American dignity in refusing to receive Slidell. She . . . and then, almost as he was leaning back to contemplate the next phase, word arrived from Taylor that Mexican cavalry had crossed the Rio Grande and had annihilated an American patrol.

Polk reconvened the cabinet, redrafted the message: "I invoke the prompt action of Congress to recognize the existence of the war." The message was read to both chambers on May 11. The House promptly voted the declaration, 173 to 14. The

80

Senate debated acrimoniously for twenty-four hours and then concurred, 42 to 2. The bill appropriated $10,000,000 for military purposes and authorized the President to raise up to fifty thousand twelve-month volunteers for the Army.[1] No one supposed that any such numbers would be necessary.

Incredibly, although relations with Great Britain as well as with Mexico had steadily deteriorated, the government still had undertaken no preparations to wage any kind of struggle. Now a belated series of high-level meetings began, to discuss urgently the ways and means of bringing Mexico to terms.

One overriding problem was the selection of a commander to direct field operations. Secretary of War William Marcy pointed to the logical choice, the general in chief of the Army of the United States, Winfield Scott.[2] Sixty years of age (two years younger than Zachary Taylor) and six feet four inches tall, Scott cut an imposing figure, carrying himself with an assurance that came from long years of command. He was careful about detail—fussy, his critics said. One rasp-tongued army wife remarked that his prim mouth, habitually pursed, could have been covered with a button.[3] He was ambitious. At the Whig convention of 1839 he had received sixty-two votes to be the party's nominee for President. He wanted to try again. A war could be the making of his candidacy. And that alone was enough to raise serious reservations about him in the mind of the civilian commander in chief, President James K. Polk, an intensely partisan Democrat.

An alternate choice to conduct operations was Zachary Taylor. He was already on the scene with more than half of the regular Army. But how sound a commander was he? As yet Polk knew nothing more of affairs on the Rio Grande than that the Mexicans had attacked. Taylor quite possibly was in danger of being isolated. No general, Polk complained in nervous suspense, should move as far from his base of supplies into exposed territory as Taylor had moved from Point Isabel.[4]

Furthermore, although Taylor had never voted in a presidential election, he too was nominally a Whig.

There seemed no way of avoiding a politically undesirable appointment. And after all Scott *was* the Army's ranking general. On May 13, the day Polk signed the war bill, he notified Scott verbally of his assignment to conduct all land operations against the enemy.

Marcy skimmed through some travel books on Mexico and examined such maps as existed. Polk and Scott interviewed men who had been in that country on diplomatic errands. With these scraps of information as their principal background, they met with the cabinet on May 14 and May 16 to formulate plans for raising and deploying their country's troops.[5]

Quotas for volunteers were assigned to every state in the Union, in the hope that this would bring a sense of direct involvement in the war to the entire nation, even reluctant New England. The quotas given the eastern and northeastern states were for "reserves," however. The call for immediate service was placed on the southern and western areas where expansionist sentiment was strongest—some twenty thousand twelve-month men to be provided by Georgia, Alabama, Mississippi, Tennessee, Kentucky, Ohio, Indiana, Illinois, Missouri, Arkansas, and Texas. Enlargement of the regular Army by increasing the size of each company to one hundred men was also authorized, but because the term of enlistment was five times as long as that of the volunteers and perquisites very little better (the volunteers, for example, had to provide their own accouterments, whereas the rank and file of the Army did not) results were meager.

Strategy revolved about seizing northern Mexico as quickly as possible and then using the captured territory as a lever for bargaining about the part of it that Polk really wanted—California and the Southwest. Colonel Stephen Watts Kearny was ordered to add two thousand volunteers to his First Dragoons, capture Santa Fe, and continue to California, there to cooperate with the Pacific Squadron and with Frémont's topographical engineers. Another four thousand volunteers were to rendezvous during the summer in San Antonio, Texas, and march under General John Ellis Wool toward distant Chihuahua. No one was sure that Wool's army could actually traverse the deserts or, if it could, how it was to be supplied over so long a route, but Wool should start anyway. The third and largest strike, calling for fourteen thousand volunteers in addition to the regulars already on the Rio Grande, was to be led by Maj. Gen. Scott against Monterrey.

Integral to the planning was the fuzzy hope that the inhabitants of northern Mexico, dissatisfied with the central government, would welcome the invaders. During the previous October, instructions had been sent to the U.S. consul in California, Thomas Larkin, to foster movements toward independence among the people there, a scheme that contemplated a Texas-style annexation of California to the United States. As soon as war was declared Polk called on John Hughes, a Roman Catholic bishop in New York, for help in sending Spanish-speaking priests into northeastern Mexico to reassure the native clergy about the honorable intentions of the Americans and thus enlist their neutrality, if not their open support.[6]

Intrigue, indeed, became one of the President's principal reliances. Even while the hasty invasion plans were taking shape, he recalled a wild plot that had been broached to him the previous February by a certain Colonel A. J. Atocha, one-time United States citizen of New Orleans but more recently an intimate of Santa Anna, currently exiled in Havana.

In February, it will be recalled, Taylor had received orders to advance to the Rio Grande, partly in order to put pressure on the Mexicans. According to Col. Atocha, that wasn't pressure enough. Let Taylor cross the Rio Grande, a move that would stir deep reverberations among the federalist factions in Nuevo León and Tamaulipas—factions who were opposed to President Paredes. Let U.S. naval forces threaten Tampico and Veracruz. As the Paredes government began to totter under the squeeze, arrange for a secret conference with certain Mexican patriots led by Santa Anna and offer them $30,000,000 for what is now the United States Southwest. The recipients would use the money to settle the government's debt to the Church and to give the Army its overdue pay. Only with the support of those two powerful elements could any regime gain the acquiescence of the country to the sale of some of its territory.[7]

This was so obviously a ploy by Santa Anna to obtain funds, or at least a promise of them, that in February Polk had given Atocha no encouragement. In May, however, he reconsidered. On the thirteenth, the day he verbally appointed Scott commander in chief, he signed an order to Commodore Conner, authorizing him to pass Santa Anna through the blockade. He entrusted a copy of this order to Alexander Mackenzie for delivery to Santa Anna himself. Mackenzie was to suggest that the United States hoped that the warmongering Paredes would be overthrown and that his successor, presumably Santa Anna, would sell to the Americans, on generous and honorable terms, the land they desired.[8]

Two motives prompted Polk's offer. Santa Anna just might keep his word and end the war on the President's terms. Even if he did not, so Polk evidently reasoned, he would prove a disruptive element as soon as he landed in his home country. This alone would justify passing him through the blockade.

Hindsight would show the guess to be unsound. Santa Anna, to be sure, was amply endowed with enemies. Just the same, he was the one man south of the Rio Grande who had even a faint chance of rallying his countrymen against the invaders. He did not disrupt Mexico. He united it as well as anyone could have, which, in truth, was not very tightly.

It would not do, of course, for the United States to hold back until Santa Anna showed his hand. Pressure had to be applied immediately, and Scott was instructed to start the Rio Grande campaign moving at once. But instead of hurrying there on the instant, as Polk thought he should, the new general sat down at his desk in Washington. He had heard from the men whom he had interviewed that yellow fever would make campaigns in northeastern Mexico hazardous before fall. In the interim there was plenty of essential work with logistics to occupy him: equipping, organizing, training, and slowly transporting several thousand volunteers to the Rio Grande over routes still to be determined.

Polk was furious. At that rate, the volunteers' term of enlistment would be one-third spent before Scott got under way. The impatient country—and the Democratic party—needed quick victories before the Whigs could start their pettifogging objections. At Polk's insistence Marcy, without a word to Scott, presented to Congress a bill that would enable the Chief Executive to appoint new generals as commanders of the volunteers. Instantly suspicious, Scott asked Polk to confirm in writing his verbal appointment as commander in chief. One thing led to another until finally, on May 21, eight days after the declaration of war, Scott snapped to Marcy in writing, "I do not desire to place myself in the most perilous of all positions:—a fire upon my rear, from Washington, and the fire in front, from the Mexicans."

Hard on the heels of this unfortunate remark came word of Taylor's victories at Palo Alto and Resaca de la Palma. The country was electrified. Taylor no longer seemed nearly so incompetent to Polk. On May 25, under the President's orders, Marcy relieved Scott of the field command and told the short-term general of the Army of the Rio Grande to confine himself to the paper work in Washington; Taylor was to be the commander of field operations. Though Scott tried to placate Polk with an abject letter of apology, the President refused to re-consider.[9]

Taylor, rewarded for Palo Alto and Resaca de la Palma with the brevet rank of major general, was notified of his new responsibility and asked his opinions on the quickest way, as Marcy put it, to "conquer a peace." (The phrase became the Mexican War's equivalent of "making the world safe for de-mocracy.") "Shall the campaign be conducted with the view of striking at the city of Mexico? or confined, so far as regards the forces under your immediate command, to the northern provinces of Mexico?" Could an invasion of the interior of Mexico be mounted from the Rio Grande?[10] Or would a strike at the capital be more favorable through Tampico or Veracruz? Were adequate supplies for an army obtainable within Mexico? And so on, including urgings in a later letter, that Taylor try assiduously to have the northern provinces "declare their in-dependence of the central government of Mexico, and either to become our allies, or to assume . . . a neutral attitude."[11]

Mails were slow. Taylor did not receive Marcy's first letter until July 2. Meanwhile he had gone plodding ahead on the assumption that Monterrey was to be his goal. Lacking maps to tell him the least thing about routes, he had spent his first days reconnoitering. Perhaps part of his army could march directly overland from Matamoros—he sent a whirlwind party of Rangers under Ben McCulloch to find out[12]—but heavy sup-plies could not, for no roads existed. The bulk of his freight would have to go as far up the Rio Grande as possible by boat—if he could find suitable craft.

He wrote urgent letters to Quartermaster General Jesup asking for shallow-draft river steamboats. On May 28 he sent one of his own officers, Captain John Sanders, to New Orleans to hurry along procurement. On June 6, he dispatched troops upstream to occupy the little river towns of Reynosa, Camargo, and Mier. From what these men and the Mexicans themselves told him he decided that the practical limit of navigation was Camargo, near the junction of the Rio Grande with the San Juan River, some hundred and thirty miles above Matamoros as the river twisted.[13]

River craft that could be adapted to the Rio Grande's swift current were hard to find. Sanders and his staff had to go as far as Pittsburgh on their quest, and there was more delay while the boats were refitted. In the meantime the need for shipping increased. McCulloch reported that lack of water, wood, and forage would prevent any march directly across country toward Monterrey. The troops as well as the supplies would have to follow the river, as many as possible by boat to spare them the crushing heat, which on some humid noons approached 120 degrees, and the rest by foot only if water transport could not be found.

The number of men to be moved increased with dismaying swiftness. The first arrivals were the unexpected result of Taylor's April call on the governors of Texas and Louisiana for five thousand three-month volunteers. In his Louisiana letter Taylor had suggested that sixty-nine-year-old General Edmund P. Gaines, then in New Orleans, help organize the enlistees. Panicked by rumors of trouble that were blowing up out of Texas, Gaines lost his head and rushed appeals for six-month recruits throughout the South—a flat violation of the nation's three-month limit on militia enlistments. By thunderous proclamation, drum rolls, band music, and bonuses for signing, he and his staff brought a rush of twelve thousand men to the colors. In a joyous frenzy of zeal Gaines formed these men into regiments, appointed officers, ordered transports. On May 18 the War Department learned what was going on: a program bound to injure its own call for twelve-month volunteers. Peremptorily it canceled Gaines's work and ordered him to Washington for an investigation.[14]

By then thousands of men were already on their way to the

Rio Grande with no provision for their housing or supply. Hard on their heels came the twelve-month men from the Midwest, where recruiting had succeeded phenomenally. They called themselves by splendid names: Grays, Greens, Eagles, Tigers, Avengers, and what not. They designed uniforms and headgear in whatever gaudy hues and bizarre shapes struck their fancy and, totally without training, started south for a summer of fun and adventure.

Reality turned out to be other than they had imagined: sand flies, spiders, mosquitoes; crashing thunderstorms that blew down acres of tents at a puff and were followed by steaming heat; warm, muddy river water to drink; beans, pancakes, and pork to eat in a blistering climate. Shortages were chronic. Just one instance: canvas for so many tents did not exist in the United States; in desperation, Quartermaster General Jesup substituted muslin and drew down Taylor's wrath.

Instead of concentrating his energies on overcoming the confusion, Taylor let himself be plagued by distractions. And indeed it would have been strange if his head, unused to adulation, had not been turned. His victories at Palo Alto and Resaca de la Palma had given his country its first military hero since the War of 1812. Imaginative lithographs of the battles filled shop windows everywhere. Taylor's likeness was painted on dishes, scarves, and brooches. Latin odes and resolutions of gratitude poured in from dozens of hamlets. A Louisiana delegation arrived with a promise of a gold sword. In the North, Whig politician Thurlow Weed, seeking a presidential candidate who might restore his party to power in 1848, sent up a trial balloon labeled "Taylor."

All this was fostered by the general's son-in-law, Robert Wood, who was in charge of the military hospital at Point Isabel. Wood collected clippings of newspaper paeans, and of editorials advocating Taylor's candidacy, and forwarded them in batches to headquarters at Matamoros. At first Taylor snorted. High office, he wrote Wood, "I would decline if proffered & I could reach it without opposition." He continued in that vein throughout most of the summer.[15] Nevertheless, the idea had been planted, and as more and more journalists flocked to the Rio Grande to interview him, Taylor began granting them more time than he could well afford.

His suspicions of the Democratic administration grew in direct ratio to the number of Whig newspapers that joined his band wagon. He thought it "strange, passing strange" that he should receive Washington newspapers containing stories of the battles of Palo Alto and Resaca de la Palma a week before letters arrived from either Polk or Marcy congratulating him on his victories.[16] He took the delay as a slight. Furthermore, from the experiences of other army officers in the Seminole campaigns, he knew how quickly civilians blamed the military for not producing victories. Yet how could he fight when he received insufficient supplies for the hordes of untrained volunteers pouring in on him? Brooding in the sticky heat, he began to wonder whether the breakdown in the Quartermaster's department might not be deliberate. If he were a candidate for President, he growled by letter to Wood, this neglect could well be part of a calculated plan to destroy him.[17]

Meantime he was guilty of negligence of his own, particularly in regard to the health of his men. Sickness killed so many new recruits in unsanitary camps all the way up the river to Camargo that mockingbirds learned from the bands to trill the death march. Boredom, too, was all-pervading. A theater flourished in Matamoros but could hardly suit the tastes of, or provide seating for, the thousands of disillusioned, restless men. Brothels, saloons, and gambling houses sucked off pay as fast as it appeared. Mexican females willing to exploit the troops flocked to Matamoros and led some of the contemptuous soldiers to suppose that all Mexican women were of that stamp. Many of the idle troops passed swiftly from rudeness to rape.

They pillaged, disobeyed orders, and brawled continuously, either with the Mexican men or among themselves. The Texans, remembering the outrages of the Alamo, Goliad, and the march from Mier, were so notorious that Taylor singled them out for particular reproof.

Whig newspapers opposed to war spread exaggerated tales of the misconduct before the nation.[18] Squirming, the Democratic administration told Taylor to exercise better discipline. Testily he retorted that the War Department was as much at fault for sending him so indigestible a mass of untrained, unsupplied men. He seems not to have called the volunteer officers to strict account, however, and they in their turn were reluctant to chide men who had voted them into their positions and who could easily vote them right back out again.

Into these confusions came a surprise visitor: Polk's special emissary to Santa Anna, Alexander Mackenzie. Mackenzie had seen the exiled former president of Mexico in Havana on July 5 and had learned from him Santa Anna's own version of what was going on in his home country. The Paredes government was unpopular. Its constitution gave undue representation to the propertied classes as opposed to the workers. Salaries and pensions had been cut, taxes had been raised, the press had been muzzled. Republicans suspected Paredes of plotting to establish a monarchy. Late in May the city of Guadalajara had revolted. And so on.

Santa Anna was diligently fomenting the unrest by promising federalists in Mexico a return to the Constitution of 1824, if he was restored to power. (Calming the federalists of northern Mexico would undercut American efforts to foster separatist movements there, but in view of other gains that Santa Anna held out the matter seemed immaterial.) The thing for the United States to do, Santa Anna continued, was to increase pressure everywhere. Taylor should capture Monterrey and Saltillo. The fleet should take Tampico and possibly Veracruz.

Paredes would fall, Santa Anna would be summoned back to save the nation, and negotiations could begin—the same story, pretty much, that Atocha had presented to Polk in February.[19]

Mackenzie was so taken in by what he heard that he disobeyed instructions and hurried to the Rio Grande before returning to Washington. He arrived about July 20 and stayed only long enough to urge Santa Anna's plan on Taylor.

It could hardly have fitted more neatly into what the general had been aiming at for two months. At last he was ready to move. Steamboats were appearing on the river for his freight, and his tough regulars were already marching by land toward the staging depot at Camargo. So it would be stretching matters to suppose that Mackenzie's talk initiated anything new in Taylor's thinking.[20] Still, the memory of the interview must have been fresh when along came a second letter from Secretary of War Marcy, dated July 9, wondering why Taylor had not replied to the first and repeating the questions the first had asked about strategy. Should Mexico be invaded from the Rio Grande, from Tampico, from Veracruz, or what? The matter was so important, Marcy said, that Taylor should reply directly to Polk himself.

This Taylor did on August 1. (He had answered Marcy's first queries on July 2, but the letter took a month to reach its destination.)[21] Both letters, the second especially, displeased Polk as being vague and showing, in the President's mind, a culpable lack of intelligence and initiative. Yet it is hard to see how Taylor, isolated on the Rio Grande, could have learned much more about Mexico than Washington could. He said that he doubted the suitability of Tampico as a starting point for an invasion because of the probable dangers from yellow fever and the lack, so far as he knew, of roads to the interior. As for an attack on Veracruz, he could not even offer a conjecture.

He was not much more definite, on August 1, about his own prospects. He said he could reach as far as Saltillo but could suggest nothing about a deeper penetration until he had actually experimented with the problems of supply. He seemed to think that his best move would be to take Monterrey, capital of Nuevo León, and Saltillo, capital of Coahuila, and then link up with Gen. Wool, who was to capture Chihuahua. The two of them would then establish defensive lines across northern Mexico for holding the upper provinces until future developments suggested their next course of action.

Polk's initial idea had also been to seize the northern provinces and use them as a lever for forcing Mexico to sell California and the Southwest. This may have been the genesis of Taylor's idea. But his opinions may have been confirmed by what he had so recently heard from Alexander Mackenzie: take Monterrey and Saltillo and topple Paredes. That would be war enough, for then Santa Anna would return to power and make the deal Polk wanted. Naturally, therefore, Taylor talked about defensive operations (or so one speculates in the absence of written evidence). And that is irony, for this apparent passiveness, though implicit in Polk's own intriguing, was one of the things that helped turn the President against his general.[22]

Clumsily, meanwhile, the Army was dragging itself toward the stone and clay town of Camargo. There again Taylor was luckier than he realized. Unprecedented rains had flooded the river. The seasonal low water that in most years would have stranded his transports did not trouble the groaning paddle wheelers in 1846. There were other vexations, however. Green mesquite wood, cut each night, was slow and undependable fuel. Smoking craft often ran out of steam in awkward spots and had to tie up to the sun-smitten shore until they could store enough energy to flounder on to the next halting place. Several missed the shifting channel, went aground on sand bars, and were extricated only with enormous labor. One sank.

Such troops as could not be ferried had to march. Generally

they fell in at midnight and stopped in midmorning, to avoid the terrible heat of the afternoons. They plodded between dense walls of chaparral where no breeze stirred. Bandits lurked on the flanks to pick off stragglers.[23]

Camargo brought no relief. The town, which stood beside the San Juan River three miles above the Rio Grande, had been severely damaged by the unusual floods. Mud left by the receding water dried to a powdery dust that swirled blindingly on the endless wind. Sun glanced from the naked ridges of limestone to strike with searing heat against the mile-long rows of tents. On many nights fog crept clammily along the valley. As company after company dragged into this desolate spot, fresh epidemics broke out, and new corpses were rolled each day in blankets and deposited with scant ceremony in shallow, sandy graves—1,500, by one estimate.[24]

By this time the problem of Gaines's illegal six-month volunteers was becoming acute. They were strung out in various camps from the mouth of the river to Camargo, griping at conditions and thoroughly disillusioned about the romance of war. What should be done with them? Legally they could not be held longer than three months. That limit was nearing. Yet if they went home now they would have brought their government nothing but trouble and expense. Recruiting agents went among them, trying to prevail on them to extend their enlistments to the authorized twelve-month term of the regular recruits. Except for one group of eighty Louisianans under Captain Albert Blanchard, few listened.[25] Most of the short-termers went rejoicingly home—and Taylor quite possibly watched their exodus with no real regret.

Even with those troublesome units gone, he had more men at Camargo than he could move away from the river. According to one estimate he would need at least 2,000 wagons for the advance on Monterrey. Only 180 were on hand. Seeking substitute transportation, he sent purchasers through the countryside after mules—mostly unbroken ones, since they were cheaper. By the end of August he had assembled about nineteen hundred head. To manage them he hired picturesque Mexican *arrieros*. The outside seams of their green broadcloth trousers, flaring open from knee to ankle, were decorated with silver buttons. More buttons gleamed on their tight jackets. Silver braid brightened their wide-brimmed, high-crowned sombreros. They knew their business. They rode like fiends, were expert with lassos. Even so, packing up and stringing nearly two thousand ill-broken mules out along the trails every morning was an exercise straight out of Wild West fantasy.

Which route should they travel? Monterrey lay on the Santa Catarina River, one of the upper tributaries of the San Juan. This suggested a march from Camargo straight up the San Juan Valley. Taylor again sent out McCulloch's Rangers to check conditions. They swept south sixty miles to a town called China, fell on it like Comanches, returned, and reported unfavorably. This left only one way: on up the Rio Grande to Mier, of infamous memory in Texas minds, and then southwest across flat, dull plains toward the mountain passes that guarded the desired city.

Reconnaissance along the Mier route turned out to be inadequate. Roads were reported to be poorer than they really were. Although Taylor was moving against a fortified city and would have found siege guns useful, he decided, incorrectly, that he could not drag his 18-pounders through the rough country and left them at Camargo. In the end his heavy artillery consisted of one 10-inch mortar and two 24-pound howitzers.

Because of inadequate transportation he also had to pare down the number of men he took, leaving about three thousand of his volunteers behind to garrison Camargo and other river points. He added another three thousand to his regulars, so that the marching force consisted of 6,220 men and 425 officers.[26] None of the volunteers in the army had seen action.

He organized the force into three divisions, dividing the

regulars between the 1st Division, commanded by Twiggs, and the 2nd, commanded by Worth. The 1st he fleshed out with the best of his volunteer units, a snappily trained Baltimore battalion; the 2nd with Blanchard's re-enlisted Louisianans. Each division was accompanied by two batteries of light field artillery.

The 3rd Division was made up of 2,800 volunteers commanded by Major General William Orlando Butler, a popular and able administrator (and a Democrat) whom Polk had placed in charge, under Taylor, of the volunteer part of the army. Butler's 3rd Division was divided into two brigades, one under Brigadier General Thomas L. Hamer of Ohio, totally inexperienced in military matters, and the other under Brigadier John Quitman of Mississippi, a lawyer and a swaggering demagogue who roared from various platforms that the Mexicans were a "bastard and robber race . . . only fit for servitude and military rule."[27] Commander of the First Mississippi Regiment under Quitman was Colonel Jefferson Davis, Taylor's erstwhile son-in-law, recently remarried, who had resigned his seat in Congress to return to the Army for which he had been trained at West Point. Another unit of the 3rd Division, but formally attached to neither brigade, were two regiments of mounted Texans, one commanded by Ranger Jack Hays. Hays's second was Lieutenant Colonel Samuel Walker, who, with his guerrillas, had recently been mustered into the more formal unit.

It was not a large force, yet putting it onto the road to Monterrey had taken Taylor three months. The country wanted faster action than that. A compromise settlement had just been reached with Great Britain about the Oregon boundary, and with that problem out of the way only Mexico remained. Why was chastising that country taking so long? Critics, mostly Democrats, began to sneer at Taylor's slowness. Their carpings, now that he was a presidential aspirant, however undeclared, got under his skin. On September 1, while the

vanguard of his army was at last stringing out toward Monterrey, he exploded in an acrimonious letter that blamed his delays
on the clumsiness and inefficiency of the Quartermaster's department.[28]

It was an injudicious philippic. Written out of temper and
harassment, it badly overstated his case, which otherwise had
considerable justice to it, and it gave the *coup de grâce* to
his already fast expiring friendship with Quartermaster General
Thomas Jesup. Jesup was in Washington and had Polk's
ear. Like his subordinates, he sought to excuse his own short-
comings in providing matériel by finding fault with the requi-
sitions from the field.

For instance, on September 5, well before Taylor's blast
reached the War Department, Jesup happened to be talking
with the President about the problems of supply. Wouldn't the
wagons Taylor wanted be a burden to a fighting army? the
President asked. Indeed they would, said Jesup, and added that
mules were always used in Mexican wars. Polk fell to brooding
about this. Why didn't Taylor use mules? (Actually, for lack
of anything better, Taylor had 1,900 of the animals on the
road at that very moment.) It all went to show, Polk told his
diary, that the man was incompetent.[29] Later, when Taylor's
blistering letter about supplies arrived, it had little effect other
than to arouse Jesup, who retorted with an equally blistering
recrimination about Taylor's inadequacies in preparing orders.[30]

Slowly the Army moved with its mules through Mier and
swung southwest across dreary plains. Near Cerralvo they
caught glimpses of the lilac peaks of the Sierra Madre Mountains. Frequent stream of sparkling waters splashed across their
path. Spirits lifted, and about that same time they began to
hear heartening rumors of trouble farther south in Mexico.

On August 3 the army garrison at Veracruz had mutinied
and had declared in favor of Santa Anna. That triggered Paredes' downfall. General José Mariano Salas seized control of
the country with a ringing cry of "Federation, Santa Anna,

and Texas." The last word sounded belligerent, but with an invasion of his country already under way Salas could hardly have sounded otherwise. Matters might change when Santa Anna arrived after being passed through the American blockade of the coast by Polk's own orders.

At this point the schemers' plans ran into trouble. In Veracruz Santa Anna was met with more sullenness than he had anticipated. He decided to make haste slowly. Saying that he was in pain from the stump of the leg he had sacrificed for his nation, while fighting the French, and that he needed rest, he retired to his country estate near Jalapa. From there he declared to the Mexicans that he had no ambition for public office. His sole desire, he trumpeted, was to drive away his country's enemies—a wish nurtured perhaps by his discovering among the Mexicans a stronger sentiment in favor of the war than he had anticipated when talking to Mackenzie in Havana. This patriotic pronouncement of his was accompanied by a ringing plea for enlistments in the army he would lead.[31]

Simultaneously he caught the government of the United States in a trap of its own making. Shortly before Mackenzie's return from Havana, the cabinet had begun to wonder whether the war could not be ended by negotiation even if Santa Anna failed in his attempt to return to power. To that end Secretary of State James Buchanan wrote the Foreign Minister of Paredes' government, suggesting peace talks. This letter too was passed through the blockade by Commodore Conner.

By the time it arrived, Paredes was out and Salas was Acting President. Buchanan's letter was immediately shown to Santa Anna. So! The gringos were playing both sides, were they? Frostily, through Salas' new Minister of Foreign Affairs, he snubbed the proposal—but, as usual, left the door open an inch by saying that final action could not be taken until the Mexican Congress reassembled on December 6. For the time being, however, the war was to go on.[32]

In September Taylor knew none of these details. But he

did learn, through Mexican sources, that Paredes was out and that Santa Anna was back in Mexico, making warlike noises. Were the threats real, or just part of the game that Santa Anna had outlined to Mackenzie and that Mackenzie had passed on to Taylor? There would be no telling until the Americans actually reached Monterrey and tested reactions there. It was Taylor's opinion, though, that there would not be much fighting.[33]

On they marched, getting glimpses of Mexican cavalry now and then but never making solid contact. On past little flat-roofed towns, many deserted by inhabitants frightened out of their wits by the grim plundering of the advance guard of Texans. Tall peaks showed ahead, more than five thousand feet in elevation and named for their shapes: Miter and Silla, or Saddle, Mountains. Reports flashed through the ranks that Miter Mountain stood seven miles beyond the western end of Monterrey, overlooking the road to Saltillo, and that Saddle Mountain guarded the town from the east. And then, on September 19, they saw Monterrey itself, tiny box houses dominated by a cathedral with two towers. Out on the northern edge of the city, which was reputed to contain between twelve and fifteen thousand inhabitants, was a huge building that had started to be another cathedral. Unfinished, it had been turned into a fort, grim looking with weather-blackened walls. It faced straight toward the road the Americans were following.

They did not take it seriously but crowded ahead, those who were near the front of the columns, for a closer look. The Rangers sashayed off, single file, on a wild, weaving ride, taunting the enemy. Suddenly cannon smoke bloomed. A solid ball, landing in front of Taylor, ricocheted over his head. He ordered the advance elements to draw back.

Perhaps there was going to be a fight after all.

6

BITTER VICTORY: MONTERREY

THE MEXICAN WAR EFFORT was even more confused and mismanaged than the American. Following the disastrous retreat from Matamoros to Linares, generals Mariano Arista and Pedro de Ampudia were summoned to the capital to explain. Command of the demoralized remnant of the Army devolved on Francisco Mejía, a small pock-marked man who habitually wore blue sunglasses. Acting under orders from the Minister of War, Mejía first sent engineers to Monterrey to prepare plans for fortifying it against the expected thrust by the Americans. On July 9, he followed with his troops. In Monterrey he began building redoubts at strategic locations, turning certain strong buildings into forts, and preparing street barricades. Money and food were short, however, and progress was slow until finally he received permission to conscript the labor and supplies he needed. After that the pace picked up.[1]

In Mexico City, fast-talking Pedro de Ampudia shifted full blame for the defeats at Palo Alto and Reseca de la Palma onto Arista—where, to be sure, the onus belonged—and won Arista's vacated place as commander in chief. Early in August he started north. Along the way, in San Luis Potosí, he picked up some three or four thousand men whom Paredes had originally gathered there for a march against the revolting city of Guadala-jara. By government order these soldiers were now diverted to the defense of Monterrey.

The deserts north of San Luis Potosí are fearsome. As the troops were marching glumly into them, word arrived that Santa Anna had landed at Veracruz. The marchers were thrown into confusion. What did this portend? Where did their loyal-ties lie? One brigade defied Ampudia and turned back to San Luis Potosí. Scores more used the turmoil as an occasion to desert and escape the barrens ahead. Cracking down on the rest with more resolution than was customary for him, Ampudia pulled the rest together and continued north. On one day he pushed his ragged battalions an incredible forty-eight miles.[2]

Despite the achievement, the march drew sharp disapproval from Santa Anna. In his opinion, so the former exile told Acting President Salas, Monterrey should be abandoned. Instead of advancing, the troops should retreat into the desert, scorching the earth and destroying the wells as they went. The Ameri-cans, he argued, would then overextend their supply lines in pursuit. With unfriendly Nature as the ally of the Mexicans, the invading enemy could then be isolated from his bases and destroyed.

Santa Anna was so devious that one cannot be sure what he meant by offering this plan. Perhaps he really believed in it. On the other hand, he may have intended it merely as a means of delaying a decisive battle until he could assume command and win the glory of the victory for himself. Or possibly he was still considering the wisdom of bargaining with Polk's emissaries after the Mexican Congress had met and was trying to avoid a major clash until the stage could be set for a peace deal that would bring him the funds he needed to win full con-trol of the government. Or, more probably, he simply wanted to create a fluid situation that would let him improvise as op-portunity suggested. In any event, he won Salas to his proposed strategy. Off went orders to Mejía and Ampudia to demolish Monterrey's fortifications and retreat.

They refused to obey. Taylor, they pointed out, had already started his advance and might catch them before they could finish moving or destroying Monterrey's hard-won, carefully hoarded store of almost irreplaceable matériel. Furthermore, was it not dangerous to assume the Americans would pursue them into the desert? The enemy might be content to simply accept the gift of Monterrey and Saltillo and dig in so solidly that the cost of driving him out again would be prohibitive. Worst of all, the generals insisted, the Army's withdrawal might so poison the morale of the northern provinces that they would revolt and join the Americans—a defection the enemy was already trying to bring about.[3]

They rushed their protest to the Minister of War. He countermanded Salas' instructions and ordered Monterrey defended. Meanwhile the last of Ampudia's San Luis Potosí troops limped into Monterrey, so that by September 10 the city's garrison numbered 7,303 officers and men of the regular Army. Another 3,000 irregulars were conscripted in the surrounding countryside, so that approximately ten thousand men of varying degrees of training and equipment awaited the approach of Taylor's 6,645 Americans.

As he had at Matamoros, Ampudia met the attackers first with pamphlets urging Roman Catholics among them to desert. A few responded, to join John Riley's Matamoros defectors, most of whom were engaged in refurbishing and emplanting the thirty or so cannon of different sizes collected for the battle by the defenders. The city's nervous inhabitants were inspirited meantime by sonorous proclamations and lively band music and by the arrival of quantities of powder. Earthworks and barricades grew steadily.

Underneath this apparent energy lay serious weaknesses. Money remained short. Many officers were bitterly jealous of

Ampudia: why should *he* have been rewarded with command after Palo Alto and Resaca de la Palma? His own sneers at some of the preparations Mejía had made did nothing to repair these feelings. Adding to the basic uneasiness were doubts sown by Santa Anna's question concerning the advisability of defending the city. Was this stand really wise?

For the Americans the dissensions proved useful. The Mexican staff did not fully and wholeheartedly capitalize on Monterrey's natural advantages for defense. Even so, the works that faced Taylor were dismayingly formidable.

Lofty mountains, marked by steeply pitched strata of limestone, girded the city west, south, and east. The land to the north, across which the Americans must come, was more open but difficult to approach for other reasons. Here lay the fields which supported the town's economy—orchards, grain, cotton, sugar cane; one principal export was *piloncillos*, little cakes of unrefined brown sugar that made up a staple item of the Mexican foot soldier's diet.[4] Most of these crops grew to considerable height and made the masking of strong points relatively easy.

The southern border of the town was the Santa Catarina River. It ran from west to east. In September, the rainiest month of the year, it flowed about three feet deep, cold and swift. The road from Saltillo, over which supplies and reinforcements would have to reach the defenders, came down out of the mountains along the river's north bank. Just before reaching the western extremity of the town, both the road and the stream passed between two high, broad-topped, steep-sided ridges.

The ridge to the north of the creek and road was the larger —some three thousand feet long. Its highest point was somewhat west of the middle. From this apex the ridge top sloped gently east by south toward the city for a quarter of a mile, then dropped off into the suburbs.[5] At the lip of this drop and overlooking all Monterrey was the old Bishop's Palace, built in 1786 to provide employment for the Indian victims of a severe drought.[6] During the War of Independence against Spain, the heavy stone structure had been turned into a fort and was one of the reasons the city had never been taken by government forces. As a memento of the war the ridge was named Independence Hill. To strengthen the hill still more against the Americans, the defenders built a strong redoubt below the Bishop's Palace or, as the Mexicans called it, El Obispado.

The ridge southward beyond the river and the Saltillo road was named Federation Hill in honor of the Constitution of 1824. On the eastern, or town, end of Federation Hill was another fort, smaller than El Obispado, called El Soldado. The guns of these two forts and of the redoubt below the Bishop's Palace dominated the western end of Monterrey so completely that an attack on the city from that sector was almost out of the question. There was one oversight, however. None of the artillery in the permanent emplacements pointed toward the rear of the guardian ridges.[7] Such coverage did not seem necessary to the Mexicans. The western sections of both hills were between eight hundred and a thousand feet high, and their slopes were almost perpendicular in places. Convinced that infantry alone could hold off any assault from the rear, the defenders built no redoubts at all on the western end of Independence Hill and only a single small one one on Federation.

The city extended from the base of Independence Hill eastward along the north bank of Santa Catarina River for about one and three-quarter miles. The river then made an L-like turn, not quite a right angle. The central part of Monterrey lay boxed inside this reclining angle. The streets were straight, narrow, and lined solidly with flat-roofed houses. One square back from the river but otherwise near the center of the main downtown section loomed the Cathedral, by far the most imposing building in Monterrey. Although work on it had begun in 1600, the last touches still had not been added, in 1846, to the impressive Renaissance-style bell tower. (There were two

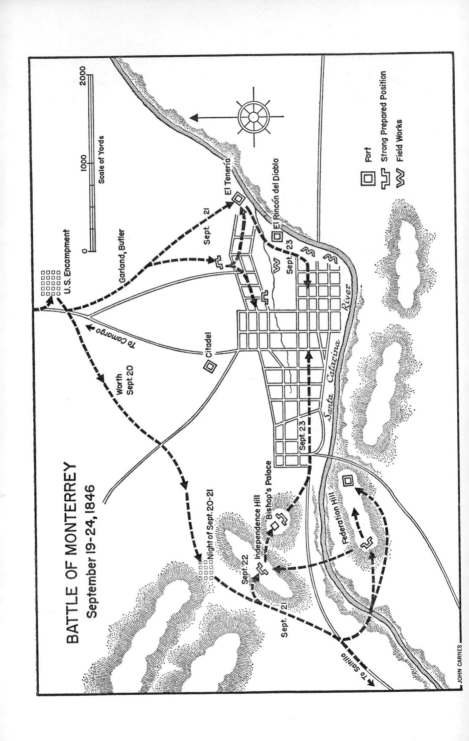

BATTLE OF MONTERREY
September 19-24, 1846

Scale of Yards
0   1000   2000

U.S. Encampment

Garland, Butler

Sept. 21

El Teneria

El Rincón del Diablo

Sept. 23

Sept. 23

To Camargo

Citadel

Worth
Sept. 20

Night of Sept. 20-21

Independence Hill

Bishop's Palace

Sept. 22

Federation Hill

Sept. 21

Sept. 23

Santa Catarina River

To Saltillo

Fort

Strong Prepared Position

Field Works

JOHN CARNES

towers, one domed and one flat-topped.) The façade, highly ornate, faced west toward the Bishop's Palace. Because the Cathedral was in the heart of the city and had the strongest walls, it became the storage place for ammunition.

A wall surrounded the grounds in front of the Cathedral. Due west of these grounds spread a large plaza and market square, surrounded on three sides by the only two-story buildings in the city. Half a dozen blocks farther west, at the edge of the closely built part of the town, lay a cemetery called Campo Santo.

The central portion of the city was about twice as long, east to west, as it was wide—approximately eleven blocks long by five wide at the broadest section. (The blocks varied considerably in size and even shape, few of them being true rectangles.) Embracing the town west and north were "suburbs" —irregular rectangles formed by intersecting lanes. Each rectangle contained a scattering of houses, gardens, and fruit trees. The different bits of property were separated by thorn hedges and stone walls four feet or so high. Together with the outer fields of corn, cotton, and sugar cane, these plots could have created serious obstacles in the way of attacking troops. The Mexicans, however, did very little to turn these advantages into a consistent line of defensive works but relied instead on a series of forts strung around the northeastern perimeter of the city.

A deep ravine, whose principal crossing was a stone span called Purísima Bridge, ran from west to east between the city proper and the northern suburbs. Beside the outer, northern, side of Purísima Bridge stood a *tête-de-pont* equipped with a 12-pounder cannon. East of the bridge on the town (south) side of the creek were two stout redans—fieldworks whose parapets met in salient angles. Each mounted a light fieldpiece and was capable of holding sixty men. Farther downstream at the northeast corner of the town, where the ravine entered

Santa Catarina River, was a strong redoubt called El Rincón del Diablo, garrisoned by 150 men. Diablo mounted three cannon.

Northeast across the ravine was El Tenería. Its eastern approach, like Diablo's eastern side, was protected by the river. As its name indicates, this stone fort had once been a tannery building. Because of vacillation among the defenders, the moat surrounding it had not been finished. Sheds, trees, and cornstalks that might shelter attacking skirmishers had not been cleared from the field of fire. It was a powerful obstacle nonetheless. It sheltered two hundred men. Earthen star points extending from the corners of the stone wall surrounding the tannery yard would enable the defenders to enfilade any assault. It was only after the Americans had appeared, however, that four guns, ranging from a 4-pounder to a 12-pounder, were dragged inside El Tenería and hastily mounted *en barbette*—that is, placed on mounds of earth.[8] Freshly piled, the mounds would turn to mud in a rain and make the guns difficult to manage.

Chief reliance of the defenders was the Citadel, an unfinished church building at the edge of the fields north of the central part of the city. Its massive, rectangular walls, twenty-five or thirty feet high, were stained so dark by weather and neglect that the Americans called it the Black Fort. Earthworks eleven feet tall, faced with soft tufa for absorbing shot, surrounded the stone edifice. Outside was an uncompleted ditch originally designed to be twelve feet deep. There were embrasures for thirty-four guns, ranging from 4-pounders to 18-pounders, but only twelve were in place.[9]

Shells from three of these guns met the first appearance of the Americans. Turning aside, the invaders went into camp three miles away in the finest bivouac they had yet seen: a picnic ground cleared of underbrush, fenced against livestock, and watered with several cold springs. The Mexicans called the spot Santo Domingo. The Americans named it Walnut Springs from its moss-hung nut trees, though in reality they were pecans.

While the *arrieros* corralled their fractious mule herd and the soldiers set up their rows of tents, a detachment of dragoons and engineers under Captain Joseph F. K. Mansfield (now brevetted major) edged out into the fields to probe the enemy's strength. Captured Mexicans added more bits of information. Adding the data together, Lieutenant George Gordon Meade compiled a rough map. Although it failed to show several of the enemy works, notably the fortress of Rincón del Diablo beyond the ravine, the matter it did present was sobering. The overlapping trajectories of the guns in the tannery, the Citadel, and the Bishop's Palace covered the entire arc of fields east, north, and west. The south Taylor could only imagine, but that too was discouraging; an attack there would have to be launched across an open, waist-deep stream against probable earthworks along the river banks and behind them a solid row of stone houses whose roofs and windows undoubtedly would be manned by thousands of infantry.[10]

As he was contemplating alternatives, in came Captain W. G. Williams of the engineers with a report that troops could move beyond range of the Citadel's guns westward along the foot-hills and reach the Saltillo road behind Independence Hill, thus isolating Monterrey. It might even be possible, Williams said, to storm the hill from behind. The back flanks were dismay-ingly steep but did not appear to be fortified. As for Federation Hill, south of the road and across the river from Independence, Williams knew nothing of it.[11]

On the basis of this imperfect information, Taylor decided to split his force in defiance of standard tactics and send General William Jenkins Worth's 2nd Division around behind Independence Hill to attack from the west.[12] He added to this force and to its batteries of fieldpieces under Captain William Mackall and Lieutenant James Duncan the brigade of mounted Texans commanded by James P. Henderson, who was governor of Texas as well as general of his state's volunteers. The bulk of one of Henderson's regiments were former Rangers led by

Colonel Jack Hays and Lieutenant Colonel Samuel Walker. All told, Worth's force amounted to about twenty-two hundred men, five hundred of them mounted.

At 2:00 P.M. on Sunday afternoon, September 20, the column moved slowly ahead through alternating stands of chaparral and dry, rattling cornstalks. Guessing its purpose, Ampudia belatedly realized that he should have protected the western ridges against assault from the rear. Hastily he ordered the garrison in the Bishop's Palace to move two of their 12-pounders back to the highest point of Independence Hill. A single 9-pounder was simultaneously hauled into the little redoubt at the western edge of Federation Hill.

Because of the intervening bulk of Independence Hill, the movement on Federation went undetected by the Americans. They did see, however, that reinforcements were moving out of the city toward the west. In order to deter the Mexicans from shifting too many troops in that direction against Worth, Taylor marched what remained of his army into view so that the enemy would realize that his northeastern flank was still strongly threatened. A desultory cannonading on the part of both opponents accompanied the maneuver, but no casualties resulted.

Worth's engineers had to bridge ditches and tear down walls for the artillery. By evening the column had advanced only six or seven miles from Walnut Springs. They halted when darkness caught them, supplementing their meager rations with pigs and chickens appropriated from humble *jacales* nearby. By the light of torches twisted out of corn husks Worth wrote a dispatch to Taylor, saying that he had definitely decided to storm Independence Hill in the morning and asking for a strong diversion against the northeast.[13]

A light drizzle fell during the night. It was a relief to leave the cold camp at 6:00 A.M. and start on around the hill toward the Saltillo road. Behind them they soon heard the boom of heavy guns. Under cover of darkness Taylor's artillerymen had moved their only heavy guns—the two 24-pound howitzers and the 10-inch mortar—into a depression some fifteen hundred yards from the Citadel and had started shelling the enemy fort. The bombardment lasted only twenty minutes and did no damage, but to Worth's nervous men it signaled that the diversion had begun.

As the column bent slowly around the far corner of Independence Hill, Henderson's mounted Texans in the van, it was met by 1,500 Mexican lancers under Lieutenant Colonel Juan Najera. Worth rushed orders ahead for his outnumbered riders to dismount and take cover behind a handy fence. Before the message reached Ben McCulloch's company of Rangers at the very head of the column, the Mexicans charged. The Rangers spurred their heavier horses straight ahead against the enemy's wiry little mustangs. The crunching impact scattered and slowed the charge. Then weight of numbers bore the Rangers back. As they retreated, fighting desperately hand to hand, the Texans who had dismounted behind the fence opened fire on both of the enemy's flanks. Duncan wheeled his battery into position and began dropping grape on the lancers. Wheeling in confusion, the Mexicans fled, leaving a hundred dead behind. Incredibly, Worth lost only one man killed, two wounded. Without further hindrance he pushed on to the Saltillo road, and there are commentators who think that at that moment the Mexicans lost the battle of Monterrey.[14]

For some reason the 12-pounders on the high point of Independence Hill did not bother Worth's force, either because the guns were not yet planted firmly or because the strike of the land was such that their muzzles could not be depressed far enough. But as the column came out on the road the immunity ended: the 9-pounder that had just reached the western end of Federation Hill began hurling round shot across the stream. The shock of the shells was Worth's first knowledge of the emplacement.[15] He sent his men scrambling back along the road out of range, then set up headquarters in an old sugar house and contemplated the problem. To keep from being surprised from the rear he ordered McCulloch's Rangers three miles up the road toward Saltillo to act as lookouts.

The din of battle on the other side of the city told him that Taylor's diversion was proceeding apace, and therefore it was up to him to justify the effort. He decided to attack Federation Hill. Its sides were neither so steep nor so high as Independence's, and spyglasses suggested that it was lightly defended, in spite of Independence's silence earlier that morning.

A few experimental shots from the gunners on Independence soon showed that they would not stay silent. Keeping carefully out of their range, Captain C. F. Smith took six companies of dismounted Texans and four companies of artillery serving as infantry south through cornstalks and brush to the waist-deep river. They waded across under fire from Federation and then dashed through the chaparral to the rocks at the western end of the hill. There, sheltered by a hodgepodge of boulders, they paused to catch their breath and peer upward, uncomfortably, at the Mexican infantry deploying along the brow of the hill to meet them.

Support under Captain D. S. Miles hurried across the river to help, and the combined groups began to clamber up the slope. A third wave, regulars of the Fifth and Seventh Infantry Regiments and Blanchard's Louisiana volunteers, swung around to the south side of the hill and began to ascend at an oblique slant toward El Soldado, the main redoubt at the ridge's eastern point. Soldado's guns and the 9-pounder at the west banged nervously away at them, but the Americans were close in and the shells swished harmlessly overhead.

The defenders were badly outnumbered. There were only 175 of them on the hill—one of Ampudia's grave errors lay in not reinforcing Federation promptly in spite of Taylor's diversion—and to them it looked as if the western and southern slopes were acrawl with an invincible horde of attackers. The officer in charge of the 9-pounder ordered his gunners to drag the weapon back to El Soldado. In their haste they upset it, fell into a panic, and took to their heels.

With a shout of triumph Worth's artillerymen-turned-infantry righted the cannon and began pumping shells at El Soldado. At this the American regulars coming obliquely up the slope at the redoubt raised a cheer and pressed harder. The dismounted Texans pushed ahead along the ridge top. The squeeze was too much for the Mexicans. Abandoning El Soldado's two guns, they fled down the snout of the ridge and across the river into the city.

The Americans hoisted their flag over the captured redoubt, swung the Mexican pieces around, and dueled across the canyonlike gap between the ridges with the heavier guns on Independence Hill until darkness and a fresh rainstorm halted the action. The Texans retired to care for their horses; the others huddled down wet and hungry inside El Soldado to wait for dawn. It had been a signal triumph, won at a modest cost of twenty men killed or wounded.[16]

The story was far different at the other end of Monterrey. At about 8:00 A.M. Taylor had deployed his forces for the diversionary attack on the city's northeastern section. The 1st Division took the left flank. (Its general, David Twiggs, was ill, and Lieutenant Colonel John Garland was commanding.) Major General William O. Butler's 3rd Division of volunteers made up the rest of the line—Quitman's brigade of Tennesseans and Davis' Mississippi Rifles next to the regulars and, on the right, Hamer's Kentucky and Ohio volunteers.

Engineer Mansfield led skirmishers ahead through cornstalks and across stone walls toward El Tenería, keeping far enough to the left to avoid the guns of the Citadel. Garland was to come in after Mansfield with his regulars and the Baltimore volunteers, ready to attack as Mansfield directed. Somehow directions got fouled up. Garland's 1st Division slid off too far to the right and ended up in a tangle of huts and stone walls and irrigation ditches. One of the redans beyond the ravine hammered them from dead ahead. The tannery enfiladed them from the left. One of the Citadel's big 18-pounders slammed out grape and canister from the right. And beyond the ravine, firing murderously between the redans and the tannery, was a fort they had known nothing about until its shot came smashing into their faces: El Diablo.

Most of the Baltimore volunteers broke and ran. Bragg's battery was ordered out into the open, exposed to all the enemy cannon, to support the attack. But support what, exactly? The American line had fragmented into confused clusters of men flattened behind walls and under trees or running along the lanes in search of something solid to grip.

Carried almost blindly ahead by their own momentum, a hundred men under Captain Electus Backus burst across the ravine between the redans and El Diablo and found shelter among the buildings there. Cut off so, they did not receive Garland's order to retire. Finding the houses empty, they crawled experimentally up onto the roofs. Peering over the two-foot parapets, they found they could see down inside the earthen walls of the nearest redan to the west and into parts of the tannery yard as well. Methodically they began picking off the enemy in the redan, interrupting themselves now and then to snipe at Mexicans on the roof of a distillery nearby. More Taylor luck: he had a toehold without knowing it. Nor did the Mexicans in the redan and in the tannery, distracted by the crash and smoke of their own guns and by the flitting wraiths out front, realize at first where the damaging fire was coming from. Before the awareness dawned, a brand-new set of circumstances came into being.

Having committed almost his entire 1st Division to this

"diversion" Worth had requested, Taylor now had to bail it out. As Garland's men began to withdraw, Taylor sent Quitman's brigade ahead toward the tannery to steady them. It, too, took a terrible beating from the different forts and was ordered to fall back.

Again, not everyone received the order. Some of the Tennessee and Mississippi volunteers had crossed the ravine and were linking up with Backus' men, whose fire had at last been spotted by the Mexicans in the exposed redan.[17] The discovery came just as the defenders found themselves running short of ammunition.[18] They panicked. Young Barna Upton saw, or thought he saw, two officers jump atop the redan's wall and hold out their swords by the point to signify surrender. One was shot; the other leaped back inside the works and fled with his men for El Diablo.[19] The survivors in the distillery followed. Part of the attacking force swarmed inside the vacated strong points. More slanted off toward El Tenería, finding cover behind the buildings Ampudia had failed to remove. Disheartened by the sudden collapse of the redan and of the distillery, the tannery's garrison yielded. In swept the Americans, to capture three officers, thirty or more men, and four small cannon.[20]

The limited success was not matched farther out in the suburbs among the cornfields and orchards, the hedges and ditches. Terrible confusion prevailed there. Some of Quitman's men were retiring as ordered. The withdrawal became a rout as lancers pursued them, pausing now and then to discharge their carbines between the shoulders of slow runners or to thrust their lances through wounded men they found huddled helplessly against the wall and hedges.[21] At that point Taylor realized that the tannery had fallen. He countermanded the order to retreat. Colonel Jeff Davis of the Mississippians and Colonel W. B. Campbell of the Tennesseans rallied their men for a scattering charge toward the strong points masking El Diablo. Hamer's Ohioans came in on the right, but got smashed hard both by the unsuspected *tête-de-pont* at the Purísima Bridge and by the enfilading guns of the Citadel.

Driven back, the Ohioans joined the mixed mass of regulars and volunteers who were re-forming to join the thrust against El Diablo. Driving past the captured redan and distillery, they swung into the outermost streets, hoping to take the enemy fortress from the rear. Taylor was with the attackers, cool as frost under fire. Butler was there, too, but not so lucky: he was shot painfully through the fleshy part of one leg.

Ridgely came up with his field battery and unlimbered. Fieldpieces, however, were not adapted to fighting in the narrow streets. Working out of sight behind a corner, gunners would load and level one of the 6-pounders. Men across the way pulled the piece into the street with ropes. The gunners leaped after it, turned it, fired, then ducked back and pulled the gun after them with more ropes.[22] The effort did not accomplish much. The little shells merely chipped the stone barricades stretched across the street openings. Meantime Captain Lucien B. Webster's men worked a 24-pounder within range of El Diablo but caused no appreciable damage to that stoutly walled fortress.

Unable to enlarge his bridgehead, Taylor ordered his men out of town as evening came on, save for some regulars, who garrisoned the captured redan and the liquorless distillery, and for the Kentuckians and Ridgely, who stayed in El Tenería. It was a tough night. Heavy rain fell, and they had neither food nor blankets to soften their vigil. Now and then the Citadel lofted a shell off in their direction through the inky darkness. In the main the desultory bombardment caused no harm, except for one ball that chanced to land among a small party strengthening an outer breastwork; it beheaded one man and injured another.[23]

All told, the diversion cost Taylor 394 officers and men killed or wounded. Small wonder that Ampudia considered it the main attack and Worth's column the distraction. To that extent the American strategy succeeded. The Mexicans failed to brace themselves against Worth as stoutly as they should have.

At twilight, just as Taylor's bedraggled fighters were returning to their camp in Walnut Springs, Worth ordered Lieutenant Colonel Thomas Childs to take five hundred men, including two hundred of Hays's and Walker's dismounted Texans, through the rocks and brush to the northwestern base of Independence Hill. Crouching there, they kept the locks of their muskets covered against the rain until 3:00 A.M. Then whispered commands passed down the line to start the prearranged assault. Two columns formed in the darkness and inched up opposite rear flanks of the hill. Their intent was to converge on the summit strong point at dawn.

The slopes were almost a thousand feet high at that point and almost perpendicular. The shivering, rain-drenched attackers had to grope for handholds, drag themselves from thorn bush to thorn bush, boost and pull each other. The drip of rain and rumble of thunder helped cover the sound of their floundering but also increased awkwardness, for the slipping, panting men had to keep the priming of their guns dry as they climbed.

They fell behind schedule. At the first glimmer of daylight on Tuesday morning, September 22, startled Mexican pickets, who deemed the hill unassailable, spotted the advance when it was only a little more than halfway up the slope. Grimly the Americans held their fire and quickened their pace up the cliff-like steeps, dim shapes in the dawn. The persistent Mexican error of firing their overloaded cartridges too high saved the attackers once again. Almost untouched, they reached more level ground, came to their feet with a yell, and charged the summit redoubt.

The Mexicans threw one of their two cannons down the hillside. The other they managed to drag with them along the broad, open ridge top to shelter inside El Obispado, the Bishop's

Palace. Too winded to pursue, the Americans sank down inside the captured strong point. Fortunately for them, the Palace had been constructed in such a way that none of its guns could be brought around to sweep the ridge at its rear.

Down at the base of the hill James Duncan's artillerymen dismantled a 12-pounder, then carried it piece by piece up the back end of the ridge—a two-hour job. During the same two hours attack parties moved up the sides, mostly out of sight of the defenders in El Obispado.

No diversion protected them this morning. Save for relieving the wet, hungry garrisons in the captured redan and tannery (a movement uncomfortably exposed to shelling from the Citadel and El Diablo), Taylor kept his men in camp at Walnut Springs, licking their wounds. Taking advantage of the lull, Ampudia ordered lancers and infantry up the gentler east slope of Independence Hill to reinforce the Palace. From there the fresh troops were to sally along the ridge top and retake the summit strong point.

The cavalry came through the back gate boldly, lances fluttering. But they were badly crowded on the ridge top, and they had no accurate idea of how many Americans had also reached the summit. Charging clumsily, they ran into a crossfire from Texans crouched on either flank. Tumbling back on themselves, they fled either around the Palace and into Monterrey or through the gate they had just left. The barrier slammed shut, but Duncan's newly assembled 12-pounder quickly blew it open. American infantrymen poured through, bayonets busy. By four o'clock that afternoon the second ridge was completely in American hands at even lighter cost than the first: six killed and six wounded. The two-day total of thirty-two was less than one-tenth of the losses Taylor had incurred during Monday's attack on the northeast.

Ampudia was demoralized. The western end of Monterrey was now completely indefensible. A breach had also been made in the northeast. So long as both El Diablo and the Citadel held, this northeastern wedge was not irreparable, but Ampudia's fear led him to decide that he would have to make his final stand in the central part of the city. During the night, accordingly, he pulled his puzzled and resentful troops out of El Diablo and put his men to work erecting more parapets on the rooftops and strengthening the network of barricades at the street corners.

Incredibly, the attacking generals at either end of the town spent the night without communicating. Worth supposed, naturally, that Taylor had sent orders but that they had miscarried. (Actually, none were dispatched.) Should he attack or not? His uncertainty increased when reports arrived that Mexican reinforcements were advancing down the Saltillo road. He ordered a force back toward the mountains to set up a road block. (The Mexicans were in the vicinity but never came into sight.) Finally, hearing guns beyond the city, he decided he had better resume his assault.[24]

From the flags rippling above the captured fortresses, Taylor knew that Independence and Federation Hills were in American hands. Assuming that Worth would continue the attack without further instructions, he determined on Wednesday morning to renew his diversion. Quitman's skirmishers poked cautiously ahead and about 10:30 A.M. discovered that El Diablo was empty. Swinging wide to avoid the fire of the Citadel and the *tête-de-pont* at Purísima Bridge, Taylor's field batteries and infantry pushed into the eastern tip of the city.

The 6-pound shells of the field guns proved no more effective this morning against the masonry barricades than they had on Monday. To increase the frustration, snipers on the roof tops cut down the gunners whenever they exposed themselves. The load had to be carried entirely by the infantry.

Fire from the roofs galled them the most. Since they had brought no scaling ladders, the only counter was to batter down each house door and work up through the building's interior to the top. It was slow, heart-chilling business—but better than Monday had been. Cannons did not bother them, and the cover was more solid than it had been in the fields. The Mexicans as a whole were notoriously poor marksmen, especially under pressure, and as the Americans beat their way slowly ahead, casualties were far lighter than they had been during the first day of the battle.

Taylor stayed close to the front of the fighting. He personally directed the smashing of some of the doors. At one point Private Upton saw him calmly munching a piece of bread and sugar he had taken from a captured grocery. But though his courage inspired his men, it could not stitch the confused, widely separated little combats into a coherent pattern. In midafternoon he gave orders to withdraw. His intent, he wrote later in his report, was to make contact with Worth, coordinate efforts, and launch a general assault in the morning.[25]

Worth, meantime, was fighting desperately on the other side of the Cathedral. On hearing Taylor's guns he had sent a charge down the hill from the Bishop's Palace, Hays's and Walker's Rangers in the lead. They had no trouble at first; the captured guns behind them had led the Mexicans to abandon the western suburbs. But at the cemetery, Campo Santo, they ran into barricades and, like Taylor on the east, had to fight ahead house by house.

Taylor's withdrawal let Ampudia throw heavy reinforcements into the western sector. Worth's men ducked from the streets into the houses. Using picks and bars from the captured hill forts, they broke holes from one building into the next. Artillerymen taught them how to set a three-second fuse on a six-inch shell, toss it through the opening, drop flat for the blast, and then crawl ahead into the reeking room. By dark they were within a block of the central plaza.

Other developments frightened Ampudia still more. Some of

Childs's artillerymen dragged a cannon off Federation Hill to a point on the south bank of the river from which they could shell the plaza. Webster pushed his 24-pounder howitzer into El Tenería, and he too could probe the plaza with grapeshot. A mortar crew managed to work its weapon around the Citadel to the cemetery. Three lighter pieces had been hoisted onto a roof near the post office.[26] Thus the plaza, the market place, and the Cathedral were exposed to cannon fire from every direction except the north.

Townspeople were jammed with the army and with hundreds, even thousands, of cavalry horses into the open squares. Powder was stored in the Cathedral. A few probing shots fired by the Americans just before dark spread panic through the crowds. In despair Ampudia sent Colonel Francisco Moreno under a flag of truce to Taylor with a proposal that for the sake of the noncombatants the Mexican Army yield the city and retire with all military matériel. Taylor replied with a demand for unconditional surrender. Ampudia then requested a personal interview. The upshot was a meeting of commissioners from both sides to work out an armistice. The American representatives were Worth, Jefferson Davis, and James P. Henderson, commander of the Texas volunteers.

The Mexicans got the best of the bargain.[27] Their army retained its small arms, a field battery of six guns, and twenty-one rounds of ammunition. They agreed to retire within seven days beyond a line running from Linares northwest through Rinconada (the mountain pass between Monterrey and Saltillo) and on toward Monclova, roughly the course of the Sierra Madre Oriental range. Both sides promised to fight no more for eight weeks, unless their governments ordered otherwise.

Why was Taylor so generous? For one thing, he did not know how close to sheer terror the people inside Monterrey were. But he did know how badly he himself had been hurt, and so did Ampudia. The Mexican general (who of course was trying to make his own case look good) estimated American casualties at 1,500, an exaggeration, no doubt. Still, persistent whispers at the time said that Taylor never revealed the full story of his losses.[28] Be that as it may, the official figures were stark enough: 142 dead, 16 of them officers, and 364 wounded. (Only 77 of the total were from among Worth's men.) The Citadel still held out, and to storm it even after the city proper had fallen would have been expensive indeed. He was short of supplies and probably could not have held the Mexicans if they had decided to break out of the city and escape. Certainly he could not fight another battle without time to bring up new strength. With all these arguments, his staff agreed.[29]

Later, after the terms of the armistice had been criticized, Taylor offered additional explanations. Civilians would have been the chief sufferers in further fighting. Ampudia assured him that Santa Anna wanted peace, and that more bloodshed was unnecessary. Familiar through Alexander Mackenzie with Polk's intrigue, Taylor was inclined to credit Ampudia's statement. "It is not unknown to the government," he wrote testily on November 8, "that I had the very best reason for believing the statement of General Ampudia to be true."[30]

Ampudia's troops began their withdrawal on September 25. They did not halt at Saltillo, the nearest city beyond the armistice line, and start preparations for more fighting. Instead they marched on past Buena Vista and through the bleak deserts to San Luis Potosí arriving in the middle of October. So perhaps Ampudia really did believe there would be peace. Or perhaps he hoped to lure Taylor out into the killing deserts beyond. No one, including Taylor, could be sure.[31]

Santa Anna had reached San Luis Potosí only a day or two before. He had been moving very cautiously, since his landing at Veracruz, and had not entered Mexico City until September 14, to the huzzahs of a carefully staged welcome. On September 17 Salas officially named him commander in chief of the Army of Liberation. Santa Anna made a flaming speech: "Every day that passes without fighting in the north is a century of disgrace for Mexico!"[32] On September 28 he started for San Luis Potosí, there to gather troops for what he promised would be his climactic effort.

7

SHIFTING STRATEGY

URING THE SUMMER OF 1846 Washington hungered for good news. The war, begun so brightly at Palo Alto and Resaca de la Palma, seemed to have died in its tracks. Silence obscured events in California. In Texas, Gen. Wool was having trouble gathering supplies for his march against Chihuahau. Taylor was bogged down on the Rio Grande. With malicious satisfaction, Whig critics of the administration took to labeling the stagnant state of affairs as "Polk's War." Unless matters improved, the November elections for Congress were likely to go against the Democrats.

The first break in the gloom came September 1 with reports that California had been occupied.[1] Expresses from Taylor added welcome word that at long last he was on the point of moving toward Camargo, first step on the way to Monterrey. Clutching at these straws, the members of Polk's cabinet began wondering what other sections of northern Mexico might be readily acquired. The more pressure that could be applied to the enemy, so the strategists believed, the sooner its government—whether Paredes or Santa Anna, they did not yet know—could be persuaded to start negotiations.

The logical area to invade next, the map studiers decided, was Tamaulipas province, a long stretch of land below the Rio Grande, between the mountains and the Gulf coast. Its capital

was the inland city of Victoria, 160 miles southeast of Monterrey. Its principal port, Tampico, lay at the province's southern
extremity, 250 miles below Matamoros. Once the Navy had
seized Tampico, might not fifteen hundred or two thousand
infantry and cavalry be able to gain control of the rest of the
coastal state?

On September 2 a letter was sent to Taylor, asking his
opinions. Mexican scouts intercepted the dispatch and sent it to
Ampudia, who forwarded it to Santa Anna.[2]

Prospects of expanded activity in Mexico delighted General
Winfield Scott. Following his demotion at the beginning of the
conflict, he had attended dutifully to his desk work in Washington and felt he had earned reinstatement. On September 12
he asked for command of the Army in northern Mexico. "I do
this," he wrote, "without any hesitation in respect to Major
General Taylor, having reason to believe my presence at the
head of the Army in the field, in accordance with my rank, is
neither unexpected nor undesired by that gallant and distinguished commander."[3]

Scott was partly right about Taylor. During the harassments
of the summer, the general on the Rio Grande had written to
more people than was perhaps judicious of his desire to be
relieved so that he could attend to his plantation in Louisiana.[4]
That diffidence, however, was evaporating under the heat of his
growing but still unannounced interest in the presidency. Polk,
very suspicious of just this turn of events, had no desire either
to add to Taylor's stature or to put Scott in a position where
the presidential boomlet could be shifted to him. Coldly he
ordered Marcy to deny Scott's application.[5] But no method of
sidetracking Taylor had yet occurred to him.

At that point, on September 19, Santa Anna's rejection of
Buchanan's offer to negotiate with Paredes reached Washington. The cabinet members, naïve in the ways of intrigue, were
shocked. This—from the man they had boosted back into

power so that he could help them! But the letter also contained its small loophole: no final action could be taken until after the Mexican Congress had assembled on December 6, 1846.

The speculation about Tamaulipas now solidified to determination, in the hope that its seizure would influence the enemy legislature as well as the American electorate. Furthermore, Brigadier General Robert Patterson was to command the campaign. Only after Taylor had provided Patterson with the troops he needed was the ostensible commander in chief of the army in northern Mexico to march a subordinate column as far south toward San Luis Potosí as seemed feasible.

Robert Patterson's military experience consisted of a brief army hitch, at the age of sixteen, in the War of 1812. Since then he had become a highly successful Philadelphia merchant —and a loyal Democrat. On those grounds Polk had named him, early in the war, a general of volunteer troops. His particular charge was the sprawl of noisome volunteer camps from the mouth of Rio Grande to Camargo.

So long as he was in the area, Zachary Taylor was his commander. That being so, Marcy showed singular lack of judgment when, following Polk's directive and disdaining prior consultation with Taylor, he ordered Patterson, on September 22, to implement a land invasion across Tamaulipas to Tampico.[6] Commodore Conner was simultaneously instructed to prepare a naval assault against the port city.

By another letter of that same date, September 22, Marcy directed Taylor to provide Patterson with four thousand troops. As he had in his letter of September 2, the Secretary requested specific data about Tamaulipas and then asked whether Taylor could move the rest of his men toward San Luis Potosí.[7]

Elections were near, and there was no time to wait for the general's answer. A great bustle began in Washington. Quartermaster General Jesup prepared to go in person to New

Orleans to undo the snarls in forwarding supplies. Armchair planners, spreading out their maps, let their eyes slip easily down the coast to Veracruz, Mexico's principal port, and suggested increasing the pressure on the enemy Congress still more by capturing that harbor as well as Tampico. Scott was asked for a memorandum on the possibilities—just an attack on Veracruz, for no one supposed yet that an advance against Mexico City might prove necessary. Warmed by its own exercise, the cabinet grew confident that this display of vigor would surely put the country in a Democratic mood for the balloting on November 3.

Into this glow of anticipation came, on October 11, one of Taylor's aides, bearing the general's reports of the three-day battle for Monterrey and of the armistice that had ended the fighting. Throughout the country, bells pealed and more Whig editorial writers climbed aboard Taylor's presidential band wagon.

Monterrey was no victory in Polk's eyes, however. For one thing, the eight-week armistice completely upset the Tamaulipas time schedule. For another, the Tamaulipas invasion might not have been necessary at all if only Taylor had pressed harder. Angrily the President wrote in his diary, "He had the enemy in his power & should have taken them prisoners . . . and preserved the advantage he had obtained by pushing on without delay." Now the Mexicans could regroup and fight again.[8]

At its meeting the next morning, October 12, the cabinet was not quite so acidulous. Some of the members suggested that the Mexican general, Pedro de Ampudia, may well have led Taylor to believe that the intrigue with Santa Anna was still simmering. Or perhaps Taylor's small army had not been strong enough to contain the enemy—though if there were mitigating circumstances, it was strange the general had neglected to mention them. The thing to do, the group finally decided, was to censure Taylor only by implication. The War Department should order him to terminate the armistice immediately. Furthermore, although Marcy should praise the army for its valor at Monterrey, there was to be no specific mention of the commanding general.

Polk, who possessed the normal human failing of interpreting decisions in the light of his own desires, considered the letter that Marcy wrote after the meeting to be a stern rebuke.[9] Actually, save for what Taylor might choose to read into its silences, it was comparatively mild and concerned mostly with ending the armistice so that the Tamaulipas and possibly the San Luis Potosí campaigns could proceed without further delay. Marcy also mentioned in this dispatch the newly proposed idea of an attack on Veracruz.[10]

During this time of planning in Washington, three long weeks away from Monterrey as dispatches traveled, Taylor was busy establishing a military government for conquered Nuevo León province, sending out patrols, and pleading by mail with the Quartermaster's department for supplies of all kinds. Knowing from painful experience how ill-disciplined his volunteers were, he confined them as closely as he could to the camp at Walnut Springs and turned the patrolling of Monterrey over to Worth's regulars. This brought the troopers into fresh contact with Mexican priests. As other Irish, English, and German Catholic immigrants had done at Matamoros, several dozen deserted to join the earlier defectors in what soon took formal shape as the San Patricio Battalion.

When the mounted Texans proved completely unruly, Taylor disbanded them.[11] He had special assignments for a few of the leading Rangers, however. He asked Ben McCulloch to keep himself in readiness for further scouting activities when hostilities resumed.[12] He sent Jack Hays and Sam Walker east to find Samuel Colt and contract for a thousand revolving pistols, to be modified according to Walker's specifications from the original model. (Walker never got to use one of those famous Walker-model Colt revolvers he designed. After his visit in the East, where he and Hays called on President Polk, he rejoined the Army for the thrust against Mexico City. On October 11, 1847, he was killed by a lancer during mopping-up operations in Huamantla. Meanwhile, a consignment of the new pistols had arrived at Veracruz and was being held on the docks for Walker to pick up.)[13]

On October 12, 1846, Taylor received Marcy's letter of September 22 assigning four thousand men to Patterson for moving against Tampico and asking Taylor about the possibilities of a march toward San Luis Potosí. Because of the interception of the letter of September 2, this was the first Taylor had heard of either proposal. To him the manner in which Marcy asked for his opinion about "conducting the [Tamaulipas] enterprise" was so offhand as to amount to little more than an insulting afterthought—especially since the enterprise had already been assigned over his head to someone else.

Still, in his reply to his superiors he had to be at least outwardly correct. He began his answer by pointing out that neither campaign could be launched until after the expiration of the armistice on November 19. Santa Anna, meanwhile, was assembling a huge army at San Luis Potosí. Taylor could not push south across the deserts against that formidable gathering with fewer than twenty thousand men, half of them regulars, plus another five thousand for keeping his supply lines open.

Those objections raised, his letter began to ramble in spite of skillful editing by his adjutant and future son-in-law, William Bliss. Concerning the Tamaulipas project: it was probably feasible in spite of the danger of yellow fever. However, any thinning out of American strength might tempt Santa Anna to strike. As it was, Taylor had only thirteen thousand effectives scattered between Matamoros and Monterrey. With so few troops at his disposal to face Santa Anna's very real threat, he could hardly spare three or four thousand men for Patterson's use in Tamaulipas. Actually, if strong offensive operations were wanted, why not raise an additional twenty-five thousand men in the United States and drive through Veracruz at Mexico City? But of course such an expedition would be costly. His own preference would be to forget San Luis Potosí. If necessary he—not Patterson, notice—would of course join the Navy in an assault on Tampico. From that port he would then run a long defensive line northwest through Victoria, Monterrey, and Saltillo. He might hook up with Wool in Chihuahua. Perhaps he could make contact with the forces in Santa Fe. All told, this defensive operation seemed to him the best idea, even though the line he was proposing stretched a staggering fourteen hundred miles in length.[14]

Long though this rambling discussion was, it practically ignored Marcy's request for geographic information about Tamaulipas, a paucity that would enrage Polk when the letter reached Washington. Part of the vagueness arose because Taylor had failed to collect very much data about the area, not having anticipated an advance in that direction. But underneath this surface cause rumbled the deep resentment out of which the general wrote his answer. His suspicions of the administration were growing cancerous. With considerable bitter accuracy he saw Marcy's letter as the opening gambit of a Democratic plot to take the control of the war away from him. For was not Marcy presenting him, a Whig, with an impossible campaign against San Luis Potosí while at the same time giving the campaign which might succeed, the one through Tamaulipas to Tampico, to good Democrat Patterson? Were these things entirely inadvertent?[15]

Taylor could not voice such thoughts to the War Department, of course. But he could object to the way in which he, the commander of the entire northeastern theater, had been short-circuited. Military protocol clearly required that the instructions to Patterson should have gone through him; saving time was not an adequate excuse, for Patterson was at Camargo, only a few more days away by express. Bluntly, Taylor concluded his discursive letter by chiding his superiors. "While I remain in command of the army against Mexico, and am therefore justly held responsible by the government and the country for the conduct of its operations, I must claim the right of organizing all detachments from it and regulating the time and manner of its service."[16]

That blast off his chest, he settled back to reading the newspaper clippings that his son-in-law, Robert Wood, sent him periodically from Point Isabel. He talked at length to favorable newspaper reporters, notably George Kendall of the New Orleans *Picayune*. And he planned assiduously how to counter the Democrats and bring the war back into his own hands as soon as the armistice ended.

The termination came more abruptly than he had anticipated. On November 2, Major John Graham arrived from Washington bearing Marcy's orders, dated October 13, for Taylor to give the Mexicans "requisite notice that the armistice is to cease at once, and that each party is at liberty to resume and persecute [*sic*] hostilities without restriction."[17] Hostilities meant the Tampico campaign. A separate letter went from Marcy to Patterson, telling him to push preparations. Hints were again dropped in both letters that Veracruz might be next.

Not a word of thanks for Taylor's victory at Monterrey accompanied the instructions. He was furious.[18] Politics! he exploded to Wood.[19] Still, he had no choice but to obey. Promptly he dispatched a note to Santa Anna, saying that the armistice was to end on November 13, by which time, so he calculated, his communication would have reached the Mexican general.[20] The change in dates was hardly shattering, for in the normal course of events the ending would have come in less than a week anyhow.

By this time Taylor was beginning to suspect that members of his own army—among them Worth and Brigadier General Gideon J. Pillow, a Democratic wheelhorse and former law partner of Polk's—were mailing home private letters that criticized both the armistice and his handling of the war. To counter their accusations and the implied censure of the administration, he wrote on November 5 a long and (as it would prove to be) injudicious defense of the cease-fire to old General Edmund P. Gaines. In the same letter he salved his wounds by sneering at the administration's still unformulated plans for attacking Veracruz. On November 8 he repeated his justifications of the armistice more formally to Washington: after the hard fighting at Monterrey, he had lacked effectives enough to force a complete capitulation from Ampudia. Besides, he had supposed peace with Santa Anna was in the offing.[21]

Simultaneously he matured his plans for mastering the flow of events. First, he would take Saltillo, fifty-some miles southwest, where he would leave Worth in charge, safely sidelined. Returning to Monterrey, he would join the advance on Tampico, marching through Victoria, the capital of Tamaulipas, while Patterson moved directly south from Matamoros. Patterson's forces would be those the President had requested, and thus Taylor would be meeting the letter of the law. But the orders Patterson followed would be Taylor's.

As Taylor himself had pointed out in his rambling response to Marcy's letter, this shift of a considerable part of his army into Tamaulipas could be risky. If Santa Anna struck northward, Worth would be dangerously exposed in Saltillo. But Taylor, who at that time underestimated the marching abilities of the Mexican foot soldiers, did not really believe that the enemy could cross the desert from San Luis Potosí with enough force to bother Worth seriously.[22] Besides, the Taylor luck was running again. Three thousand hardened reinforcements had unexpectedly become available: General John Ellis Wool's column that had started out from San Antonio late in September to conquer Chihuahua.

The core of Wool's small army was six companies of regulars from the Sixth Infantry. Their immediate commander was Major Benjamin L. E. Bonneville, whom Washington Irving had made famous a few years earlier through a book about Bonneville's adventures as a fur trader in the Rocky Mountains. Supporting these regulars were Captain Enoch Steen's hard-bitten dragoons and a very efficient flying battery of eight small field guns commanded by Captain John M. Washington. Among the topographical engineers was a captain named Robert E. Lee. So much for quality. Quantity was provided by two regiments of Illinois volunteers and one regiment of volunteer cavalry from Arkansas, the last commanded by another personal friend of Polk's, Colonel Archibald Yell, one-time governor of the state and, at the outbreak of hostilities, a member of the national House of Representatives. A handful of Texans served as scouts. Their most notable member was Daniel Drake Henrie of the ill-fated Mier expedition of 1842, who had tunneled out of the massive fortress of Perote near Veracruz and with seven others had escaped to the United States, a spectacular feat the Mexicans had not forgotten.

Supplied by an awkwardly segmented train of five hundred wagons, Wool's men marched in sections westward to the Rio Grande and crossed the river unopposed on a pontoon bridge the engineers had prefabricated in San Antonio.[23] As they entered the dilapidated old town of San Juan Bautista (today's Guerrero), a delegation of Mexicans told them of the fighting at Monterrey and of the armistice that had ended it. Because of the cease-fire, the Mexicans said, the Americans must proceed no farther.

Wool defied them. So far as he could tell from his inadequate maps, the armistice line followed the Sierra Madre Mountains. He was nowhere near them yet and thus was free to keep on moving. But in what direction? Chihuahua, his appointed goal, lay some four hundred miles due west of San Juan Bautista. The best information that he could glean, however, said that there was no direct route across the stark mountains and waterless deserts. To find usable roads he would have to detour far to the south.

Unopposed, the marchers set out. Most of the way their sore feet stirred up choking clouds of dust. Occasionally, however, they encountered streams swollen so deep by heavy rains in the distant mountains that the teams drawing the wagons could not keep their footing. It was up to the men, then, to hook long ropes onto each of the five hundred vehicles and haul them inch by inch through the punishing fords. On October 29 they took unresisted possession of the city of Monclova, population 7,000, beautifully situated in a green valley at the foot of bold mountains. There they halted, for at Monclova the armistice did prevail.

By that time Wool had begun to doubt the wisdom of continuing to Chihuahua. To get there he would have to push on south almost as far as Saltillo. And to what end? Reports told him that there were very few enemy troops at Chihuahua. Rather, Santa Anna was calling in every available man to San Luis Potosí. If Wool clung to his original goal, so he wrote Taylor plaintively on November 1, "all that we shall find to conquer is distance."[24] Would it not be better for him to pose a direct threat to San Luis Potosí by capturing Saltillo? He did not know, of course, that Taylor at that very time was planning to do exactly the same thing, using Worth's regulars as his striking force.

This letter came as a happy surprise to Zachary Taylor. During Wool's march there had been no communication between the widely separated commanders, and Taylor supposed that the Chihuahua army long since had passed westward out of reach.[25] Instead it had bobbed up in the nick of time at

Monclova, giving him men enough to mature his own plans.
(He ordered Wool to sit tight in Monclova, until he had decided where the unexpected reinforcements would be most
useful.[26]) With eager new briskness he then assigned twelve
hundred men to Worth and prepared to march with him to
Saltillo, which reconnaissance indicated would not be defended.
From there he would hurry straight back to Monterrey to
assume charge of the operation against Tampico.

On November 11, just before operations began, a special
emissary arrived from Secretary of War Marcy, bearing dispatches dated October 22. Because of Santa Anna's zeal in
declaring for federalism, the missive said, there was little chance
of a revolt in the north, and therefore strategy had changed
once again.[27] Tampico was no longer the main goal; Veracruz
was. The administration had decided that four thousand troops
could land on the coast either above or below that port city
and seize it from behind without the necessity of battering
down the coral-reef fortress of San Juan de Ulúa. Gen. Patterson was to have charge of this newest expedition—if Taylor
could spare fifteen hundred to two thousand more troops, in
addition to those needed in Tamaulipas, without danger to
himself.

The last remark, as Taylor realized, was lip service to his
dignity. The truth came out in Marcy's next paragraph: Taylor could afford to send the troops to Patterson because the
commander in chief himself was not going to need very many.
He was to cancel any plans he may have made for an advance
toward San Luis Potosí and remain in Monterrey. Furthermore,
he was to get in touch with Wool, if possible, and ask him
to help provide the troops Patterson would need for the Veracruz expedition. These troops were to be represented as part
of the Tampico campaign, so that the Mexicans would not
suspect the eventual strike farther south.[28]

Taylor, coldly furious at this interruption of his own

schemes, chose to obey only those parts of the directive that suited him. He wrote Marcy that he had already halted Wool's march toward Chihuahua. He said that it would be folly for him to remain in Monterrey and that he was going to push forward as far as Saltillo; that city, besides being an important breadbasket for Santa Anna, was a vital road hub for highways radiating to San Luis Potosí, Chihuahua, Monclova, and Monterrey. If Santa Anna were allowed to entrench himself there, the entire American line in northern Mexico would be endangered. He concluded this letter with remarks that edged toward insolence. In proposing to send only four thousand men against Veracruz, he said, his superiors were showing neither prudence nor foresight.[29]

This remarkable letter sent on its way, Taylor marched with Worth to Saltillo, occupying that city on November 16. While there he heard that Tampico had been abandoned by its Mexican garrison. At first he did not believe the rumor, but on returning to Monterrey, November 23, he received confirmation. Santa Anna, having learned through the intercepted letter of September 2 that the Americans planned to attack the city, had ordered it evacuated. Tampico was next to indefensible against naval cannon. Furthermore, the Mexican general meant to reorganize his entire army at San Luis Potosí for a grand onslaught against the invaders, and he did not wish to fritter away bits and pieces of his potential force in widely scattered, inconclusive actions.[30] In obedience to his orders, the Mexican garrison had marched away from the city toward San Luis on October 27. On November 12, American naval vessels inched into the harbor without opposition.

Knowledge of the effortless conquest caused Taylor to adjust his thinking. The need for a land attack on Tampico, ultimate goal of the Tamaulipas campaign, had vanished—yet he had six thousand troops ready to move. He decided to concentrate them against Victoria, the provincial capital, which in his earlier planning had been only a way station on his proposed march to Tampico. Still, the Victoria campaign was not il-logical—at least on paper. A strong American base there would threaten the flank of any advance Santa Anna might make northward from San Luis Potosí toward Saltillo or Monterrey. If adequate roads to the interior existed—that unreconnoitered "if" about transport was the great weakness of the whole Victoria scheme—the provincial capital might even be developed into a staging point for an attack on Mexico City through the interior. More importantly, in Taylor's thinking, Victoria might be developed into an important bastion in a holding line across northeastern Mexico.

This last was a stubborn clinging to the concept with which the war had begun: seize territory in the north and then sit on it until the Mexicans were ready to bargain. Marcy's letters about Veracruz were clear indications that the administration was at last abandoning that fruitless idea. Taylor, though, still felt that the plan was sound. Fuller and swifter communications with his civilian superiors in Washington might have cleared the air, but that is conjectural. Both he and Polk were men of narrow vision, suspicious and obstinate. Closer contact might simply have resulted in a quick explosion and Taylor's removal from command. As it was, he stayed just far enough ahead of the slowly traveling directives to manipulate matters as he thought best for the country . . . and for himself. If the Mexicans resisted his advance against Victoria, he might not only deal them a crippling blow but also brighten his image in American newspapers. Staying obediently in Monterrey would do neither.

Quite unintentionally, General Wool gave him more cause to defy Marcy's orders. The situation in Monclova was touchy. Prevented by the armistice from moving ahead, Wool had been forced to let his entire army and its sprawling wagon trains congregate in the little city. Soon upwards of three thousand idle soldiers and teamsters were at loose ends among a supine enemy. The same sort of arrogance and disorder that had plagued Taylor on the Rio Grande now began to strike sparks of resentment from the inhabitants. In their own way the officers proved as offensive as the rank and file. On Sundays they rode in full regalia, escorted by dragoons, to the doors of the cathedral, dismounted, brushed the humbler worshipers out of their way, and strode inside, spurs and swords and pistols clanking in the hushed sanctuary.[31]

An able commander but an unyielding martinet, Wool did not let discipline slip as far out of hand as Taylor had on similar occasions. But his heavy-handed methods created their own forms of trouble. W. H. L. Wallace, adjutant of one of the Illinois regiments (and not to be confused with Lew Wallace of Indiana), wrote caustically that the old general was so vain, senile, and unpopular that the War Department had been "criminally foolish for putting him in command."[32] Colonel William S. Harney grew so infuriated at Wool that he requested permission to withdraw but was refused, unless specific orders came from Taylor. Just when tempers were hottest, Inspector General Sylvester Churchill arrived from the Rio Grande. A colonel by actual rank, he had no command of his own. But he was a regular. Wool gave him precedence over the volunteer colonels in the line, a flaunting of their dignities that turned them almost purple.[33]

Harried by the crumbling of his army's morale, Wool was dismayed to receive Taylor's orders that he sit tight in Monclova. He bombarded the general with pleas that he be allowed to take his men deeper into Mexico, where there was some chance of seeing action. Finally he sent his aide, Lieutenant Irvin W. McDowell, to Monterrey to enlist the cooperation of Taylor's adjutant, Perfect Bliss. By letter, Wool importuned Bliss, "This is a favorable time for operating against the enemy. Take time by the forelock and push on before the enemy collects a large force against us. Urge the general to concentrate his forces. . . . Urge the general not to leave us here. Go we must; and when an opportunity occurs, we will do good service."[34]

The plea stiffened Taylor's determination to create a powerful holding line in direct disobedience of Marcy's order to stay in Monterrey. He directed Wool to advance south and east to the agricultural town of Parras on the roundabout road between Saltillo and Chihuahua, 180 miles beyond limits Washington had specified. Monclova meantime was not to be abandoned but garrisoned by three companies under Captain W. M. Warren.

McDowell carried these orders full tilt back to Wool, who had already anticipated them by sending reconnoitering parties out into the mountains beyond Monclova. The main body of troops followed on November 24. Although it was a cold, rigorous march between towering peaks and along echoing gorges, it did not end the squabbling among the men. Protesting that his Arkansas cavalry always received the poorest campgrounds —skimpy grazing downstream from the rest of the army's filth —Colonel Archibald Yell one night refused to accept a designated spot and picked his own. Before the affair was finally settled, Yell, his lieutenant colonel, J. S. Roane, and Major Solon Borland had been placed under arrest and their regiment had come to the verge of mutiny three hundred miles deep in enemy territory.[35]

On December 5, the grumbling column marched into Parras. It was a long strip of town, located in a valley where springs came sparkling down out of the mountains. Mud walls enclosed some of the best vineyards in Mexico—*parras* means vines. Farther out were fields of grain. The inhabitants were sullen but curious. After the troops had set up camp, even high-born ladies thronged out to look, riding in huge, ornate carriages pulled by tiny mules tinkling under silver trappings.[36]

Wool issued stern orders about respecting noncombatants. This did not sit well with his men. Mexican *vaqueros* sometimes roped and beat stragglers whom they caught outside camp. According to Sam Chamberlain's lurid reminiscences, *My Confession*, one American soldier "was stripped naked, and dragged through clumps of cactus . . . his privates cut off and crammed into his mouth." Sam was given to exaggerations, but perhaps that tale approximated the truth, for another Illinois volunteer also reported the molestation of stragglers and added grimly, "The old Gen. tries to keep the Volunteers under the strictest subjugation but we will do a great deal as we please in spite of the old Woolly Devil."[37]

To keep such attitudes under control, Wool drilled the men hard. He sent out far-ranging reconnoitering parties, and he foraged diligently to provide provisions both for his own men and for parts of Taylor's army farther east. More importantly, he was depriving Santa Anna of a principal source of foodstuffs.[38] And, without knowing it, he was, just by being there, furthering Taylor's private strategy.

So much for the western end of the holding line. The one point remaining to make it solid was Victoria.[39] Then, just as Taylor was about to march, he learned that the Navy had interfered. Fearful that the quiet in Tampico might hide a trap, the commodore of the invasion fleet had sent a request to Matamoros for a thousand reinforcements. Without consulting Taylor, Gen. Patterson prepared to dispatch the men by sea from the pool he had been collecting for his and Taylor's invasion of Tamaulipas province.

Taylor flew into a passion.[40] It was high time that this underling learned his place, even though Patterson was a pet of the President of the United States.[41] On November 28 Taylor sent an express at breakneck gallop to the Philadelphian, ordering the troops held and voicing his "entire disapproval" of Patterson's action. He followed this letter with an icy rebuke to

Washington, protesting Patterson's "direct and unwarrantable interference with plans . . . for a combined movement upon Victoria" and insisting that hereafter his subordinate not be encouraged to "mischievous meddling"—strong words to lay before Polk himself, especially from a man who himself was hardly being obedient to his own superiors.[42] But conceivably he did not expect them to remain as his superiors. On December 10, during the height of the Patterson tempest, he at last admitted to Robert Wood that he would probably consent to serve as President "if the good people were inprudent enough to elect me."[43]

And, he might have added, if the newest strategy shaping up in Washington did not succeed in diminishing him to full obscurity.

8

OUT ON A LIMB

Partly because of the unsatisfactory progress of the war, the November elections went against the Democrats, and the Whigs gained tenuous control of the House of Representatives, 117–110. To Thomas Hart Benton of Missouri, the leader of the Democratic bloc in the Senate, the reason was clear. "Ours is a go-ahead people," he told Polk impatiently. Conquering outlying provinces that possessed little essential value to the enemy and then trying to outwit the Mexicans was not the way the American nation should handle the problem. Nor was Taylor a go-ahead general. As evidence, Benton cited the rambling, uninformative letter Taylor had written on October 15, during the first discussions of a campaign in Tamaulipas, which the senator from Missouri had been permitted to read. He joined Polk in deploring the armistice with Ampudia. Clearly, as Polk already had said, Taylor was "unfit for command."[1]

What was needed, Benton continued, was a "bold blow." First, Veracruz should be seized—a drive that the administration had already determined to make. Next there should be a "rapid, crushing movement" toward Mexico City—a thrust that Taylor had touched upon, not very enthusiastically, in the same discursive letter Benton and Polk were so roundly condemning.

Polk nodded his complete agreement. He was growing more

and more displeased with Taylor. Recent letters from Gideon Pillow and others in Monterrey said that the general was being controlled for political purposes by "cunning & shrewd men": by Adjutant Bliss; by Kendall of the New Orleans *Picayune*, who was openly promoting Taylor's presidential boom; and by Bailie Peyton of Worth's staff, who had been an outspoken and violent political opponent of Polk's in Tennessee.[2] Under their aegis Taylor had turned hostile to the administration and thought only of himself. "This is most reprehensible on his part," Polk complained to his diary early in November, "for I have not only treated [him] with kindness, but have given him his present promotion. I have known nothing of politics in my treatment of him, but am forced to believe he . . . has suffered political feeling to have more to do with his conduct than he should have done."[3]

Such a Whig manifestly was not to be entrusted with a climactic campaign against Mexico City. How about Scott. Another Whig? Benton waved in disparagement: "no confidence in him."

Who then?

Benton was ready with his answer—Thomas Hart Benton, naturally, provided that Congress would create for him the new rank of lieutenant general, so that he would be clearly superior to both Scott and Taylor. He further nominated himself to be chairman of a bipartisan peace commission that would travel with the army, prepared to come to terms with the Mexicans as soon as the rapid, crushing movement had produced, as it inevitably would, fatal rifts "between the Spanish who monopolize the wealth and power of the country, and the mixed Indian races who bear its burthens."[4] Those modest proposals offered, he listened complacently while Scott, in obedience to the President's request, presented to the cabinet on November 12 a memorandum concerning the forces he deemed necessary to advance from Veracruz to Mexico City.[5]

The numbers of men and the cost involved frightened the President's advisers. Furthermore, the vanguard of the force would have to be assembled rapidly in order that Veracruz could be taken before the advent of the yellow-fever season. One way to save time and some money would be to draw the men from Taylor's command, for they were relatively near the scene of the proposed action and could be shipped out through both Matamoros and Tampico.

By Scott's figures (which were too high), Taylor had twenty thousand regulars and volunteers available in northeastern Mexico—assuming he had succeeded in halting Wool, a matter not yet known in Washington. Nine thousand men could be taken from him for launching the southern campaign. This would leave him 8,500 volunteers and 2,500 regulars for holding a shortened version of the defensive line Taylor himself had proposed in his rambling letter of October 15. Faced with that many men in the north, Santa Anna would not dare leave San Luis Potosí unguarded and would have to split his forces in order to meet the attack on Veracruz.

Reluctantly, because of the cost, the cabinet accepted the plan in principle. They were unanimously opposed to Benton as general in chief, however.[6] After the Missouri senator had left the room, the secretaries pointed out to Polk his lack of military experience and the opposition that the creation of a special rank for him would stir in Congress.

Who then?

Marcy suggested Scott. Polk bristled and quickly raised alternative possibilities: Major General William Orlando Butler of the volunteers and, after Butler had been rejected, Brigadier General Robert Patterson.[7] The cabinet declined him too. (Two days later, on November 20, Taylor's letter protesting the War Department's going over his head in giving orders to Patterson about the Tamaulipas campaign reached Washington. In chill anger Polk termed the rebuke "bad-tempered" and interpreted it as clear evidence that Taylor was trying to provoke a quarrel. "He is evidently a weak man . . . giddy with the idea of the Presidency . . . narrow-minded, bigotted. . . . I have no prejudice against him, but think he has acted with great weakness and folly."[8])

Marcy meanwhile had swung the rest of the cabinet behind Scott. Battered by the full body and unable to find anyone else who could handle the obstreperous Taylor, Polk yielded. On November 19 he summoned the big six-foot four-inch general into his office and officially told him that he was to lead the attack on Mexico City. "He was grateful," the President told his diary, "& so much affected that he almost shed tears."[9]

Politicians were instantly suspicious of Polk's motives. Some thought that the President had made the appointment so that Scott and Taylor would split the country's plaudits and so cancel out each other as potential Whig candidates. Calhoun's suggestion was even more cynical: Polk probably hoped that when Scott drew on Taylor for troops the latter would resign in disgust and so cut his own political throat.[10] No hint of such scheming appears, naturally enough, in Polk's diary. Still, the President was not fully candid with Scott. He did not tell the new general about Benton's proposal, although he had not given it up. In January, after Scott had hurried to Mexico, Polk actually presented Benton's nomination to Congress, but the legislators declined to act on it. Hearing of the double-dealing, Scott was furious and declared passionately that James K. Polk, President of the United States, was "an enemy more to be feared than Santa Anna with all his hosts."[11]

For the time being, however, all was benign. Scott submitted a final memorandum concerning the number of troops he would need from Taylor—the figure jumped from nine to eleven thousand[12]—and hurried to New York to catch ship for New Orleans and the Rio Grande. Knowing Taylor would resent what was happening, he tried to placate him with an oily letter written from New York on November 25.

I am not coming, my dear general, to supersede you. . . . My proposed theater is different. . . . But, my dear general, I shall be obliged to take from you most of the gallant officers and men (regulars and volunteers) whom you have so long and nobly commanded. I am afraid that I shall, by imperious necessity . . . reduce you, for the time, to stand on the defensive. This will be infinitely painful to you, and for that reason distressing to me. But I rely on your patriotism. . . .[13]

In a follow-up letter, written December 20 from New Orleans, Scott explicitly repeated his orders about standing on the defensive, so that every soldier possible could be shifted to the new offensive planned for the south—an offensive in which Taylor was to play no part. He then suggested, as he had in his November letter, that Taylor meet him in Camargo toward the first of the new year, 1847. In neither case did he put the request for a conference as a flat order.

Even before receiving these letters, Taylor was feeling badly put upon. Although clippings regularly forwarded by Wood indicated that the people of the United States were still giving him "an ample share of credit for my sacrifices," he feared, touchily, that the good opinion might not last. For he knew by then that he was being actively denigrated in his own army by "numerous letter-writers & others, envious & sycophantic, who envy acts they cannot emulate."[14] Friends of the chastened Patterson were criticizing Taylor's abrupt handling of that affair. Worse, the self-styled victors in newly occupied Tampico were giving themselves such airs over the capture of that undefended port that they were making Taylor's own elaborate preparations against Victoria seem anticlimactic and unnecessary.

Actually he was running a calculated risk, should Santa Anna choose to strike during the movements. Together he and Patterson were assembling at Monterrey and Matamoros, six thousand of their best men for the attack. Worth had taken another twelve hundred to Saltillo. Finding replacements for those men meant stripping the garrisons along the Rio Grande. Monterrey, for instance, was to be controlled by two regiments of raw Indiana volunteers called up from the mouth of the river. A third regiment of Indianans, left behind, appealed to Patterson for permission to join the others. Haplessly he granted the request and brought more of Taylor's wrath on his head.[15] Would that meddling Democrat never learn whose war this was?

The orders for the Indianans to move came so quickly that transportation was not available for them at Camargo, and the troopers, all but blinded by dust-laden winds, had to break wild mules on the spot in order to move their gear. As rumors of Santa Anna's force at San Luis Potosí grew, some of the officers looked over the tenuous lines of supply and felt misgivings. Lew Wallace, future author of *Ben Hur*, wrote gloomily to his father that with a single battery of four guns the Mexicans could sweep the river and cut Monterrey and Saltillo completely off from all supplies.[16]

Ignoring the criticisms, Taylor went stubbornly ahead. He placed Butler in charge at Monterrey. On December 12 he sent Twiggs's regulars and Quitman's volunteers south along the road to Victoria. On December 15 he followed with an escort of dragoons, pushing hard through the cold, dusty days. On the seventeenth he overtook the main part of his troops at the village of Montemorelos, not quite sixty miles along the road to Victoria. Simultaneously, he himself was overtaken by urgent dispatches from Worth in Saltillo. What they had feared was happening: Santa Anna was about to attack!

In spite of the message's alarmed wording, Taylor still did not believe that a large army could cross the desert from San Luis Potosí. Unconvinced, accordingly, that the danger was acute, he split his forces. The regulars and part of the volunteers continued toward Victoria. Taylor himself turned back with only May's dragoons and his favorite group of volunteers, Jefferson Davis' Mississippi Rifles, brightly clad in white duck trousers and crimson shirts.

In Monterrey, General Butler was more stirred. He rushed orders to the Indianans at Camargo to hurry their preparations. Then, in spite of the unhealed wound in his leg, he marched with what men he had available over the mountains to Saltillo. Behind him came Colonel Humphrey Marshall's regiment of mounted Kentuckians, summoned by Butler away from what they considered their humiliating duty of guarding wagon and mule trains.[17]

Still another messenger raced with the alarm from Worth's headquarters in Saltillo to Gen. Wool in Parras. Haste seemed imperative to prevent Santa Anna from driving in between the two armies. In a swirl of confusion tents were struck, teams harnessed, wagons loaded, and the sick sent to the hospital in town, where nuns agreed to care for them.[18] Within two hours Steen's dragoons were on the road, followed by Bonneville's regulars and Washington's flying artillery. Nearly five hundred wagons strung out behind. The two regiments of Illinois volunteers brought up the rear. It was a difficult march through desolate country. The men were up at three-thirty each morning and did not halt until close to dark. The mountain nights were bitterly cold. For their fires the shivering volunteers ripped up fences, stole furniture, and even wrenched doors off the little mud *jacales* that they passed.

By December 20, Wool's scouts, Robert E. Lee among them, had concluded that the alarm was groundless. Some Mexican troublemaker, perhaps hoping to create just this sort of confusion, evidently had whispered to Worth that Santa Anna was hurrying north to take advantage of the shift of troops toward Victoria. Worth's imagination had done the rest. There was going to be no battle.

Once the movement toward Saltillo had started, however, momentum kept it going. Wool's marchers kept tramping on

as fast as they could through the thick dust and at 1:00 P.M.
on December 21 reached the walled hacienda of Agua Nueva,
some twenty miles south of Saltillo on the road to San Luis
Potosí. There they halted, well pleased with themselves. In less
than four days they had covered 116 miles. This feat, coming
on top of the long walk from San Antonio, led one of Wool's
historians to exclaim that the entire movement was unprecedented in history, "not surpassed by the march of 10,000 Greeks
under Xenophon." A less literary trooper actually on the scene
was more impressed by the fact that twenty horses died of
exhaustion after reaching the last camping ground at Agua
Nueva, but that not a man was laid up.[19]

Taylor had passed through Monterrey on his way to Saltillo when he learned that the alarm was false. Rather than
try to check the centripetal forces Worth had put into motion,
he let them spin on toward their center, Saltillo. He ordered
Wool not to return to Parras but to stay at Agua Nueva, astride
the San Luis road. He told the Second and Third Indiana Regiments to continue on through Monterrey to the Saltillo plains.
(The First Indiana, which was already nearing Monterrey, he
ordered back to the Rio Grande, to punish it for having asked
Patterson for preferential treatment.[20]) Since these dispositions
concentrated most of the troops on the northeastern theater in
the Saltillo region, he told Butler to shift his headquarters to
the same city. He then wearily wheeled his dragoons and Mississippians around and marched once more toward Victoria. He
was sixty-two years old, and the unending miles in the saddle
were beginning to gall.

Wool disliked his assigned location. It offered conveniences,
to be sure. Agua Nueva was a prosperous hacienda, boasting
several flat-roofed buildings useful for many purposes and a
picturesque chapel whose adobe façade rose well above the
walls to a typical Mexican crown of triple arches. There were
several fine springs nearby, ample pitch pine for fuel in the

mountains, and almost limitless flat ground for drill. Strate-
gically, however, the spot had little to recommend it. It was
at the southeastern corner of a broad triangular plain whose
northern apex was the approach to the narrows of La Angostura. Although the ranch did control the main road up from
the south, there were other roads, both east and west, by which
an enemy army could enter the flanks of the plain and cut Wool
away from Saltillo. And, finally, those broad expanses of open
ground were ideally suited to the hard-riding Mexican cavalry,
which Santa Anna was reputed to be assembling in overwhelming numbers.[21]

Wool decided, accordingly, to ride to Saltillo on the afternoon of December 22 and discuss the problem with his fellow
generals. He was accompanied on the trip by his aide, Lt.
McDowell, and by captains Robert E. Lee, George W. Hughes,
and James H. Carleton. Dark and fog caught the small party
in La Angostura. Pinched between the bluffs to the east of the
road and the deeply gullied stream on the west, they had to
dismount and feel their way ahead. Delayed thus, they did not
reach Saltillo until nearly midnight, too late to interrupt either
Worth or Butler, both of whom were ill.

The only satisfaction Wool could obtain from Butler the
next morning was a promise to ride to Agua Nueva and examine
the situation personally as soon as he felt up to it. Somewhat
disconsolately, Wool and Capt. Carleton started back to exposed Agua Nueva. The problems of defense were very much
on the general's mind, and he kept evaluating the terrain they
passed. The pretty hacienda of Buena Vista caught his eye.
Grazing for hundreds of horses, ample water, and acres of flat
ground for tents lay between the ranch and the soaring, saw-
tooth mountains to the east, where firewood was available.
A bit farther on, in the narrows, he halted to examine what
darkness had hidden from him the night before. Steep bluffs
fifty to seventy feet high rose to his left. The dusty road

stretched ahead for more than a mile in plain view. To the right an extraordinary network of gullies twenty or more feet deep coiled down from the eastern hills to the main gulch, only a few paces away from the road.

The pass was a natural barrier: a few cannon placed between the bluffs and the gullies could completely bottle the road. It could not be turned readily to the right because of the deep gulches. But how about the top of the plateau on the left?

He and Carleton reined that way up a ravine to see. A short climb brought them onto an inclined tableland. Strewn with sharp pebbles but almost devoid of vegetation, the ground climbed gently southeastward to the base of precipitous mountains, somewhat more than a mile away from the road. This softly tilted plateau was bordered north and south by two long, broad ravines. These headed well up in the mountains on either side of an outthrusting ridge, whose high point looked like a kind of minor peak standing slightly detached from the more massive summits behind it.

The southern and widest of these bordering ravines slanted from the mountains a little south of west until it reached the north-flowing stream in the narrows. The northern and by far the longer of the ravines took a more northwesterly course to the stream. The distance between them at the base of the mountains was less than half a mile. Where they broke through the bluffs bordering the road, they were close to a mile apart. This wide western section of the plateau, bordering the road, was fringed with four smaller ravines, none of which reached halfway to the mountains. The shortest of these ravines creased the extreme northwestern corner of the trapezoidal tableland. Between it and its neighboring short ravine to the south was a long, narrow, crooked finger of land, its tip touching the road just opposite the most intricate section of the stream's network of gullies.

Wool pointed. There, he told Carleton, at the exact tip of

the finger was the place to put artillery.[22] Infantry support, dug in on the top of the promontory, could see along the road for well over a mile. Other troops stationed at the heads of the subordinate arroyos and along the high ground just back from the edge of the main ravine to the south could keep the enemy (if enemy ever appeared) from striking across the plateau. Indeed, he grew so intrigued with the strong points of the position that he ignored the weaknesses at the base of the mountains.[23] The main ravines were shallow there. Mexican cavalry protected by riflemen on the slopes above might very possibly work their wiry little mustangs along the toes of the hills, come down on the hacienda of Buena Vista from behind, and completely isolate the guns on the road. Without considering this, Wool rode on.

Jitters continued almost daily at Agua Nueva. Mexican patriots, hoping to deter their disloyal countrymen who were supplying the invaders with beef, told the *vaqueros* that Santa Anna was on the way and would soon attend to them. The contractors rushed the tale to headquarters; bugles sounded—and nothing happened. On Christmas morning dust from an American patrol caused another "stampede," as the alarms were called. A bit later Captain Robert E. Lee discovered that rows of white objects glimmering in the moonlight were not the tents of an enemy army, as reported, but a flock of bedded sheep.

Though ludicrous enough in hindsight, the alarms led Butler to appraise Agua Nueva more critically than might otherwise have been the case. Conceding its dangers, he ordered Wool to pull north to the apex of the plain, at the beginning of the narrows, where there was a small hacienda called La Encantada, the Enchanted. During winter La Encantada's spell seemed entirely evil. Fuel was scarce. Cold dusty winds howled continually through the pass, rattling the tents that were the men's only shelter. Disgusted, Wool marched his little army on through La Angostura to the preferable campground near Buena Vista, pleading in justification both its comforts and the advantages of the adjoining battlefield. Irritated by Wool's arrogation of authority, Butler refused to listen. If there was any fighting, he snapped, it would be on the plains near Saltillo, where his engineers were about to prepare redoubts and breastworks. Wool meantime must do as he was told and camp at La Encantada.[24]

During these periods of uncertainty at Agua Nueva, Taylor was receiving a succession of shocks of his own. The first, which overtook him on December 24 while he was riding toward Victoria, was Scott's unctuous letter of November 25, requisitioning troops and putting him on the defensive. He read it with mortification. Another man had been given command of what was to be the decisive campaign against Mexico City! Yet this was not a thing against which he could openly object. Had he not been advocating the very sort of defensive operations to which he was now assigned?

With more mildness than he felt, he replied to the unsettling letter that he was happy to receive any of Scott's orders and would place his troops in position so that the new commander could draw on them as needed. But, he added, he could not meet Scott at Camargo as suggested. Rumor said that the Mexicans were concentrating heavy forces of cavalry at Tula Pass between Victoria and San Luis Potosí, and he wanted to investigate.[25]

Taylor reached Victoria on January 4. That same day Patterson marched into the provincial capital from Matamoros with 1,600 men. Anticlimax—Quitman's volunteers had taken the city without opposition a week earlier, on December 29. Taylor reviewed his united forces, drew their cheers, and then slowly came to the realization that he had put six thousand of his best troops in what might prove to be an uncomfortable cul-de-sac.[26] Enemy cavalry were indeed massing at Tula under Generals Urrea and Valencia. Brevet Colonel May's dragoons, scouting in that direction, bumped into a squadron of them and lost his baggage and his rear guard of ten men as prisoners.[27] Larger forces of the same Mexican cavalry could easily block the long, wretched roads from Monterrey and Tampico by which Victoria had to be supplied. Nor could six thousand men subsist on the countryside. So this grand movement, which Taylor had designed in November as a way to bring himself back into the war, had turned into a fiasco. On January 14 he ordered Victoria abandoned, grumpily aware that even to his admirers he could hardly look, at this juncture, like a conquering hero.

To Scott he had long since ceased looking like one. Taylor's letter of December 26, declining to come to Camargo, reached the general, waiting impatiently at the dilapidated river town, about January 2, 1847. It raised his eyebrows more than a little. Rumors of cavalry, indeed! Twice he had told Taylor to come to Camargo to discuss the all-important business of collecting troops for the Mexico City campaign. Actually Taylor had not yet received the letter of December 20, and would not until January 20. And the directives had been phrased, out of politeness, as requests, not flat orders. Nevertheless, it appeared to Scott's touchy vanity that Taylor was using the most flimsy of pretexts to disregard instructions and avoid confronting the man who had vaulted into the saddle ahead of him.[28]

Well, he could afford to be magnanimous, and he couched his reproof to Taylor in relatively gentle terms. But he could not afford to wait, for he had to land his army at Veracruz before the season of black vomit came to the aid of the enemy. Without consulting Taylor, therefore, he wrote on January 3 directly to Maj. Gen. Butler in Saltillo, demanding 4,500 volunteers, 4,000 regular foot soldiers (including Generals Twiggs and Worth), 500 dragoons, and two field batteries.[29]

This requisition, totaling somewhat more than nine thousand men, probably did not seem unreasonable to Scott. Six weeks earlier in Washington he had proposed taking eleven thousand. That plan, however, had been based on an assumption that twenty thousand men were available in northeastern Mexico. Actually the figure was high by at least three thousand, probably more. To Taylor, therefore, the appropriation would not seem modest, for it would leave him roughly seven thousand men, a mere eight hundred of them regulars, for holding a line two hundred miles long.

Scott sent two copies of the requisition to Taylor. One went by way of Monterrey. Between that city and Victoria, the bearer, Lieutenant John Ritchey, halted, on the evening of January 11, at the hamlet of Villa Gran, near Linares. Unaccompanied by his small escort of dragoons, he went out into the twilight for a stroll. Mexican *vaqueros* lassoed him, dragged him to death, and took his dispatch case. Although the captured papers bore information of highest importance, there is, incredibly enough, no certain proof that they ever reached Santa Anna.[30] Once the loss was known, however, the American commanders had to assume the worst. Although they acknowledged the possibility of Santa Anna's striking at Taylor's weakened army, the consensus, shared by Taylor, was that the Mexicans probably would shift their strength to meet Scott's movement against Veracruz.[31]

The other copy of Scott's orders went by way of Matamoros and reached Taylor about the middle of January, just as he was preparing, unhappily, to abandon Victoria. His resentment bounded. The defensive line to which Scott was relegating him was so enfeebled as to be almost untenable if Santa Anna should choose it as an objective. Furthermore, Taylor had not been given adequate warning that so ruthless a stripping was planned. To him the whole business smacked of political intrigue. Only months ago Scott had been in disfavor. Now he was soaring without restraint. Why? The only explanation that Taylor permitted himself to see was a deliberate plot by Polk and Marcy—and Scott, too—to scuttle his presidential aspirations.

He let his feelings boil over in an angry answer to Scott's letter of January 3. He denied Scott's hint that he had avoided a meeting by not going to Camargo. He called his treatment "unprecedented in our history," and said bluntly, "I cannot misunderstand the objects of the arrangements. . . . I have lost the confidence of the government." Then he struck a martyr's pose. In spite of being sacrificed, he would remain loyal and do his duty.[32]

At least he knew what to do with the six thousand men in Victoria. He sent forty-seven hundred of them off to Scott's rendezvous on Lobos Island below Tampico. With the rest—some field artillery and, as usual, May's dragoons and Davis' Mississippians—he started back toward Monterrey.

Before he arrived, the troops Scott had ordered began leaving the area. Knowledge spread simultaneously that the letter of January 3 outlining American strategy had been captured by the Mexicans. Now what? Fresh alarms shivered throughout the area. Spies told Maj. Gen. Butler, who had been left in command in Saltillo, that an attack was imminent. Had not the wealthier citizens quietly pulled out of the city? Were not the streets filling with cutthroats, obviously sent there to help the Mexican Army when it arrived? According to a related rumor, Santa Anna had recently ordered the alcalde (or mayor) of Saltillo to open the jail so that the prisoners could join the cutthroats. When the alcalde refused, the prisoners rioted. That much at least was true: there was a disturbance in the jail. A sentry fired through the night. The uproar spread. Thinking the promised attack had come, citizens barricaded their houses. Couriers clattered through the narrow streets, the long roll sounded in the barracks, sleepy soldiers caught up their guns and poured into the main plazas. From Saltillo the fright swept to Monterrey. The military governor there (Taylor had not yet arrived) ordered all American civilians—contractors, sutlers, merchants, newspaper correspondents and plain camp followers—to take up arms or be expelled from the city.[33]

Butler decided to concentrate what forces he had left. He pulled his only available reserves, Marshall's Kentucky cavalry and Colonel William R. McKee's Kentucky foot regiment, close to Saltillo. He ordered the small garrison at Monclova to rejoin Wool. Yell's outposts of Arkansas cavalry were drawn back to La Encantada. Listening at last to Wool's arguments about Buena Vista as a defensive strong point, Butler let him establish his camp beside the hacienda. Signals were arranged: two cannon shots from the town if it was attacked, two from Buena Vista if the enemy appeared there.[34] A strong redoubt was finished at the southeast corner of Saltillo, on a slope that commanded both the city and the approaches from Palomas Pass, named for the haunting sound of its doves, to the east, and a pair of 24-pounders were dragged into place. Suffering then from the wound in his leg, Butler prepared to return to Monterrey and named Brigadier General Joseph Lane of Indiana as military governor of Saltillo. Briskly Lane barricaded the streets and prepared the churches as defense bastions in case the Mexicans managed to reach the city proper.[35] Reconnaissance intensified. Major Solon Borland, later a United States Senator from Arkansas, led fifty men across the mountains and deserts beyond Agua Nueva to a big walled hacienda called La Encarnación. Their guide was Daniel Drake Henrie, who had covered this same stretch with the Mier prisoners of 1842. The day after the patrol reached Encarnación, along came thirty Kentuckians, who had gone east out of Saltillo through Palomas Pass and then had ridden south along the other side of the mountains to the same hacienda. Commanding officers of the Kentuckians were Major John P. Gaines and Captain Cassius Marcellus Clay.

Hearing from *vaqueros* at La Encarnación that a party of Mexican lancers was camped several miles farther south, the combined patrols decided to raid them for prisoners from whom they could extract information. A heavy rain soon cooled their enthusiasm, and they returned to La Encarnación. After locking their horses inside the walled yard, the men, neglecting to post sentries, sought shelter within the houses. A bugle sounding charge awoke them at dawn, and they found themselves ringed by Mexican cavalry under General J. V. Miñon, to whom they surrendered without a fight.

The day after the capture they were started south under heavy guard. All were dismounted except the officers; as a mark of courtesy they were allowed to retain their horses. Maj. Gaines also kept his two ornate, single-shot pistols, carrying them in holsters slung across the pommel of his saddle.

After they had marched a considerable distance, a guard who had been studying Henrie finally recognized him as having escaped from Perote four years earlier. The excited Mexican officers decided to have him shot. Gaines, who understood Spanish, overheard the discussion. Biding his time, he sought out the commander, said that Henrie was sick, and asked permission for the invalid to ride the major's own fine mare.

Seizing a favorable opportunity, Henrie broke for safety, losing his hat at the mare's first leap. Suspecting a general rush, the Mexican commander clapped a pistol to Gaines's chest. The cavalry presented their lances at the rest of the walkers. Capt. Clay snapped a command for them to drop to the ground to show that they had no intention of running. After the excitement faded, they were shackled two by two for the rest of the march to the prison at Perote.

Half a dozen riders were meanwhile pursuing Henrie. One wild tale says that he killed two of the pursuers with Gaines's pistols, clubbed a third with one of the empty guns, swooped up a fallen lance, and charged the others, scattering them.[36] In any event, he got clear but in doing so rode the mare to death. He cut several steaks from the fallen horse and trudged on afoot, hatless under the blazing sun, anxious not only to escape but to report the menace of several thousand cavalrymen, whose presence might portend—who could say?

Before Henrie reached Saltillo, fears were current that something had happened to Gaines's and Borland's overdue patrols. Seeking information, seventeen or eighteen Kentuckians rode through Palomas Pass. Mexicans lured them into a ranch, got them drunk, and sent word to Miñon, who captured them, too. About the same time Col. Yell heard from Mexican cowboys that Borland had been taken. With two hundred Arkansas volunteers Yell rode toward La Encarnación, saw a thousand or more enemy cavalry, and fell hastily back. Almost immediately thereafter in came Henrie, "dreadfully lacerated and with his face burned to a perfect blister."[37]

Taylor arrived in Monterrey in the midst of these excitements, looking as rumpled and calm as an old farmer going to market. Officers, wagonmasters, and newspapermen rushed to him with their fears and outrages. What was the matter with the government? One of Taylor's aides, Lieutenant Robert Selden Garnett, voiced what was quite probably the general's own feelings. Either "the administration . . . was a junta of damned fools, or they looked with *indifference* [Garnett's italics] upon Genl. Taylor's probable defeat. . . . In my own mind I am satisfied that the administration sent Genl. Scott to this country to strip Genl. Taylor of his forces, with this covert hope, that disaster might break Genl. T. down, and that by giving Genl. Scott sufficient rope he would, by his own follies and vanity, hang himself."[38]

Reporters in Monterrey picked up variations on this line. After interviewing Taylor, Josiah Gregg, a merchant, doctor, and part-time correspondent for Arkansas and Kentucky newspapers, told his journal and his editors that because of yellow fever Scott could not possibly advance against Mexico City in the time available. In Gregg's opinion, Scott should have added his troops to Taylor's for an advance through the interior. As matters stood, the withdrawal from Parras and the removal of the bulk of the troops from Victoria, Monterrey, and Saltillo would look to the enemy like a retreat and might well tempt him to attack. Thus failure loomed both in the north and the south. Such bad judgment, Gregg concluded after interviewing the newly arrived general, could be explained only as an administration scheme concocted for the sole purpose of ruining both Taylor and Scott.[39] In his own letters Taylor was even less generous and included Scott among those who were plotting against him.[40]

In the self-righteous frame of mind brought about by these "persecutions," he wrote an open letter to Senator Crittenden of Kentucky, declaring publicly what he had written privately to Robert Wood more than a month earlier: he would consent to be a candidate for the Whig presidential nomination.[41] He followed this on January 27 with a stinging letter to the Adjutant General in Washington, knowing that it would be immediately laid before both the Secretary of War and the President. In it he boldly rebuked the administration for continually acting over his head. (If he had been punctilious, he said, he might with perfect right have refused to let Scott take any troops whatsoever.) Washington evidently was endeavoring to keep him in the dark about its intentions, else why had a special messenger not been sent him concerning the new strategy, so that he and his men could have been spared the long and unnecessary march to Victoria? The President, he finished, might just as well relieve him of his command as put him "in a position where I can no longer serve the country with that assurance of confidence and support so indispensable to success."[42]

He had not yet been relieved of command, however, and the

problem of the Mexican cavalry at La Encarnación (reports
of the captured patrols reached Monterrey the night of January 25) was still his to handle as circumstances seemed to war-
rant. Advice arrived shortly thereafter that Santa Anna was
marching his main army north from San Luis Potosí. (The
Mexican general actually was on the road, having left San Luis
on January 28. But authentic reports of the departure could
not possibly have reached Taylor by January 30; what he heard
was a mere rumor that chanced to be true.) Beset on all sides,
he wrote grimly to Wood, "We now begin to see the fruits of
the arrangement recently made at Washington, by an intrigue
of Marcey [sic], Scott & Worth to take from me nearly the
whole of the regular forces under my command."[43] But at least
a Mexican army was something a man could grapple with. Come
what might, he would ride to Saltillo and face the enemy with
such strength as he had.

He reached the mountain city on February 2. After consulting with Wool and Lane, he decided to convert Saltillo into a
supply base, its main dump to be a few miles southeast of the
city near Arispe's cotton mills, where Yankee girls were teaching
Mexican señoritas how to spin. He would then take his troops
on past the defensive position at Buena Vista and reactivate the
camp at Agua Nueva. His reasoning: there was no water along
the thirty-five-mile stretch between La Encarnación and Agua
Nueva. If Santa Anna risked that desolate road, his troops
would arrive too parched to fight.[44] Or so Taylor wrote. But
quite possibly his stand there was part of a calculated attempt
to restore his popular image as a rough and ready warrior,
marching out to meet the enemy. The risk did not seem to him
unreasonable. He still did not believe Santa Anna could move
twenty thousand troops across the desert and therefore he
thought Santa Anna would turn the bulk of his forces against
Scott at Veracruz.[45]

The administration in Washington was meanwhile doing its

inadvertent best to foster the image Taylor wanted. Early in January the War Department received his November dispatches stating that he had ordered Wool to Parras and that he himself was going to advance on Victoria. Polk was furious. These advances were in flat disobedience of Marcy's instructions of October 22, directing Taylor not to go beyond Monterrey—instructions which the general had received in time to check the deployment. Furthermore, the defiant general had stupidly divided his forces into small groups stationed too far apart to be able to support each other, or so it looked to Polk, who did not yet know that both Parras and Victoria had been abandoned.[46]

On January 4 the President angrily directed Marcy to request that Scott, as commander in chief, order Taylor to pull all his troops back into Monterrey. Scott complied on January 26. After saying quite gently that he would overlook the abusive remarks in Taylor's letter of January 15, he went on, "I must ask you to abandon Saltillo, and make no detachments, except for reconnaissance and immediate defense, much beyond Monterrey. I know this to be the wish of the government, in which I concur."[47]

The directive reached Agua Nueva on February 6 or 7. By that time Taylor was having second thoughts about wanting to be relieved of his command. Indeed, so he wrote Wood, it looked to him as though the administration had reduced him to impotence in the very hope that he would resign out of sheer disgust. "But I shall disappoint them, as I have determined to remain here & do my duty."[48]

If he were allowed to remain. . . . Belatedly and uncomfortably he began to realize that his rash letter of January 27 to the Adjutant General might well furnish the War Department with grounds for recalling him.[49] Unknown to him, meantime, other indiscretions were rising to plague him. Although his letter to Senator Crittenden declaring his candidacy had not

yet reached the United States, discussions about him were rife
everywhere. Democrats were countering Whig enthusiasm by
decrying Taylor's conduct of the war in general and the Monterrey armistice in particular. Hoping to answer the accusations, Gen. Gaines on January 22 allowed the New York
Morning Express to publish Taylor's long letter to him of November 5, in which Old Rough and Ready defended the truce,
questioned the wisdom of a campaign against Veracruz, and
extolled his own plan of seizing territory and then digging in
for a Mexican counter.

Other newspapers copied the letter and Polk went into a
fury, declaring that the publication of the letter would let the
enemy know of American intentions concerning Veracruz.
Taylor's indiscretion, the President sputtered to his diary, was
the result of his having fallen into "the hands of political man-
agers . . . and after all the kindness and indulgence I have shown
him." No more! Gaines was put on the carpet in Washington.
Taylor was not quite recalled. But Marcy did send him a stern
rebuke, warning the general of an army regulation that decreed
dismissal from the service for publishing reports about military
operations.[50]

It would be March before Taylor learned of these developments. For the time being, Scott's order to retire to Monterrey
gave his anger plenty to feed upon. He flatly refused to comply, unless he should receive specific orders direct from Washington and not roundabout through Scott.[51] To Wood he
added that he and Scott now understood each other perfectly.
Henceforth there would be no communication between them
save of an official nature.[52] To the Adjutant General he was a
little more restrained, arguing only that it would be fatal to let
Santa Anna gain Saltillo, where water and food were plentiful
and natural defenses were strong.[53]

The implications he offered the nation were clear and stirring—the doughty old warrior, shorn like Samson, bravely

defying his enemies inside the Democratic administration in order to stand firm against the enemy outside. One small crack runs through the picture, however. Taylor never really expected that Santa Anna would come at him full force. His activities at Agua Nueva during the next several days impel a conclusion that he anticipated nothing more than a small battle with a diversionary force dispatched from San Luis Potosí to mask Santa Anna's real intentions concerning Veracruz.

Even small battles might restore prestige, however. In order to achieve that, Zachary Taylor, presidential candidate, was willing to climb out on the end of a military limb—way out. For at that very moment Santa Anna was marching rapidly north with every man he could muster.

9

DEPLOYMENT

S ANTA ANNA had reached San Luis Potosí, the staging point
for his army, on October 8. His progress thereafter was
shackled by Mexico's chronic shortage of funds. Grandilo-
quent appeals for patriotic donations produced only a fraction
of what the general required. The one untapped source of
revenue remaining to the bankrupt nation was church property,
but levying on it was so ticklish that the cautious government
merely skirted the edges of the issue and hence raised no
money.[1]

Beset by empty coffers, Santa Anna in November sent letters to his old emissary, Col. Atocha, hinting that he was again
ready to deal with the United States. The effort was fruitless.
The American administration, burned once before by Señor
Atocha, refused the intermediary's suggestion that it relax its
blockade of Mexican ports as an earnest of good faith. In
addition, Buchanan set such stringent peace terms that there
was no possibility of even opening the talks.[2]

Santa Anna's position meantime grew still shakier. Although
the Congress that assembled on December 6 elected him President, the margin was painfully narrow—11 to 9, each state of
the nation casting a single vote. His control over the army
was equally uncertain. By drawing in Ampudia's defeated units
from Monterrey and the untested garrison at Tampico, by

levying on the most faithful of the states, and by sending press gangs through the remote hamlets, he managed to assemble twenty thousand men. But how long could he hold them? They were inadequately clothed, wretchedly fed, and irregularly paid. Morale touched rock bottom. Though the men received drill in small units, they never maneuvered as brigades.

Ready or not, he had to do something. Word of the Atocha negotiations had leaked, and rumor flared through the country that Santa Anna was preparing to sacrifice the nation for his personal gain. Caustic newspaper editorials began asking why, after his fiery speeches about driving the enemy out of the north, he remained motionless at San Luis Potosí.[3] Battered by this barrage of discontent, he concluded reluctantly that the time had come to challenge the gringos. The decision was reached, apparently, with no knowledge of Scott's proposed landing at Veracruz or of the reduction of Taylor's army in the Monterrey-Saltillo area.[4]

In order to pay the unavoidable bills of the march, he appropriated ninety-eight bars of silver from neighboring mines and had them minted into coin. On January 26, 1847, he issued general orders concerning equipment: each soldier was to take a uniform, underclothing of Russian duck, two shirts, four rounds of ammunition, and cooking utensils. The artillery marched first, on January 27—three 24-pounders, three 16-pounders, five 12-pounders, eight 8-pounders, and a single mortar. The heavy guns were in charge of the San Patricio Battalion of American deserters, distinguished by a green flag embroidered with a figure of St. Patrick, a harp of Erin, and a shamrock.[5] Ammunition was transported by twenty-one wagons and 450 pack mules. Cavalry and infantry, totaling 19,525 men, moved out of their camps in three sections, a day apart. In addition, J. V. Miñon had approximately fifteen hundred lancers far in advance near La Encarnación. Urrea, in command of about the same number at Tula, was ordered north to cut communications between the Rio Grande and Monterrey.[6]

A sonorous general order promising booty accompanied the army's departure.

COMPANIONS IN ARMS! . . . The independence, the honor, and the destinies of the nation depend, in this moment, on your decision! Soldiers! the entire world is observing us. . . . Privations of all kinds await you; but when has want or penury weakened your spirit or debilitated your enthusiasm? . . . Today you commence your march, through thinly settled country, without supplies and without provisions; but you may be assured that very quickly you will be in possession of those of your enemy, and of his *riches;* and with them, all your wants will be superabundantly remedied. . . .[7]

The pronouncement was not entirely bombast. In all that poor, torn country, there probably was no other man than Santa Anna who could have accomplished so much with the materials available.

The order issued, he donned one of his ornate uniforms—he owned one coat embossed with fifteen pounds of gold lace—climbed into a heavy coach pulled by eight mules, and moved northward with his shivering army.[8] It was a dreadful ordeal. Along much of the route the only water was lifted in trickles from brackish wells by mule-driven wheels. Icy rains and snow lashed the underclad men and women—large numbers of wives and sweethearts accompanied the marchers to act as foragers, wood gatherers, and cooks. Dozens of both sexes froze to death. Two battalions were detached at Matehuala to patrol the supply routes. Hundreds vanished, although death had been decreed for desertion. As the army neared the end of its road it probably numbered fifteen to sixteen thousand men.[9]

Rendezvous was set for February 17–20 at the hacienda of La Encarnación, thirty-five miles from Agua Nueva, where Borland's and Gaines's patrols had been captured a month earlier. As the advance guard of Mexican cavalry neared the ranch on the seventeenth, they were attacked and driven back by a party of Texas Rangers under Ben McCulloch, who at

Taylor's request had rejoined the army as chief of scouts earlier in the month.[10] In spite of this skirmish, Santa Anna did not believe Taylor was aware of the approach of a major army. Miñon's cavalry had been in the vicinity for a month, basing themselves on the hacienda of Potosí, sixty miles southeast of Agua Nueva, and McCulloch (so Santa Anna reasoned) probably would consider his opponents in the skirmish as another of Miñon's patrols. No one (he thought) knew of his own activities. Ever since November he had checked civilian travel northward *"sin pasaporte firmado por me."*[11]

Secrecy, ingrained in his nature, was also important to his strategy. By mid-February he knew from his own agents that a mere six hundred Ohio volunteers were scattered along the American supply lines from Camargo to Monterrey and that Saltillo was guarded by no more than four companies of Illinois infantry and two 24-pounders in a redoubt overlooking the city.[12] The rest of the American troops in northeastern Mexico, not quite five thousand of them, were concentrated at Agua Nueva, hoping, it would seem, to deter the Mexicans by establishing control over the main road and, especially, over the only water in the vicinity. A sudden attack by overwhelming numbers would surely shatter them.

Santa Anna was so confident of this that he already had made preparations to decimate the fleeing Americans. He ordered J. V. Miñon to take position with his lancers in Palomas Pass, east of Saltillo, so that they could fall on the fugitives streaming north, and he appealed for guerrillas from as far away as Parras and Monclova to hurry to the Saltillo plain and help with the slaughter.[13]

Throughout this period, Taylor continued to discredit repeated reports about Santa Anna's approach.[14] The desert was too formidable; and, anyway, he had heard false alarms before. Besides, he was sure that Santa Anna had received the intercepted dispatch of January 3 and would react logically by hurrying to Veracruz to fend off Scott. Other Americans in northeastern Mexico thought so, too. Lieutenant Robert Selden Garnett of Taylor's staff reported that even after Santa Anna's army had arrived within thirty-five miles of Agua Nueva, "our military savans swore that this Could not be so, that it was against all military propriety."[15] When scare stories began rippling through Saltillo as early as February 14, correspondent Josiah Gregg, who spoke Spanish fluently and had established better contacts in the city than the military had, gave the rumors just as little credence. Possibly, he granted for the sake of the argument, Santa Anna would strike at Taylor's reduced forces while trusting to the black vomit to handle Scott—then rejected his own speculation and declared that if Mexican troops were moving north from San Luis Potosí it was a mere demonstration to keep Taylor off balance while the main army shifted to Veracruz.[16]

The Taylor luck, in short, was running again. Santa Anna should have received the intercepted dispatch and should have reacted logically. But he was acting illogically, evidently through ignorance, and as a result Old Rough and Ready was about to get the battle he wanted, albeit a more vigorous one than he anticipated.

Except for May's and Steen's dragoons and the field artillery batteries of Bragg, Sherman, and John Washington—fourteen guns all told, the biggest a 12-pounder—the American force at Agua Nueva consisted entirely of volunteers. There were two cavalry regiments—Yell's Arkansans and Marshall's Kentuckians—and six infantry: two regiments from Illinois that had marched out of San Antonio with Wool, two from Indiana, one from Kentucky, and the one from Mississippi, cocky in red shirts and white duck trousers, with razor-sharp, eighteen-inch Bowie knives strapped around their waists. Only the Mississippians had tasted battle before, at Monterrey. They were considered to be Taylor's pets, partly because his onetime son-in-law, Jeff Davis, was their colonel.

The days at Agua Nueva passed pleasantly, even though the weather was often cold and cloudy, scuffs of snow glimmering on the peak tops. The men cleared the tent grounds of mesquite and cactus, hauled pine wood five or six miles down from the mountains, drilled hard every day under Gen. Wool's frosty gaze, and still had energy left over, one Illinois volunteer wrote on February 19, for "playing ball, running foot races and horse races, jumping wrestling &c. . . . My time passed swiftly and surprisingly by."[17]

Underneath this surface amiability ran dangerous animosities. The principal officers of the two Indiana regiments were either incompetent or hated each other passionately. The colonel of the Second Indiana was William A. Bowles. At the time of receiving his commission Bowles had known nothing whatsoever of military science, and during more than half a year in Mexico he had made not the least effort to learn. His colleague, James H. Lane, colonel of the Third Indiana, had at least endeavored, with some success, to educate himself, as had the brigadier general in charge of both regiments, Joseph Lane, a Democratic appointee of Polk's. The effectiveness of the two unrelated Lanes was partly canceled out, however, by the fierce antipathies they bore each other.

On February 20, while the last of Santa Anna's troops were moving into the rendezvous at La Encarnación, Colonel James H. Lane drew his Third Indiana Regiment into a hollow square on the parade ground at Agua Nueva. General Joseph Lane was there, watching. They exchanged uncomplimentary remarks, and in full view of the entire regiment the general struck at the colonel. Col. Lane parried the blow and hit his superior in the face with his fist. As other officers pulled them apart, the general snarled at the colonel to prepare himself for a duel. Whirling away then, he strode to his tent, which was close at hand.

Col. Lane turned to the regiment, said the matter was of a private nature, and requested his men to stay out of it. Gen. Lane meantime reappeared with a loaded rifle, came within thirty yards, and shouted, "Ready!" Several of the men in the ranks, ignoring their colonel's recent request, loaded their rifles to protect him. Fortunately someone had summoned the guard. Arriving on the double-quick, they eased the general away.[18]

No disciplinary action followed. Taylor, however, did keep the regiments apart thereafter. Gen. Lane, although the commander of both regiments, stayed with Bowles's Second Indiana. The Second thus went into battle with two commanders, a dichotomy that would produce unhappy results during the ensuing days.

By this time McCulloch had reported his skirmish near La Encarnación, with cavalry that he did not believe came from Miñon's group. Other intelligence, arriving simultaneously through paid Mexicans, said that Miñon was nowhere near La Encarnación. He was off at Potosí hacienda, preparing to start north for some point from which he could strike across the mountains at Taylor's rear.

Wondering belatedly whether he had underestimated Santa Anna, Taylor ordered McCulloch and seven or eight men dressed like *vaqueros* to return to La Encarnación for more detailed information. He also told black-bearded Brevet Lieutenant Colonel May to take the American Army's entire cavalry force of four hundred dragoons, plus Lieutenant John Paul Jones O'Brien and two 6-pounders from Washington's battery, eastward toward Potosí and create a diversion that would interrupt Miñon's plans, whatever they were. At the same time he sent couriers racing to the camp in Rinconada Pass, between Monterrey and Saltillo, and on to Monterrey itself, with a request for such men and guns as could be spared. There were not very many.

McCulloch and May left Agua Nueva together at dawn on February 20, the day of the quarrel between Col. Lane and

Gen. Lane. After riding five or six miles into the mountains behind Agua Nueva, they reached a fork in the road and separated. McCulloch's small group continued south toward La Encarnación. May's larger patrol of horsemen moved east along the base of a high, rough ridge. Thirty miles out of Agua Nueva the dragoons reached, at about 3:00 P.M., the ranch of La Hedionda. Their horses were tired. The early winter dark was near, and the next food and water for the animals was a long way off. May decided to stop.

Almost at once signal fires began smoking on the mountaintops. Through his spyglass May detected a large, slowly moving cloud of dust ten or more miles out in the desert east of him. Whirlwinds? Or Miñon's lancers? He sent Lieutenant Thomas Wood and twelve dragoons ahead to entice an attack if possible, and ordered Lieutenant Samuel Sturgis and one other man to climb the high, rocky slope directly north of the ranch. From its summit, the frightened peons of La Hedionda said, one could look directly down on a fork in the road from Potosí and see whether the cavalry over there, if any, intended to march toward Saltillo or across the mountains to La Encantada, at the south end of the narrows of La Angostura. While waiting for the reports, May found several bales of cotton in the ranch's sheds and used them to barricade either end of the road that ran through the walled hacienda. Behind each barricade he placed one of O'Brien's 6-pounders.

Sturgis and his trooper rode as far up the steep slope as they could, left their horses, and scrambled on afoot. They reached the top at sunset. A Mexican patrol that had been watching them now opened fire. The two scouts emptied their guns in return and bolted toward their horses—too precipitately. Both tripped, fell heavily, and were taken.

Hearing the shooting, May put men behind the windows of the ranch buildings and on the roof tops. Darkness fell. More signal fires flared. Lt. Wood and his twelve men did not appear, but a Mexican *vaquero* did. The pickets pounced on him and dragged him roughly before the fierce-looking, enormously bearded lieutenant colonel. Chattering with fear, the captive said that he had just come from La Encarnación and that Santa Anna was there with a huge army.

May thereupon decided that it was more important to take his guns and irreplaceable cavalry back to Taylor than to push for a diversion. About ten o'clock the force started back. Signal fires blossomed ahead and to the sides. But there was no attack, a lapse on Miñon's part, and at dawn on Sunday, February 21, the dragoons reached Agua Nueva. Moments later Wood's patrol appeared. They had missed finding La Hedionda during their return through the dark.[19]

A few hours later McCulloch's group galloped in. At daylight, when smoke from thousands of newly kindled cook fires drifted like blue fog across the plain at La Encarnación, the Ranger captain and one of his men had actually ridden through the heart of the enemy camp. Twenty thousand men were there, he guessed, at least five thousand of them cavalry. (His total was too high by four or five thousand.)[20]

All or some of those thousands of Mexicans could flank the Americans on the west by a road that entered the Agua Nueva plain through San Juan de la Vaquería, eight or nine miles away. And, as May's report made clear, Miñon was already moving along Taylor's east flank, though whether the Mexican cavalry were aiming at La Encantada or at Saltillo was not yet apparent. Undoubtedly, however, the movement would be coordinated with whatever thrust developed out of La Encarnación.

Twenty thousand men across those deserts! . . . But there was no time to marvel. The position at Agua Nueva was no longer tenable. Taylor gave orders for the main portion of the troops to fall back through the Narrows to Wool's old campground beside the hacienda of Buena Vista. Such wagons as were at Agua Nueva loaded the most essential baggage and rolled out with the marchers, leaving Yell's Arkansas cavalry behind to guard the supplies for which there was as yet no transport.

As Taylor rode north he improvised. At La Encantada he dropped off Col. McKee's Second Kentucky foot regiment and part of Washington's eight-gun battery to support Yell in case the Mexicans should force him out of Agua Nueva sooner than anticipated. The rest of the force marched through the Narrows. In the broad mouth of the ravine that formed the north border of the plateau Wool had selected as battlefield, he pointed out a campground for Colonel John J. Hardin's First Illinois infantry. The rest of the troops he took on another mile to Buena Vista.

The teamsters unloaded, picked up several more empty vehicles from the wagon park at the hacienda, and returned through the dusk to Agua Nueva, fifteen miles or so away. The transport was guarded by Colonel Humphrey Marshall's Kentucky cavalry and Enoch Steen's First Dragoons—a hard push for the latter, since they had been in the saddle almost continuously since leaving for La Hedionda at dawn the day before. It looked now as if they would be on the go until the next morning as well, for their orders were to help the wagon train load as many supplies as possible by midnight, burn the rest, and return to Buena Vista without pause.

Not many people rested that cold night—or ate supper either, for no wood had been gathered at the hacienda in advance.[21] Leaving the cheerless camp after seeing the men located, Taylor rode on to Saltillo with his favorite escort, May's Second Dragoons and Davis' Mississippi Rifles, reinforced by Sherman's and Bragg's batteries. Most of his supplies were at the big dump near Arispe's cotton mills a few miles southeast of the city, and he wanted to protect them as well as he could against whatever attack Miñon might have in mind.

As his little column disappeared, the First Illinois set up their

tents, only to be ordered out straightway to fortify the Narrows. Wool, author of this battle plan, intended to move Washington's eight guns into La Angostura at dawn, and he wanted
the battery stoutly protected. Accordingly six companies of
the Illinois volunteers were set to building a breastwork along
the southern end of the long promontory that reached almost
to the edge of the road where the guns would be. Two more
companies (the remaining two were part of the garrison in
Saltillo) dug a trench from the foot of the bluffs to the stream
gully. Only the road remained open so that the supply train
could come through, and that hole could be quickly corked by
pushing in two or three wagons filled with stone and chaining
them tight.[22]

At Agua Nueva the teamsters, assisted somewhat perfunc-
torily by the troopers, were burrowing away at the heap of
supplies left at the ranch. About eleven o'clock they heard a
far-off rattle of musketry in the mountains. A little later the
pickets that had been posted along the San Luis road raced in
with word that the advance guard of the enemy was in sight.

The teamsters took fright. As fast as their wagons were
filled—and often before—they started whipping their teams
toward Buena Vista. In their haste they wrecked five vehicles
and abandoned them with their loads beside the road. The
soldiers were moving simultaneously with torches through the
hacienda, setting fire to the stacks of unthreshed grain that had
been gathered for the horses, to the barns and woodpiles, even
to the dry palms in the yard. Then, in the deep crimson glow
that seemed to light half the plain, they too fell back. By daylight on February 22, the entire force, save for a few pickets
at La Encantada, had regrouped either in the Narrows or at
Buena Vista.[23]

At the sound of the long roll just before sunrise, tents tum-
bled in twenty minutes and were stowed with other essential
baggage in wagons that drew up in parallel lines on either side
of the road just north of the hacienda. Forty rounds of ammu-

nition were issued to each man.[24] A regimental band struck up "Hail, Columbia!" Because it was George Washington's birthday, Wool set "Remember Washington!" as the day's password. The shout rolled down the ranks, and the deployment began.

Captain John M. Washington lined up his eight guns almost wheel to wheel in the narrows. Supporting them were Colonel John J. Hardin's eight companies of the First Illinois, who had spent the night in their trench or behind the breastwork on the promontory. Colonel William Bissell's Second Illinois, Steen's dragoons, and McCulloch's Texans took position to the Illinois left, angling southeast along the plateau, just beyond the heads of the two short ravines that seamed the central part of the plateau. Col. Bowles's Second Indiana, accompanied by Brig. Gen. Lane, deployed just beyond the upper end of the southernmost of the short ravines.

The arrangement left a gap of nearly half a mile between the left flank of the Second Indiana Regiment and the mountains. Whether Wool was concentrating so on the road that he did not notice the inviting hole or whether he was waiting for Taylor to make the final dispositions cannot be said. In any event he held more than half of his available men in reserve, some on a knoll to the rear of Washington's battery and the rest on the Saltillo side of the big ravine that formed the northern border of the plateau.[25]

At 8:00 A.M. pickets rode in with word that the Mexicans had reached Agua Nueva. Wool relayed the report to Taylor in Saltillo.

The situation there, overshadowed by the drama of Buena Vista, cannot be reconstructed accurately. Evidently Taylor had decided, on his arrival after dark on the evening of February 21, to have his teamsters spend the following day, Washington's birthday, moving as many supplies as possible from the dump near Arispe's cotton mills into the town's central plaza, in front of the cathedral. There Major W. M. Warren, in command of four companies of volunteers, was to guard the matériel against an attack by citizens or guerrillas by erecting street barricades around the square. Captain Lucien B. Webster's two 24-pounders in the redoubt just outside the city ought to be enough to deter Miñon if he came that way; the Mexican cavalry were armed only with lances and old-fashioned escopettes, large-caliber muskets sawed off to a length convenient for use on horseback, and were intended not to storm fortified positions but simply to harry the American rear. At least this seems to have been Taylor's reasoning.[26] He added none of the troops he had brought with him to the city's garrison—Webster and Warren would have to handle matters with the forces they already possessed—and early in the morning started back south toward Buena Vista with his same escort: May's dragoons, Davis' Mississippians, Bragg's and Sherman's guns.

About 9:00 A.M. the men on the plateau saw him coming and raised a cheer. They were in good spirits. They had gotten a lift from moving forward onto high ground, where the enemy would have to come uphill to dislodge them, and now the sight of their imperturbable commander, of more guns, and of the smart Mississippi Rifles in their white trousers and red shirts offered reassurance that all was well behind them. More encouragement came when Taylor ordered two of the newly arrived cannon, a 12-pounder under Sam French and a 6-pounder under George Thomas, to join the infantry on the plateau.[27]

While the guns were moving into position, the men who were on high enough ground to see across the far edge of the tableland detected a film of dust advancing across the plain beyond La Encantada. Underneath it, very obviously, were more thousands of steadily marching feet than any of them had ever before seen gathered into a single army. And they were the objective.

10

CRISIS

At NOON on February 21, about the time that Taylor was listening to Ben McCulloch's report of his second reconnaissance, the Mexican Army began to move out of La Encarnación. Santa Anna still believed he could surprise the American camp at Agua Nueva, and to achieve the triumph he called on his ragged men to make an almost incredible effort. They had just covered two hundred miles of desert. Thirty-five more waterless miles lay ahead, much of which the marchers must cross during the icy winter night so that they could attack at dawn. Furthermore, they must do it on almost empty stomachs. Only three rations were issued them. One was eaten the morning of the twenty-first. The second, consisting of a bit of dried meat, two biscuits, and a small hard cake of brown sugar, was to be eaten during the rest halt that night. The third was an emergency ration, to be consumed as circumstances dictated. The hope was to supplement that last skimpy meal with food seized from the *norteamericanos*.

Since the rest camp that night would be dry, canteens were to be filled and horses and men were to drink to capacity just before the start from La Encarnación. "The chiefs of corps," the order of the day read, "will pay *much, much, much* attention to this last instruction."[1]

Ampudia's four brigades of light infantry marched first,

176

strengthened by three 16-pounder cannon, ammunition wagons, and a company of sharpshooters. Engineers and cavalry followed, then the heavy infantry of Manuel María Lombardini, accompanied by the Army's five 12-pounders. Francisco Pacheco's division brought up the rear, followed by the rest of the artillery, wagons, and pack mules. More lancers under General Andrade formed a rear guard. The women who acted as cooks and laundresses straggled behind and to the sides, forbidden this day from mingling with the marchers.

The column, stretching for miles, wound slowly across the dead flat plain and into the mountains. In cold darkness it snaked over a pass and started down the other side. The advanced patrols sent the American pickets running before midnight and then halted, hopeful that the encounter would be dismissed as one more minor cavalry demonstration. While waiting for dawn, the soldiers pulled as close together as the terrain allowed, munched their cold rations, and stretched out, blanketless, to find what rest they could. It was not much. The temperature was below freezing and fires were prohibited. They could not even have the solace of the band music they liked so well.[2]

At the first glimmer of light on the morning of the twenty-second they broke camp in profound silence. When the head of the column glimpsed Agua Nueva, the hacienda was still burning. Little grass fires licked at the ends of blackened fingers; when one chanced to touch a desert palm, it raced up the trunk to the dry fronds and blossomed in a ball of yellow sparks.[3]

Santa Anna hurried to the van in dismay. The enemy had escaped! Then the peons at the ranch told him that the Americans had departed in haste. He saw the five wrecked wagons listing beside the road and jumped to the conclusion that a panic had swept the enemy camp. On the strength of that he decided to gamble. Although his men were tired, hungry, and thirsty, he would pursue Taylor without rest. Miñon supposedly was already lurking in the mountain passes east of Saltillo, ready to fall on the rabble. Irregulars from as far away as Parras were gathering in Saltillo and throughout the plain to help with the annihilation. But none of it could come about unless he pressed hard after the *norteamericanos* and increased their confusion.

He gave Ampudia's advanced battalions only time enough to fill their canteens and then sent them hurrying along the road with a regiment of cavalry as support. After leaving orders for the rest of the army to follow without halting for more than a drink, he overtook the light infantry, exhorting the last ounce of effort from them.

It was a fatal mistake. Outriders dropped back to tell him that more of the enemy, apparently, than a rear guard had halted in the Narrows and on the plateau to the east. As Santa Anna galloped ahead and swept the ground with his spyglass, his heart must have sunk. Instead of continuing its runaway stampede, the enemy had wheeled around in a position of great natural strength, ready to fight. And he had come upon them with an exhausted army.

The mistake was so glaring that commentators, reflecting on it afterward, were sure that it could not have resulted from chance. Captain James H. Carleton later declared that Taylor had planned matters just that way, falling back in simulated haste in order to lure the Mexicans into a prepared trap. Lt. Garnett compared the strategy, inaccurately, to Wellington's retreat into the Torres Vedras during the Peninsular War and said the American withdrawal led Santa Anna "into a snare, completely checkmated." No similar afterglow colors Taylor's own public or private reports. In a letter to E. G. W. Butler, for instance, he wrote candidly that he withdrew because he found his position at Agua Nueva untenable and decided to perform the military maneuver known to other commanders (he did not use the phrase in his own letter) as getting the hell out of there.[4]

Nor, as Santa Anna realized after further study, was the Mexican situation hopeless. His force, however weary, outnumbered the Americans at least three to one.[5] Moreover, Taylor lacked men enough to cover the entire plateau in strength.[6] The heaviest part of his force was concentrated either on the road or on the bluffs immediately above the road, leaving the base of the mountains unguarded. By hurling a strong diversionary attack against the battery in the pass, the Mexicans might keep those men pinned to the center while flankers worked past the American left, skirted the base of the hills to the far ravines, and came down on Buena Vista from behind.[7] Miñon, hearing the sound of the battle from his position near Saltillo, ought to have perception enough to help matters by harrying the American rear.

Santa Anna's first need was time in which to gather his men and group them in such fashion as to mask his intent. Characteristically, he gained the necessary hours by trickery, sending three messengers to Taylor under a white flag. Three American officers and an interpreter rode out to meet them. One of the trio raced the message to Taylor, who was standing near Washington's battery. It was about 11:00 A.M.[8]

The message was typically florid. "You are surrounded by twenty thousand men, and cannot in any human probability avoid suffering a rout, and being cut to pieces with your troops, but as you deserve consideration and particular esteem, I wish to save you from a catastrophe and for that purpose give you this notice, in order that you may surrender at discretion. . . ."

Taylor replied more laconically. "I decline accepting your request."[9]

His engineers meantime had occupied points from which they could watch the deployment of the Mexican troops. As their reports came in, Taylor shifted his reserves to meet the

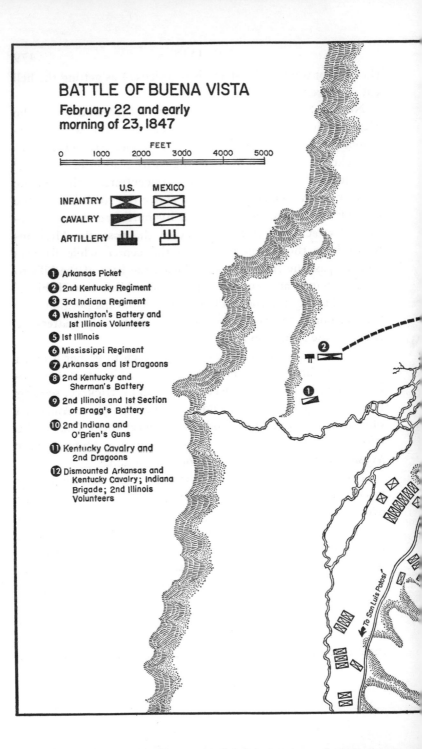

BATTLE OF BUENA VISTA

February 22 and early morning of 23, 1847

FEET

| 0 | 1000 | 2000 | 3000 | 4000 | 5000 |

	U.S.	MEXICO
INFANTRY		
CAVALRY		
ARTILLERY		

① Arkansas Picket

② 2nd Kentucky Regiment

③ 3rd Indiana Regiment

④ Washington's Battery and 1st Illinois Volunteers

⑤ 1st Illinois

⑥ Mississippi Regiment

⑦ Arkansas and 1st Dragoons

⑧ 2nd Kentucky and Sherman's Battery

⑨ 2nd Illinois and 1st Section of Bragg's Battery

⑩ 2nd Indiana and O'Brien's Guns

⑪ Kentucky Cavalry and 2nd Dragoons

⑫ Dismounted Arkansas and Kentucky Cavalry; Indiana Brigade; 2nd Illinois Volunteers

To San Luis Potosi

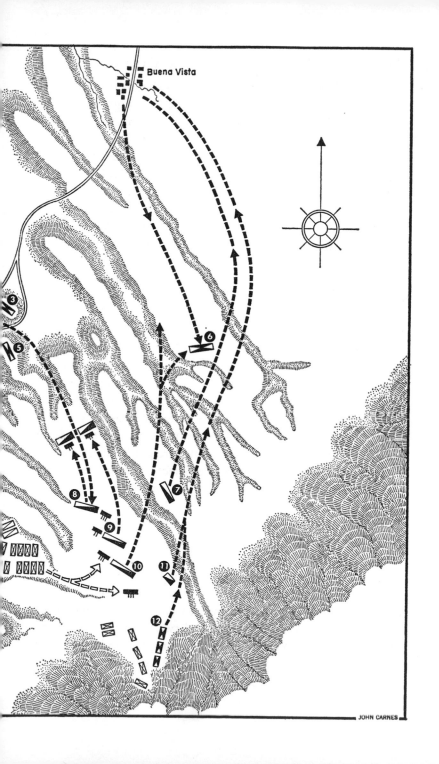

Buena Vista

JOHN CARNES

threats. An initial Mexican movement to the west led him to think Santa Anna might try to circle the stream gullies on the American right, a difficult but not impossible maneuver. Surprised yet wary, Taylor countered by sending Bragg's battery of 6-pounders, Company E of the Arkansas cavalry under Captain Albert Pike, and Colonel William R. McKee's regiment of Kentucky infantry across the stream and onto the slopes above the network of gullies. Colonel James H. Lane's Third Indiana, still in reserve, took the place McKee had vacated on the little knoll behind Washington's eight-gun battery.

So far Santa Anna had succeeded in fooling his opponent. He had no intention of striking at the west. While Taylor was shifting men in that direction, Santa Anna sent a thousand of Ampudia's infantry up the gorge bordering the southern part of the plateau. They were not detected until they climbed out of the gorge and started up the side of the mountain. Their goal was a little knoll that rose a hundred feet above the plain on the lower part of the ridge separating the main ravines that embraced the plateau. The strategy behind the move was evident as soon as the men were: to control, from the top of the knoll, a route by which flankers could circle the American left.

Taylor scrambled to adjust. He detached three guns from Washington's battery—one 12-pounder, one 6-pounder, and a toy 4-pounder—and sent them under John Paul Jones O'Brien to plug the gap between the American left and the mountains.[10] Humphrey Marshall loped the bulk of his Kentucky cavalry to the base of the knoll, dismounted the men, and started climbing, hoping to reach the summit ahead of the enemy. Seeing more Mexican infantry following the first push, Wool ordered Major Willis A. Gorman to take four companies of Indianans—two from the Second and two from the Third—to Marshall's support. Yell's Arkansas cavalry, meanwhile, backed up these skirmishers by moving up the northern ravine and deploying along the base of the hill on that corner of the plateau.[11]

The first shot of the battle came in the middle of the afternoon, when the lone Mexican mortar threw a shell at the climbing Americans. It fell far short. The unengaged volunteers, watching gape-mouthed from the surface of the plateau, hooted and jeered. The advance parties of Kentuckians reached the knoll ahead of the tired Mexicans and began firing across the ravine at them with good effect. Stung hard, the attackers veered and climbed higher, hoping to circle the head of the ravine above the Americans. Vegetation on the gully-scamed hillside was sparse, and the men below could see the intense, painful gropings of each tiny figure—a toy battle, slow motion, among the boulders and hollows. Whenever an apparent advantage was gained by the Americans, the watchers cheered wildly.[12]

Thinking that Marshall had not detected the upper prong of a new party of Mexican climbers, Wool sent a staff officer to warn him. Somehow signals were confused. Marshall thought he was being ordered to pull back. His bugler sounded a recall. At that, Wool himself galloped up, checked the movement, and told Marshall that the entire hillside engagement was under his full discretion. He also gave him command of Gorman's four companies of detached Indiana volunteers.

The latter moved too slowly when the Kentucky colonel attempted to recover the ground he had given up. Although they retook the knoll finally, the Mexicans pushed in above them, reaching the upper slopes of the dominant ridge peak on whose slopes the main ravines bordering the plateau had their origins. Cautiously the Americans squirmed along beneath them, firing carefully and inflicting heavy casualties. The trigger-happy Mexicans shot back at random. Nearly all their bullets went high, and their tremendous outpouring of ammunition wounded only seven men. Thus, by sunset, the skirmish

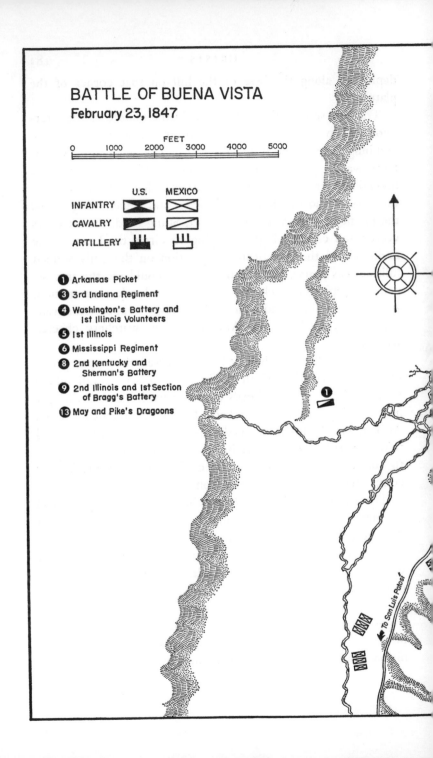

BATTLE OF BUENA VISTA
February 23, 1847

FEET

0   1000   2000   3000   4000   5000

	U.S.	MEXICO
INFANTRY		
CAVALRY		
ARTILLERY		

① Arkansas Picket

③ 3rd Indiana Regiment

④ Washington's Battery and
    1st Illinois Volunteers

⑤ 1st Illinois

⑥ Mississippi Regiment

⑧ 2nd Kentucky and
    Sherman's Battery

⑨ 2nd Illinois and 1st Section
    of Bragg's Battery

⑬ May and Pike's Dragoons

To San Luis Potosi

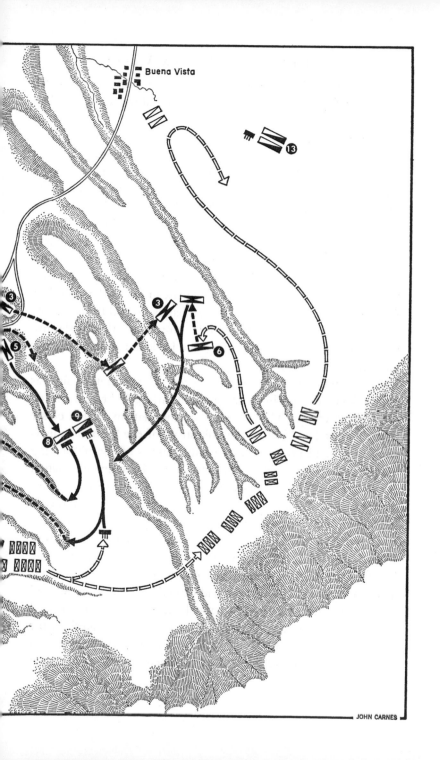

Buena Vista

JOHN CARNES

seemed to be ending in a draw, although Ampudia's dead-tired, wiry little fighters, dug in on the peak top above the knoll, had the advantage of position.[13]

Assured that no major development was likely to take place during the night and worried still about his supplies at Saltillo, Taylor once again rounded up May and Davis, added a single 6-pounder from Bragg's battery, and returned to the city. On the other side of the plateau the Mexican Army built its fires and cooked its first meal in twenty-four hours—the last one for which the men had rations. Standing on a slight elevation, Santa Anna delivered one of the bombastic speeches that were his specialty, promising food from the defeated enemy camp on the morrow. The Americans on the plateau heard the cheering. Afterward the music of the Mexican bands floated to them, soft and melancholy in the twilight.[14] Now and then rifle fire winked on the hillside, reminding one Indiana major of fireflies gleaming across a meadow.[15]

It was not firefly weather, however. The mountain air was cold. Clouds drifted in after midnight, and a light rain soaked the waiting troops. The left wing on the plateau shifted closer to the mountains. Most of the volunteers of the Second Indiana were green and jittery, and the faint sounds of the night rang loudly in their ears as they advanced toward the unseen enemy. A stir either of Texas horsemen returning from watering their mounts or of riflemen moving to or from the mountainside frightened the pickets. One of them rushed to Col. Bowles with word that Mexican lancers were probing for a way around the flank. Mushy with weariness and apprehension, Bowles gave a series of mistaken orders that completely muddled his regiment. If an attack had been developing, the Second might have been hard put to repel it. But the alarm passed and the regiment settled into its new position, blanketless, for the rest of the night, Bragg's three-gun battery just behind them. Here and there small fires bloomed briefly as the men

set fire to heaps of weeds and dry yucca stalks they managed
to gather.[16] From mouth to mouth the tale of Bowles's incom-
petence spread swiftly down the line, destroying what little
confidence the men still had in their commander.[17]

There might well have been a true alarm, however, for the
Mexicans were busy throughout the night. Just beyond the
mouth of the wide ravine forming the southern border of the
plateau was a small hill on which Santa Anna placed eight guns
to support an early morning diversionary attack against Washington's battery a mile away. Pacheco's infantry gathered in
the ravine itself, to march eastward half a mile, as Ampudia's
brigades had done, and climb out of the gulch at the foot of the
mountains. On the ridge forming the south bank of the same
ravine, Lombardini collected still more infantry and cavalry to
parallel Pacheco, whom he would join at the upper part of the
ravine for a joint assault on the American left, guarded by the
jittery Second Indiana. To support this movement, Mexican
gunners under Manuel Micheltorena, onetime governor of California, moved a battery of eight 8-pounders to the head of the
ridge Lombardini would follow and placed the cannon where
they could command O'Brien's small battery stationed on the
southeast corner of the plateau.[18]

During this same period another fifteen hundred light infantrymen clambered up the dark slopes to reinforce Ampudia's
men, clustered on the rain-swept sides of the high, steep ridge
that separated the heads of the two ravines. Detecting the
movement, American pickets fired on the dim shadows, then
withdrew. Marshall sent an express to Wool, who told Major
Xerxes Trail to reinforce the mountain troops with two companies drawn from Col. Bissell's Second Illinois Regiment. Trail
led these men onto the slopes just before dawn.[19]

Worried about the threat to his left, a threat he strangely
had not anticipated when selecting the battlefield, Wool ordered Brigadier General Joseph Lane to take immediate com-

mand of that sector. Lane arrived just before daylight, alerted the Second Indiana, who were heartened by his presence, and distributed ammunition, but did not have the regiment fall into line just yet. Throughout this period and thereafter he ignored Col. Bowles, the nominal commander of the regiment. The aloofness would result, during the opening phases of the battle, in disastrous confusions.[20]

As daylight strengthened, the American forces gulped their breakfasts cold, lacking wood for fires. At least they ate. The Mexicans formed for battle on empty stomachs. By sunrise three columns were on the march. Pacheco and Lombardini pushed six thousand infantry and cavalry toward the mountains. The latter, marching his men in full view of the ridge beyond the ravine, helped divert attention from Pacheco, keeping cleverly out of sight against the walls of the gorge.

Simultaneously the Mexican battery on its little hill beside the road opened up on the Narrows, covering General Mora y Villamil as he started the Mexican Twelfth Infantry Regiment, the Battalión Puebla, and the Guarda Costa de Tampico in a wide column toward Washington's battery. Meanwhile, Ampudia's reinforced men on the mountainside scattered out and began driving against Marshall's defenders.[21]

It was a beautiful morning, every detail showing knife sharp in the rain-washed air. The clouds broke into white puffs around the jagged peak tops; the sun gleamed on the wet rocks. The Mexicans were ragged and hungry, but they moved with snap and precision. Their flags and battle standards and the red pennants on the lance tips fluttered brightly. The red-faced blue uniforms formed undulant masses of color against the tawny desert. Bands played cockily, and the waiting Yanks felt their nerves tingle with admiration and more than a little awe.[22]

Wool's position was perilous. McKee's Kentucky foot, Bragg's battery, and Pike's company of Arkansas cavalry—

close to seven hundred men, all told—were to the right of the gullies, where obviously no action was going to occur. Taylor had another six hundred men in Saltillo. Thus Wool's force in the Narrows and on the plateau numbered only thirty-three hundred or so men, opposed to the twelve thousand who were converging on them.[23]

At this point Brevet Major Joseph Mansfield of the engineers galloped up to the headquarters marquee on the northwest corner of the plateau with word that Pacheco's division was massing in the upper ravine, ready to charge against the left. Wool sent Inspector General Sylvester Churchill to warn Gen. Lane, who was busy watching Ampudia on the mountain and Lombardini across the ravine. By another messenger, Wool ordered Bissell's Second Illinois to shift farther left and forward in support of Lane. He then sent Mansfield riding wildly across the gullies to McKee with orders to bring his Kentuckians to the plateau and help Bissell. Though no specific orders went to Braxton Bragg, stationed on the right with McKee, he and Mansfield decided that Bragg should bring his guns into the fray, although this meant a long detour to find a spot where he could take his caissons across the gullies. Wool, meantime, dropped off the plateau to be with Washington's battery, threatened by Mora y Villamil.[24] From the beginning he had assumed the guns in the Narrows would be the Mexicans' main target. The preconception remained unshakable even after the heavy concentration of strength on the left became fully apparent—a line of thinking Santa Anna had hoped to foster with Mora y Villamil's formidable diversion.

As these shifts were taking place, four companies of Yell's Arkansas cavalry left their horses near the upper part of the northern ravine and slanted on foot across the mountainside to help relieve Ampudia's heavy pressure on Marshall. O'Brien unlimbered his 12-pound howitzer and in spite of the elevation succeeded in dropping a few shells among the lower section of the Mexican skirmishers. The cannonade accomplished little; the men simply scrambled up the hillside out of range. At the same moment Micheltorena's 8-pounders beyond the ravine began pumping round shot at the American battery. O'Brien fell back behind the protection of a slight rise. At that point Churchill's orders to re-form against Pacheco arrived. As part of the maneuver, Gen. Lane placed O'Brien's three guns to the right of the Second Indiana, where they could form a link with Bissell's advancing Second Illinois.[25]

Washington's battery, with Wool watching, now opened on Gen. Mora y Villamil's advancing column of cavalry and infantry. The first shots fell short, bumping up curtains of dust that obscured the attackers. The Mexican battery near the road, elevating its muzzles to shoot over the heads of the assault column, did no harm either to Washington's guns or to the supporting infantry in the trench and succeeded only in killing a few horses tethered near the Third Indiana, held in reserve on the hillock behind the American battery. On their part, Washington's gunners quickly found the range. W. H. L. Wallace, watching from his position on the promontory above, saw "fragments of men and horses . . . flying in the air." For a few heart-stopping moments the Mexicans held. Then, under a hail of canister, they broke back and fled for safety into the ravine up which Pacheco's division had just marched.[26]

Matters on the plateau developed less happily. Having put the Second Indiana into line, Gen. Lane rode to the front of the regiment and ordered, "Forward, guide center!" hoping to gain the top of the ravine before the Mexicans could clamber up its sides. He then loped to the rear without explaining to Col. Bowles, who was at the other end of the line, what prompted the maneuver.

The advance started moments too late. The first wave of Mexicans poured out of the ravine along a broad front. Each Indianan—there were 360 in the ranks—dropped to one knee and began firing coolly. All this was quite unexpected by Bowles. Stories told afterward said that he dissolved into a complete funk. Leaping from his horse, he swung it around broadside between himself and the Mexicans.

O'Brien pumped out canister. But Micheltorena's battery, ahead and to the left beyond the ravine, raked the Americans with grape. Lombardini's cavalry began flowing across. Another wave of Pacheco's infantry came howling over the rim— four thousand or more men against four hundred, including O'Brien's gunners. Or, rather, against 310, for within minutes the defenders had suffered ninety casualties.

A slight rise of ground hampered the firing of Lane's extreme left. To bring them into place for more effective action and to move, if possible, out of range of the Mexican battery, the general ordered O'Brien to limber and advance obliquely ahead and right. The artilleryman obeyed, pushed sixty yards against heavy musketry, unlimbered, and opened fire again. The Indiana infantry slanted after him.

The maneuver was executed before Lane's intended support —Bissell's Second Illinois, McCulloch's Texans, and Steen's dragoons—were close enough to be of help. No word of Lane's purpose reached Bissell. To the Illinois colonel the advance looked like an insane push onto untenable ground, an opinion shared by Col. Marshall, who was watching the Indiana advance from the mountainside.[27]

Some of Lombardini's infantry and cavalry, slicing in between Lane's left and the mountain, opened an enfilading fire on the Indiana flank. And in spite of the Americans' shift, Micheltorena's guns beyond the ravine could still reach the line. Meantime, more of Pacheco's men swarmed out of the ravine, pushing their fellows, who had dropped to the ground in the face of O'Brien's point-blank cannonading.

At that juncture Bowles, standing at the right rear, bawled, "Cease firing and retreat!" A battle madness was on the men, and they did not heed at first. He shouted the command twice more. Confused by this direct contravention of Lane's order to advance, the right half of the Indiana line stirred uncertainly and then started falling in little groups to the rear. As soon as their backs were turned to the enemy fire, confusion swelled to panic and a rout developed. The left held for a while, then caught the fear. Peeling away company by company, they joined the panting flight back across the plateau into the lower part of the northern ravine.

O'Brien, who had been loading his three guns with double charges of canister, was completely exposed. Every horse of the 4-pounder lay dead; every one of its gunners was killed or wounded. Most of the other animals and men were casualties too, but by abandoning the 4-pounder, the lieutenant was able to disengage the 12 and 6 and take them back to Washington.[28]

Cheering frenziedly, Pacheco's attackers rushed ahead. Some leaped into a gully just ahead of Bissell's six companies of Illinois volunteers and used its banks as a parapet. Others followed their officers in a sharp turn against the Americans on the promontory that guarded the road. McCulloch's Texans were driven for shelter into the northernmost of the short ravines, and affairs looked dismal. Fortunately McKee's winded Kentucky foot arrived at that moment. Supported by Sam French's 12-pounder and George Thomas' 6-pounder, the strengthened line stood its ground. The wave of Mexicans advancing down the plateau against the American center faltered and slowed.[29]

All this while the whole upper third of the plateau gaped wide open. Lancers and infantry poured along the base of the mountains, the horsemen trotting hungrily toward the wagon park at the hacienda. To exploit the break fully and crack the stubborn center, Santa Anna started the grimly rejoicing San Patricio Battalion of deserters up the south ravine with three big guns, two 24-pounders and a 16.

The American skirmishers on the hillside, fearful of being

isolated by the breakthrough, gave way before Ampudia's infantrymen and raced down the slope. Most of the dismounted cavalrymen reached their horses and galloped off the plateau. They crossed the north ravine, climbed out over its bordering ridge, and swung down the gentler draws leading to the campground beside Buena Vista. Those who failed to gain their mounts joined Gorman's fleeing Indianans and Trail's scattered Illinois volunteers and streamed after the panicked men of Bowle's Second Indiana. Ampudia's men, who had been up all night, were too tired to follow. If the advantage was to be pressed home, Lombardini's advanced units of cavalry would have to do it.[30]

About a thousand men were involved in the flight from the plateau.[31] Wool frantically sought to shorten the lines of those who were left, sending Churchill to order Bissell and McKee to fall back to the northwestern corner of the plateau, above Washington's guns, and re-form north and south, facing the mountains. The volunteers retired in good order, turning now and then to fire on command at the enemy, who were again advancing toward them. Meantime Thomas W. Sherman and John Reynolds had brought up two more guns from reserve. Bragg climbed out of the gullies with two 6-pounders.[32] Though Sam French was badly wounded, Lt. Garnett took over command of his 12-pounder and continued the fight without skipping a shot. The six swiftly firing guns made a formidable barricade across the newly occupied corner of the plateau, and the Mexicans paused again.

How long the re-formed line could hold was problematical. The lumbering San Patricio Battalion had struggled up out of the ravine and was unlimbering on the upper central part of the plateau. Six thousand or more Mexicans, their weariness briefly forgotten, were massing at the foot of the slopes, ready either to finish the push against the center or to follow the vanguard of cavalry across the north ravine and swing in several prongs down the ridges and draws beyond, overwhelming the ranch and wagon park and isolating the battery on the road. In the opinion of some strategists, only one thing looking toward success was omitted: there should have been another strong Mexican push along the road against Washington's battery. Santa Anna had reserves enough to make the drive, but he either overlooked it or thought it would be too costly.[33] In any event, the order was never given and the full weight of the attack had to be carried by the Mexican soldiers already on the plateau.

At this point—it was about 9:00 A.M.—Wool saw Taylor approaching. The commanding general had already noticed the masses of Mexican blue on the hillsides and instantly surmised what had happened. Giving Davis instructions about what to do next, he left the Mississippi Rifles at the little stream that flowed out of Buena Vista spring and galloped ahead with May's dragoons. Wool met him at the northwest edge of the plateau. A persistent story, mentioned in no official account, says that the dismayed Wool recommended a general withdrawal.

Taylor shook his head. A retreat with those green volunteers would turn into a rout involving not just a regiment but the entire army. Somehow they would have to rally and hold.[34]

11

RECOVERY

BACK IN SALTILLO, Taylor had discovered that a considerable part of his supplies had not yet been transferred to the
plaza. Miñon was still sitting in Palomas Pass. Although his cavalry might concentrate on helping Santa Anna's main push
against Buena Vista, the booty in the dump near Arispe's mill
might prove to be an even stronger magnet. Taylor dared not
let the supplies sit undefended, even though he knew he would
need every man possible on the plateau. He ordered what
wagons he could find arranged around the dump, bolstered the
barricade with Captain William Shover's single 6-pounder, and
detached two companies of red-shirted Mississippi riflemen
with orders to defend the camp against all odds—not an unduly
severe assignment, in view of Miñon's primitive equipment.
Then, shortly after sunrise, he started back to the battlefield
with May's dragoons and the remaining eight companies of
Davis' foot soldiers.

A little before noon a handful of fugitives appeared in the
wagon-guarded camp from the battlefield and gasped out that
the American lines had broken. Simultaneously an advance
squadron of Miñon's cavalry rode out of Palomas Pass and
cut directly between the supply camp and the redoubt overlooking the city. Shover fired twice at them, but the distance
was too great for his 6-pounder. The Mexicans seized in their

turn a few more fugitives from Buena Vista and heard from them the same story of disaster to the Americans.

More cavalry appeared. Inside the city, Maj. Warren manned the street barricades with three companies of volunteers and sent the fourth into the redoubt to support Webster's gunners. Lieutenant Bowen of the Mississippi Rifles wanted to sally out of the wagon camp with the 6-pounder and drive Miñon back, but Capt. Shover, in command, felt that if the American Army was fleeing a last desperate stand would have to be made in front of the city, and he had better wait on call until he learned what was likely to develop. He harnessed his horses to the gun carriage and caisson, ready for instant improvisation. Then he climbed onto a nearby elevation and peered toward Buena Vista. Guns were still booming, and he could see no sign of a rout.

Miñon was equally perplexed. The report of the captives led him to think the whole American Army would soon be pelting in terror down the road. Hoping to intercept them as directed, he moved his entire force of fifteen hundred or so riders out of Palomas Pass—Webster fired with his 24-pounders but could not reach the column—and took position beside the Buena Vista trace. No panicked rabble appeared. He wondered about moving toward the battlefield, but orders said to wait. There he stayed.

Convinced at last that no rout was making, Shover decided to drive the cavalry out of the way. He took the 6-pounder out of the wagon camp at a run, unlimbered on the plain, and peppered the Mexican flank. Seeing what he was up to, Webster sent Lieutenant James Donaldson out of the redoubt with a 24-pounder to join the harrying. In the city Paymaster Weston rounded up a hundred or so teamsters and American civilians, armed them with swords, pistols, muskets, and shotguns, and galloped forth, whooping and shouting, to help. Tangled by the ravines, the Mexicans found themselves unable to form any kind of charge against the mobile guns. After losing an estimated sixty-three men (American casualties were zero), Miñon fell back into the pass, driven from the field by less than one-tenth of his own number.[1]

It was a costly as well as an ignominious retreat. Miñon should have gone toward Buena Vista. He could have been of real help there.

When Taylor reached the hacienda, the rout of which the Saltillo fugitives had gabbled seemed well under way. Old Rough and Ready never turned a hair. Imperturbably he ordered the assistant quartermaster, Captain W. W. Chapman, to halt the wagons, whose frightened teamsters were beginning to whip their horses onto the road to escape. Chapman succeeded in restoring order and in forming a new park only half a mile north of the ranch.

Simultaneously Taylor ordered Davis to have his Mississippians fill their canteens at the Buena Vista stream and afterward march southeast up the ridge nearest the hacienda to meet the Mexicans who were forming to drive down it toward the rancho. He saw that Yell and Marshall, having checked the retreat of their cavalry from the mountain, were re-forming in good order on the campground above the road, where they would be the sole obstacle to Torrejón's cavalry, massing at the foot of the mountain to charge the hacienda and the wagon park. Taylor signaled for Pike's lone company of Arkansas cavalry to leave its useless position east of the gullies and rejoin its regiment.[2] But none of these measures was more than a stopgap. To meet the heavy numerical odds shaping up against them, the defenders had to have artillery. Putting spurs to Old Whitey, the general galloped with May's dragoons to the corner of the beleaguered plateau to see whether any of the guns there could be spared.

Wool was distraught. Either at his own request or to give

him something to do, Taylor sent him angling back across the ravines and ridges to intercept and try to rally the fugitives who were fleeing from the plateau.[3] He himself then rode ahead to evaluate the situation in the center.

It had improved somewhat. Lieutenant John O'Brien had traded his own 12-pounder to Washington for a more maneuverable 6-pounder, had replaced his wounded horses and men, and had returned to the plateau, so that now eight guns were massed there. Although the San Patricio Battalion by that time had set up its three guns, the plateau was narrow enough that the American 6-pounders could reach them, and the deserters obtained little advantage from the superior range of their heavier cannons. Their support, pounded hard by American grape, fell back. Santa Anna, who had ridden onto the plateau to witness the moment of triumph, had his horse shot under him.[4] He thereupon changed his mind about continuing the drive against the American center and ordered most of the men gathered at the foot of the mountain behind the San Patricio battery to move on south and support the attack against the American rear—or the left flank, as it had become.

As the pressure against the center lightened, Bissell and McKee pushed ahead to recover some of the ground they had lost. Mexicans sheltered in one of the central short ravines opened a fierce fire on their flanks. Hardin came up with four companies of the First Illinois to help clear out the nest. Shooting failed to do it. Grimly, the Illinois colonel then ordered a bayonet attack, the only one of the battle. Though it was the first such experience for the volunteers of the First Illinois, they roared ahead like veterans, killing, wounding, or capturing 150 of the enemy: "the most brilliant thing of the day," according to one of the participants, W. H. L. Wallace.[5]

Still more Mexicans were sheltered in the next ravine to the south, but they showed no disposition to press ahead. Deciding they could be safely ignored, Taylor took a chance and stripped his center. He sent May's dragoons and artillerymen Tom Sherman and John Reynolds, each with a 6-pounder, to join the stand on the campground beside Buena Vista. One of Bragg's men, Lieutenant Charles L. Kilburn, was dispatched with one gun to support Davis; several moments later Bragg himself followed with another. Enoch Steen and part of his dragoons were ordered to help stem the fugitives and swing them back against the enemy.[6]

Wool, riding alone, by this time had intercepted Davis, who was slanting up one of the long ridges leading to the mountains. On their march the Mississippi Rifles breasted scores of hot, dusty fugitives from the upper plateau, both footmen and riders, and tried to cajole them into returning to the fight, even offering water from their freshly filled canteens as an inducement. Only a few responded. Among them was Col. Bowles. Haggard and tear-stained at the enormity of what he had precipitated through his order to retreat, he found a rifle somewhere and fought the rest of the day as a private.[7]

A thousand or so Mexican cavalry had ridden off the plateau across the north ravine and were preparing to descend on the hacienda. More lancers, backed by what seemed a full division of infantry, were facing Davis. He had fewer than four hundred men. Weighing the odds, he asked Wool for support. The only uncommitted regiment was Colonel James H. Lane's Third Indiana, on the knoll behind Washington at the mouth of the north ravine. Wool said he would send them up and reined around.[8]

In the north ravine, well to Davis' right, and on the ridges bordering it, the officers of the Second Indiana were trying to halt their men. Here and there clusters of them came together, some with Gen. Lane, pale from the pain of a wounded arm, some with Lieutenant Colonel W. R. Haddon, a few with Major Cravens. These handfuls eventually fell in, as Col. Bowles had, with the Mississippi Rifles.

While ranging up toward the mountain to assist with the rallying, Captain Enoch Steen and Captain George Lincoln, the latter Taylor's assistant adjutant general, came within range of Mexican sharpshooters. Lincoln was killed, Steen severely wounded in the thigh. Behind them, nearer the road, Major Roger Dix, a paymaster, and Captain T. B. Linnard of the Topographical Engineers came onto a sizable group of deserters trudging sullenly along with their bedraggled regimental standard. Dix grasped the colors and waved for the men to follow him. Linnard found a drummer and fifer and fell in behind. Between them they marched the reinspired group over to join Col. Lane's Third Indiana, just departing its knoll behind Washington to join Davis.[9]

Thanks to these various efforts, all but fifteen or so of the shattered Second Indiana were recovered. Stumbling on to the hacienda, this handful fell in with some of the erstwhile fighters from the mountainside, Indianans under Maj. Gorman (hurt by the recent fall of his horse) and the Illinois relief under Xerxes Trail. A few of these retreaters rushed on past the ranch toward Saltillo, where they were picked up by Shover and Miñon. Most were checked, however, and placed inside the walled yards of Buena Vista and on the flat roofs of the houses, to help in a last-ditch defense of the rancho.[10]

Throughout this time, Davis had been advancing slowly along the ridge toward the mixed Mexican infantry and cavalry who were moving toward him. To the right of the Mississippi Rifles was a broad, steep-walled ravine. A shallow branch of it slanted off across the ridge between the approaching opponents. Near the gully's edge, Davis put his column into line of battle and commanded, "Fire, advancing!" The men charged, whooping, across the depression, Davis on horseback in the lead. A ball hit his boot, driving bits of leather, brass from his spur, and shreds from his sock into his shattered heel.[11] The Mexicans fell back slowly. They may have been trying to lure the red shirts into a trap. Cavalry were trotting down the ravine to Davis' right, looking for a way to climb out and flank him. So far as he could see, no support was on its way to help him fight them off.

Exasperated by the fact and by the agony of his foot, Davis ordered the regiment to drop back. On the way they found shelter behind a slight rise overlooking the ravine and from it fired a heavy volley that halted the cavalry. Then, picking up their wounded, they continued back across the ravine over which they had advanced only moments before. No pursuit developing, they paused there, dropping to the ground to catch their breath after an almost unbroken forced march that had begun at Saltillo shortly after sunrise.

Col. Lane's Third Indiana and some of Gen. Lane's reinvigorated Second, supported by one of Bragg's guns from the center, were marching meanwhile up the left-hand branch of the big north ravine, bound for a union with Davis. The ground was unfamiliar, and they missed their goal. When they climbed out of the ravine they discovered themselves alone on a ridge; there was still another ravine between them and the Mississippians. Moreover, they had emerged onto the high ground two or three hundred yards closer to the mountains than Davis was after his short retreat. Unhappily, the newcomers were also within two hundred yards or so of some twenty-five hundred enemy infantry. Some of these foot soldiers had evidently come down from the mountain to reinforce the group just repelled by the Mississippians; now they were re-forming for another advance. A thousand cavalrymen were grouped in solid ranks behind them. This sudden appearance of unsuspected Americans was as surprising to the Mexicans as the sight of *them* was to the hurrying Indianans.

Immediately thereafter another uncomfortable surprise met the newcomers. The San Patricio battery spotted them as they clambered out of the ravine and opened up on them. Fortu-

nately the first shot went high. Collecting themselves, the Indianans fired twenty-one carefully controlled rounds at the
Mexican infantry, who had instinctively started toward them.
The damaging volleys, added perhaps to a fear that more Americans might appear out of the ravine at any moment, checked
the Mexicans.

As the enemy infantry halted, the cavalry moved around
their right flank, intending to charge Davis, who by then had
re-formed his men and had sent to the rear for artillery, if any
was available. Lt. Kilburn seems not to have appeared, perhaps
because he was unable to get his gun carriage across the ravines.

Divining the intent of the Mexican cavalry, Col. Lane prepared to cross the ravine and join the men he had been sent to
support. He made the march double-time by the right flank
and thus came into position with the rear rank of the Third
Indiana next to the enemy. Having no time to countermarch,
the men faced the Mexicans by the rear rank. Captain Thomas
Gibson's company found itself against the ravine it had just
crossed, dressed so as to present a square front to the advancing
column of lancers. The Second Indiana, its once-disorganized
fugitives regrouped as a cohesive unit, took its stand immediately to the left of the Third. The Mississippi Rifles lined up
to the left of the Second. The combined force numbered about
eight hundred men, opposed to perhaps a thousand indifferently
armed lancers. Whether the Americans formed in a broad,
shallow V, the open middle facing the enemy, as Jefferson
Davis remembered, or in an oblique line save for the squaring
where the last company was anchored on the ravine seems a
moot point.[12]

The American officers shouted at their men to hold their
fire. The richly caparisoned lancers advanced on the silent,
waiting ranks in beautiful order, loping their horses at first,
then slowing to a trot and finally to a walk. Throughout the
advance, according to Gibson, they were "chaunting a song."
Davis first, then Col. Lane of the Third Indiana, called "Ready!"

Every musket came down. Presumably the Mexicans had hoped to draw a ragged volley from their opponents, take the losses involved, and charge while the guns were empty. But no shots came. The song of the Mexicans faded, the pace slowed. The air, tense with the electricity of a swiftly approaching thunder storm, was so still that the clicking of the gunlocks was plainly audible.

The head of the column came within thirty feet, Gibson said; thirty paces, Lane reported; eighty yards, Davis wrote. Anyway, it was close enough that a few scattered troopers lost control of their nerves and squeezed their triggers. On the sound of the reports, the commanders yelled "Fire!" The head of the Mexican column, swept by a volley of eight hundred balls, simply dissolved. Horses fell and plunged. Bodies sprawled and contorted. The survivors broke down into the ravine and fled. Tom Sherman roared up with a 6-pounder and dropped grape on their flanks—not uncontested. Although the cheering Americans were a mile away, the San Patricio battery found the mark at last and sent them hunting cover in the ravines.

Quite possibly this stand saved the day for Taylor, or so Captain James Carleton thought. In the official reports describing the battle, Taylor lavished praise on his onetime son-in-law, overlooking, so the Indiana regiments thought, some of the essential help the Mississippians received. This and the reflections he cast on the Second Indiana after its break caused long controversy and bitterness in the Hoosier state. Be that as it may, the famous V—if it was a V—turned Jefferson Davis into a military hero. He became Secretary of War, a few years later, and in 1861 President of the Confederate States of America. Throughout his handling of the Civil War he kept bringing up Buena Vista and what he stubbornly remembered as a tide-turning V. "If ever the Confederacy perishes," a Southern newspaper finally remarked in despair, "it will have perished of a V."[13]

Though perhaps the tide was turned there on the ridge, the

battle was by no means ended. The attack on Davis was only one part of a coordinated charge against the entire American rear—or left, as the thin, ragged, mile-and-a-half line then faced. Torrejón came down on Yell and Marshall and on May's handful of dragoons with a thousand men. Their head-on impact against the heavier American horses was staggering to the Mexicans, but the Mexicans could manage their little mustangs. The Americans, using light bits on big horses unused to rifle fire from their backs, could not.[14] The American horses bolted. Momentum took over, and the charging enemy swept the defenders along with them in a confused melee of shouts, shots, dust, thrusting lances, and rearing hoofs. Yell was killed at the onset. Several more dropped near him. The rest boiled in chaos into the street leading between the walled yards of the hacienda.

As soon as the American riflemen stationed there could pick out targets, they opened fire at almost point-blank range. It was a total surprise to the attackers. They panicked. Half fled back to the mountains; half bolted on ahead through a gap in the western hills and were seen no more that day. Reynolds, who had been sent with Sherman to help at the ranch (Sherman had veered off in response to Davis' appeal) arrived barely in time to throw a few 6-pound shells at their backs. The attack cost the Mexicans thirty-five dead around the edges of the hacienda and an indeterminate number of wounded.[15]

The recoil of the Mexican cavalry both from Buena Vista and from the Mississippi and Indiana rifles on the ridge took the last of the heart from the tired, half-starved infantry that should have been following on the heels of the horsemen. Confused, they fell back with the lancers into the coves on the mountainside where the ravines took shape. There they jammed up with the men whom Santa Anna had pushed ahead along the base of the hills rather than commit them against Taylor's shortened center. Soon five or six or eight thousand men and horses—an awesome eyeful, though no witnesses agreed on how many—were pinned up against the hillside like practice targets.[16]

The Americans on the left, acting without any coordinating direction, seized their opportunity. May's dragoons and what was left of the volunteer cavalry pressed hard after the remnants of Torrejón's shattered horsemen. Every one of the guns that had left the plateau to meet the Mexican charge joined the pursuit, pausing to blast out a few rounds of grape and then advancing again, the excited drivers rattling carriages and caissons over ground that conventional artillerists would have written off as impassable.

The only support the terrified Mexicans had was the San Patricio battery. It drove back an attempt by Lieutenant Daniel Rucker and part of the dragoons to ride with swinging sabers into the closest part of the Mexican huddle, but otherwise its effect was limited. Some of the advancing American guns were in draws, out of reach of the battery, and the deserters' aim at what they could see was disturbed by the fire of the three American 6-pounders remaining on the tip of the plateau.[17]

During the cannonading a burst of wind rolled curtains of dust across the battlefield. Thunder crashed, and a brief, lashing rain slowed the action. Such deluges were unseasonable, and an ancient theory (one that would be repeated a century later in connection with nuclear blasts) was trotted out in explanation: the heavy discharges of so much artillery had concentrated the moisture in the air and had brought on the storm.[18]

As visibility returned, the Americans pressed on. Just when it seemed the wriggling enemy might be chopped up at will by the flying artillery, a white flag appeared. Racing couriers halted most of the American shooting on the left, and Wool started across the plateau with a Mexican emissary for the

parley Santa Anna was represented as wanting. It was about
1:00 P.M.

On the plateau sound and motion ceased, save for the continued booming of the San Patricio battery and the dying peals
of the passing thunderstorm. Taking advantage of the pause,
Taylor dropped off the plateau to see to his field hospital,
sheltered in the mouth of the big north ravine. (There was
another hospital unit at the hacienda.) The layout had been
well arranged by Wool and was functioning with more smooth-
ness than was customary in those careless times. The wounded
were being treated promptly, though brutally by modern
standards, and those who needed further attention were being
placed in ambulances for transfer, as soon as the road was
known to be open, to the base hospital inside the Saltillo
cathedral. Supply and ammunition wagons were busy, too, a
welcome pattern of order after the deafening confusions on
the plateau. As calm as if he had just ambled in from his plantation, Taylor chatted with Washington, exchanged words
with the wounded, reassured the anxious staff officers swarm-
ing around him.

An eruption of heavy fire from above hurried him back onto
the tableland.[19] There had been no real truce. As Wool had
advanced toward Santa Anna's supposed location, the San Patricio battery had continued firing; the troops had continued
deploying. Suspecting treachery, Wool turned and galloped
back. The Americans on the field always believed that Santa
Anna used the trick to extricate his trapped right wing from
its merciless pummeling.[20] Mexicans insist that the affair was
the unauthorized work of an officer named Montoya, who
found himself within the American lines and pretended to be
a messenger in order to reach his own side.[21]

Whatever the truth, the Mexican right did use the pause
brought by the storm and by the white flag to climb out of its
trap and start streaming back south along the base of the moun-

tains. Unable to parallel them directly because of the ravines, the various American batteries dropped back toward the road. The weary Indiana and Mississippi foot soldiers trudged more directly across the intervening gullies, taking their time.

Gradually, while Taylor was relaxing below the plateau, the retreating Mexicans gathered along its upper edge. The San Patricio battery fell back to the southeast corner of the table-land to join them. And then, either improvising on the spot or executing a plan formed at the time of the white flag, Santa Anna decided on a last assault. It was well timed. The bulk of the retreaters had caught their wind and were drawing new confidence from each other as they drew together near their original base. Sizable bodies of fresh reserves lurked out of sight in the big south ravine. Taylor, by contrast, had no more untapped strength to call on. His only available reserves had been committed on his left. He had stripped his center of artillery, and the guns had not yet returned. One last hard drive, Santa Anna reasoned, would carry the field. He ordered his reserves into battle formation out of sight in the ravine, ready to join a charge launched by the refreshed men on the mountainside.

Wool's failure to reach the Mexican general had stirred suspicion among the American staff officers, but the withdrawal of the San Patricio battery helped lull the doubts for a time. They leaped alive again when the Mexican troops that had been retreating in confusion first halted and then began to reform. In an effort to keep the withdrawal going, someone (Wool probably) launched an attack by the units on the plateau. O'Brien advanced on the far right with two guns. The Second Illinois and Thomas' gun came in on his left. Beyond Thomas were the First Illinois and McKee's Kentucky foot soldiers.[22] Messengers were dispatched simultaneously to quicken the return of the rest of the artillery and infantry from the far left.

Timing was faulty. The American thrust on the plateau should not have started so soon. The soldiers there had to fight totally without backing until the tired forces north of the plateau could come up. Those men were moving slowly. Bragg's horses were so exhausted that when the order to hurry reached him he could comply only by cutting loose from his heaviest caisson.[23] Although the Mississippi Rifles and the Indiana regiments quickened their pace, they were a long way off. The Mexicans, meanwhile, were close—and in overwhelming numbers.

Instead of stimulating the enemy retreat as planned, the premature American drive seemed like a lever that swung Santa Anna's hosts straightway around, fast and fighting. Micheltorena's battery of 8-pounders pushed across the upper part of the south ravine onto the southeast corner of the plateau and joined its fire to that of the San Patricio Battalion. Supported by the barrage, lancers and infantry swarmed toward the advancing Americans. More horsemen and foot soldiers rose like evil genii out of the bordering ravine to the south. This was the uproar that brought Taylor hurrying back to the plateau on Old Whitey.

Once again John O'Brien was caught in an exposed position with his guns. He had advanced somewhat beyond the head of the southernmost of the short gullies that seamed the lower section of the tableland. Off to his left ranged the Second Illinois, Thomas' single gun, McKee's infantry, and, finally, Hardin's First Illinois. As the Mexicans charged at them from the mountains and from the big south ravine, "the most tremendous firing ensued," wrote W. H. L. Wallace, "that ever mortal man conceived! . . . The whistling of the Mexican bullets was almost sufficient to drown the report of their guns, though they were only fifty yards from us."[24]

Instinctively the foot soldiers jumped for shelter into the heads of the two short ravines nearest them.[25] Gunners O'Brien and Thomas were left unsupported on the plateau. Since O'Brien was closest to the converging masses of the enemy, they concentrated on his two 6-pounders. Though a few of his gunners fled, the great majority held fast. One horse, then another, was shot out from under him. He realized that to save his guns he would have to limber up instantly with the horses that were still alive and retire. Seconds before he could give the order, however, he saw Bragg's three guns appear over the lip of the plateau. Farther away, just dipping into the north ravine, came Davis' and Lane's infantry. Could they arrive soon enough? O'Brien decided to take the risk and trade his guns for time. He kept firing until he saw Bragg swing around to unlimber. Sherman followed with his battery, and the infantry appeared, at long last it seemed, over the north rim of the plateau. O'Brien and his wounded gunners gave the enemy one last, point-blank cannonade, abandoned the two 6-pounders, and scuttled for cover.[26]

Triumphant Mexicans in "tinseled hats" poured past the captured guns to the banks of the ravines in which the Americans had sought shelter and began aiming their muskets down at the dodging, cowering men. Remembering the horror afterward, Wallace was amazed that anyone escaped. "They are most miserable shots or they would have killed every one of us huddled as we were in the bottom of that narrow ravine."

Lancers spurred their horses into the heads of the gullies. The two principal Kentucky officers, Col. McKee and Lieutenant Colonel Henry Clay, Jr. (son of the statesman), and Col. Hardin of the First Illinois tried to rally their confused men for a stand. They failed. The soldiers melted away, and all three officers died. Survivors bolted for the mouths of the two gorges. Lancers pursued them in the gully bottoms and along the rims. More enemy cavalry came around the corner of the plateau to cut them off, so intent on the kill that they forgot Washington's battery, which for some time had been sitting quietly in the Narrows. The American gunners opened up over the heads of the stampeders. "I have heard many sweet sounds," remembered Wallace, "—the voices of lovely women and the melodious breathing of sweet instruments but the whistling of that shell was the most grateful sound that ever greeted my ear." The grape blasted the lancers apart. Those that survived fell head over heels back to the shelter of the main ravine—or back up the shorter gulches, where they worked off their frustration by methodically lancing to death, from horseback, the wounded who were lying there.[27]

Up on the plateau other waves of infantry swung toward Braxton Bragg, who was just coming into position. The first of the enemy were only steps away when his three guns roared in unison. Taylor, who was just behind the gunners, unruffled though bullets quite literally nicked his clothing, afterwards wrote dryly in his report, "The first charge of canister caused the enemy to hesitate; the second and third drove him back in disorder, and saved the day."[28] Such moments breed legend. This was the time, supposedly, when Taylor called out politely to his battery commander, "A little more grape, please, Captain Bragg!" Possibly. A rocklike calm under fire, with its stirring inspirational value on his men, was the general's greatest strength. But it seems unlikely that anyone would recall exactly what he did say during those minutes of thundering confusion—or that the family newspapers of 1847 would have printed the words if they had been accurately recalled. The quotation more probably was born during the presidential campaign, when first it was given circulation, instead of on the battlefield.

Nor did Bragg turn the tide unaided. Thomas held his ground; Sherman came up. All of them chewed great holes in the tight mass of Mexicans; surveying the field the next day, correspondent Josiah Gregg came across seven men annihilated by a single round shot.[29] Meantime, Davis and Lane, both

wounded, arrived with their riflemen. The seesaw battle—
"the hottest as well as the most critical part of the action," as
Wool put it—raged through what was left of the afternoon.[30]

The February sun dropped early behind the mountains.
Grudgingly the Mexican infantry and cavalry fell back into
the big south ravine from which they had launched their drive
that morning. While twilight lasted, the American guns dueled
in desultory fashion with the San Patricio battery. Darkness
stopped even that, and the battalion of the deserters limped off
the field. They had been a gall to their former comrades most
of the day but had suffered heavy casualties in return: two
officers, two sergeants, three corporals, and twenty-one privates
killed or wounded.[31]

The Third Indiana and what remained of the Second settled
down for the night almost where the Second had spent the
previous hours of darkness. May's dragoons moved up to the
foot of the mountains to check any repeat attempt to sneak
skirmishers around to the American rear. The badly battered
Illinois regiments reoccupied their breastwork above Washington's guns. Cold rations were distributed; the wounded were
taken to the field hospitals.[32] Though every man on the field
was numb with exhaustion, the intense cold prohibited more
than snatches of sleep. In the heavy silence, Capt. Carleton
heard with a shiver the hungry howling of wolves and the
sound of the night-flying vultures that the Mexicans called
zopilotes.[33]

About 3:00 A.M. the reinforcements that Taylor had summoned from the Rinconada and Monterrey reached Buena
Vista: two 18-pounders and three or four hundred men. Since
the American army had suffered 746 casualties—267 killed, 456
wounded, 23 missing—the newcomers did not suffice to replace
the losses.[34] Mexican casualties were more severe—at least five
hundred dead on the field, in Taylor's opinion (Wool raised
the estimate to a thousand)—but in terms of percentages the

enemy was better off. The odds the next day would still be heavily in their favor.

Many observers marveled that the Americans had not suffered more.[35] If Mexican training and equipment had matched the strategic advantages that they had seized from time to time during the day, the outnumbered American army almost surely would have been crushed.

In addition, Santa Anna's generalship had been faulty. Once the First Mississippi Rifles and the Third Indiana had been committed, the Americans had no more reserves. If the Mexicans had maintained uniform pressure at all points of the American line, a developing weakness in any one section could not have been remedied. Instead, Santa Anna had swung his full weight first against the left and then against the center. The sequence let Taylor shift what troops and guns he had from one point to another as needed, and on each occasion the reinforcements had arrived on the new scene in the barest nick of time,[36] another bit of Taylor luck that could have been precluded by proper Mexican diversions at the appropriate moment. "I tell you, Henry," one Illinois volunteer wrote his brother, "that they had us nearly whiped if they had known it."[37]

Throughout that unpredictable day of shifts and suspense, volunteer troops of the sort Taylor had learned to distrust during the Black Hawk campaign had for the most part responded magnificently to his demands. Even the Second Indiana and the troops from the mountainside had rallied after their morning panics and, either at the hacienda or with the Mississippi Rifles, had proved their mettle. In spite of the difficult terrain, the flying artillery had maneuvered with dazzling skill. In Wool's opinion, the work of the guns at each critical moment was what had truly saved the battle.[38]

So far, so good. But could the weary troops hang on and repeat their accomplishments the next day? Taylor could only hope so. Lacking men enough to try to take the initiative from

Santa Anna, he made no plans but simply let the troops rest on the cold field as well as they could, bracing themselves mentally and physically for whatever the enemy chose to hurl at them in the morning.

Tired though the Americans were, the Mexicans were more exhausted. They had been thrown straight into battle at the end of a grueling march. They settled down for their cold night without food. They had absorbed dreadful punishment and twice had seen apparent victory snatched from them by the incredible rallying power of the enemy. No spirit was left in them—or in Santa Anna. He ordered a silent withdrawal, leaving his wounded on the field.

The retreat began in good order, under the dim rays of a new moon, but soon turned into a shambles as hale men pushed the sick and wounded out of their way in a wild rush for safety.[39] Men unable to keep up dropped unattended by the wayside. Others discarded whatever equipment impeded their progress. Deserters vanished into the shadows. Losses on that dreadful march back to San Luis Potosí turned out to be far higher than those suffered on the battlefield itself—as many as seven thousand by Gregg's estimate, though Taylor's more conservative figures suggested that the battle and retreat combined cost the Mexicans fifteen hundred to two thousand in dead and wounded, two to three thousand in desertions.[40] Santa Anna himself admitted to a thousand casualties on the battlefield.[41]

At dawn the Americans realized that the enemy had vanished and that the battle was over. Almost in disbelief, they began wandering across the plateau, giving water and food to the wounded Mexicans they found, transporting them to the hospitals, and boasting meantime of what they had achieved. In front of the headquarters marquee Taylor and Wool, both of them undemonstrative by nature, exchanged exuberant hugs of relief and joy.[42]

12

RESULTS

T HE BATTLE OVER and routines re-established, Taylor on February 27 moved his army forward to the old camp at Agua Nueva. Scouts followed the heartbreaking litter left by the Mexicans as far as La Encarnación, to make sure that this really was a retreat and not an attempt by wily Santa Anna to lure the Americans out of their well-nigh impregnable position at Buena Vista.[1] More activity than that Taylor lacked strength to accomplish.

While he was at Agua Nueva he received a succession of reports that indicated what might have resulted if Santa Anna had won his gamble. The Mexican irregulars were still lurking along the roads near Saltillo. Miñon, although driven back into Palomas Pass by the minuscule forces in the redoubt and supply camp, still lurked expectantly in the vicinity. If Taylor had been forced to withdraw from Buena Vista, both groups would have fallen on him mercilessly. After the battle had been clearly lost by their countrymen, however, neither Mexican group dared show itself.

Potentially more dangerous than either of those forces were the cavalry commanded by José Urrea, whom Santa Anna had ordered to cut the American supply lines between Monterrey and the Rio Grande. From February 23 to 25 Urrea besieged a garrison of 125 Ohioans guarding the intermediate town of Marín but was driven off by rescuers summoned from Monter-

rey with artillery. Shortly afterward, in a series of raids, the
Mexican general destroyed 179 wagons, killed a few soldiers,
captured twenty-five more, and murdered forty or fifty Mexican teamsters who were working for the *norteamericanos*.[2]

These triumphs interrupted contact between Monterrey and
New Orleans for a week or so. Rumor flew through the United
States that Taylor was on the point of disaster. Polk complained to his diary that it was the general's own fault for
extending himself, in violation of orders, far beyond his capacity for defense. In his nervousness the President even began
to wonder, belatedly, whether Scott had not taken too many
troops away from the northern theater.[3]

Urrea's activities led Taylor to turn the camp at Agua
Nueva over to Wool and move to Monterrey. The raids on the
wagon trains, he wrote in happy self-vindication to the Adjutant General in Washington, showed in crystal clarity what
would have happened if he had not followed his own under-
standing of the situation, rather than the administration's, by
advancing beyond Saltillo. There he had met the enemy and
had driven him far back into the interior. "No result so decisive
could have been obtained by holding Monterrey, and our
communications would have been constantly in jeopardy."

While he was in this triumphant mood, he received Marcy's
sharp censure about Taylor's letter of November 5 to Gen.
Gaines, in which Taylor had defended the Monterrey armistice
and had criticized the administration's Tampico and Veracruz
suggestions. To the angry general, the reprimand seemed un-
merited. His letter had been of a private nature, and Taylor
himself had had nothing to do with its publication. Moreover,
at the time of writing, the Veracruz campaign, so far as he
knew, had been a mere gleam in the strategists' eyes. (He did
not learn until several days after November 5 that the speculation had turned into decision.) Why, therefore, such a stinging
rebuke?

He jumped to conclusions. The whole "abusive" business,

he wrote Robert Wood on March 20, was a "contemptable, pitiful & ungentlemanly . . . course for the purpose of insulting or outraging me." Actually, he went on, it was the administration that deserved rebuking. If Scott, Marcy & Company had left him a thousand more regulars, he could have followed Santa Anna's retreating army into the desert and have annihilated it, ending the war. In justice to the dead of Buena Vista, their friends should hold meetings throughout the United States and demand the recall of both the Secretary of War and Major General Winfield Scott. That pair, and the entire Democratic administration, he fumed, were more interested in overcoming Taylor than in defeating Santa Anna. But, he crowed triumphantly, "through the blessings of divine providence I have disappointed their expectations."[4]

Indeed he had, if such had been their hope. News of Buena Vista reached the United States late in March. That part of the country favoring the war went wild. Old Rough and Ready had won again under desperate conditions imposed by his own superiors!

As was the case following Monterrey, Polk refused to share in the rejoicing or give the victorious general credit for the results. Taylor, he wrote in his diary, was always blundering. He had brought on the battles of Palo Alto and Resaca de la Palma by advancing too far from his base of supplies. He had let Ampudia escape from Monterrey because he had attacked with inadequate supplies and manpower. He had invited the attack at Buena Vista by exposing himself in outright defiance of explicit instructions. He had not won: the hungry Mexicans had retreated. Success was not due to his generalship but to the "indomitable & intrepid bravery of the men under his command."

In his bitterness the President refused to allow the different corps of the Army to fire salutes in honor of the victory. Taylor's rashness, he said, did not deserve such recognition. When

the potent *National Intelligencer* of Washington proclaimed
Taylor the greatest general the United States had known and
declared for him for President, the gall to Polk's pride was
almost more than he could endure. Why this rejoicing? Taylor
had sacrificed hundreds of lives in his disobedience. If he had
been defeated, as by all rules of military science he should have
been, he would with justice "have been universally execrated."[5]

While the victors were sulking in this wise through the political aftermaths of their triumph, Santa Anna was limping
back to San Luis Potosí. He sent couriers ahead to announce
victory: although Taylor had opposed him with nine thousand
men and twenty-six pieces of artillery (approximately double
the actual count), he had slain two thousand of the Americans,
had captured three guns and three battle flags, and had fallen
back only because a shortage of supplies and dysentery among
the troops led his staff to demand a withdrawal.[6]

For a day or so bells pealed joyously in Mexico City, but
soon enough the truth was out. In spite of this, Santa Anna
managed, with his indefatigable resiliency, to raise another
army and march off into the mountains east of the capital city
to oppose Scott's advance from captured Veracruz. Mexican
morale had been sorely hurt at Buena Vista, however. Attitudes
and results might have been far different if he had broken
through the pass of La Angostura, opening the northeast to
Urrea's raiders, and afterward had swung south with the buoy-
ancy of victory sustaining his hard-used troops. As it was, the
Mexican rank and file resisted Scott doggedly and bravely but
with the taste of defeat in their mouths. By fall the war was
lost.

Scott received his share of plaudits for the accomplishment,
but the image that caught popular fancy was Old Rough and
Ready, unpretentious and unshakable, doing his job with un-
swerving integrity in the face of underhanded scheming at

home and overwhelming odds in the field. To be sure, as many voters were told by Democratic newspapers, luck had helped him. Still, in evaluating success, the United States electorate has seldom been critical of luck. They were not in Taylor's case. In 1848, after a campaign ruffled by the Free Soilers' fierce third-party opposition to slavery, he became the twelfth President of his country, accumulating 163 electoral votes to 107 for his Democratic opponent, Lewis B. Cass of Michigan, and a popular vote of 1,360,000 to 1,224,000.

His death in office on July 9, 1850, spared him some of the other things Buena Vista helped make inevitable: the upsetting of the precarious balance of proslavery and antislavery forces because of the nation's territorial leap across the Southwest and, after that, the cataclysmic conflict between the states, in which nearly every officer who had fought under him in Mexico became a leading figure for either the North or the South.

But that is another story.

APPENDIX

THE GUNS
AT BUENA VISTA

BOTH ARMIES at Buena Vista, and especially the Mexican infantry, fought in tight formations on a plateau that offered little shelter and was constricted on all sides by either high mountains or deep gullies. Firing by field guns and small arms was at times heavy. Casualties, however, proved lighter than circumstances would suggest to a modern reader. The reason of course was the appalling inefficiency of the smoothbore muskets and muzzle-loaded cannon still being employed in 1846–47.

Surprisingly enough, rifles of legendary accuracy were available at the time. Daniel Boone was famous for being able to knock out a squirrel's eye at a distance of several dozen paces. Mike Fink drove nails with rifle bullets and regularly shot a tin cup full of whiskey off the head of his friend Mike Carpenter—until their final murderous quarrel. Davy Crockett, who died at the Alamo, was such an unerring shot, according to folklore, that when raccoons saw him coming they climbed down from their trees and surrendered, considering themselves already as good as dead.

The weapon used by these backwoods heroes had been developed years before the American Revolution in the frontier regions of Pennsylvania and afterward had been carried across the Allegheny Mountains into Kentucky, where it became known as the Kentucky long rifle. Like all other guns of the period, it was a flintlock, a name applied to a three-part mechanism devised for igniting powder in a gun chamber without the use of a match or glowing coal. The rear part of the lock was the hammer, operated by a spring. In the upper part of the hammer was a small vise into which a piece of tawny, translucent flint could be clamped. When a pull on the trigger released the hammer spring, the flint darted forward like the bill of a pecking rooster. Hence the hammer was generally called a cock, and thumbing it into position was known as cocking the piece. At half cock the trigger was supposedly inoperable and the position safe; a gun that did go off "half cocked" was undependable and premature.

As the flint darted forward on its arc it struck, at a slant, the second main part of the firing mechanism, a steel plate called variously a frizzle, frizzen, or battery. Flint and steel—the familiar impact sent a shower of sparks downward into the third part of the device, a small shallow pan filled with powder. The resultant flash from this primer charge flared through a small vent, the touchhole, into the rear of the gun barrel, igniting the load of powder behind the ball, or bullet. If earlier shots had clogged the touchhole with residues, the sparks from the flint resulted only in a showy "flash in the pan," nothing else.

The powder in the rear of the gun barrel was a black mixture of (approximately; proportions varied) seventy-five per cent potassium nitrate, or saltpeter, and twelve and a half per cent each of charcoal and sulphur. The first touch of fire released part of the oxygen in the saltpeter. This oxygen served to burn the rest of the mixture. In other words, gunpowder was capable of burning without air, an ancient chemical discovery of enormous potential. Furthermore, the combusion released a huge volume of gas and white smoke. The rapid expansion of this gas propelled the ball through the barrel and on toward its target.

The more tightly the ball fitted into the barrel, the more efficient was the gun's performance. A loose bullet not only let some of the gas escape unutilized; it also bounced back and forth in the barrel. Its course was influenced, often erratically, by the manner of its striking just prior to leaving the muzzle. Furthermore, a round ball could not be cast so that its weight was uniformly distributed. The center of gravity never quite coincided with the spherical center, and this too imparted a wobble to the projectile. As a result, smoothbore guns that fired loosely fitting spherical bullets—the general name for such weapons was "musket"—were seldom accurate at ranges in excess of sixty yards or so.

In theory the disadvantages were easily remedied. Long before the settlement of North America, European gunsmiths had realized that spiral grooves, called rifling, inside the gun bore would impart a spin to a tightly fitted ball. Rapid spinning equalized weight distribution and eliminated wobble. Tightness did away with bouncing inside the bore and captured the full force of the powder discharge.

All this increased the rifle's range and accuracy, but it did present demerits. Driving a tight bullet down the full length of the barrel took more patience than a soldier generally possessed when someone else was shooting at him. The black powder fouled the grooves and increased the snugness unless the bore was swabbed after every second shot or so. Wooden ramrods often broke under the hard thrusts, while metal ones either harmed the rifling or dented the bullet, impairing accuracy.

Pioneer hunters padding quietly through the Kentucky woods did not find these drawbacks critical. The Indians they fought did not attack en masse, as European armies did, but stealthily in small groups. The game on which the pioneers depended, unlike the massed buffalo of the plains, was generally glimpsed at a distance through small openings. Hence the hunters desired range and accuracy in a gun more than speed of loading and accordingly devoted themselves to increasing these qualities. They found that the powder in the gun chamber burned slowly, relatively speaking. Often the ball was on its way before the last of the charge had ignited. To gain maximum thrust, barrels were elongated—but this made the guns heavy. To lighten the weapons, American gunsmiths gradually reduced the caliber (the diameter of the bore in hundredths of an inch) from the standard musket size of .69 to as little as .45. Other riflemen learned, meanwhile, that a bullet smaller than the bore could be used if the projectile was wrapped in a greased buckskin patch. This patch, which removed some of the fouling in the bore as it was inserted, fitted snugly into the grooves and imparted the desired spin to the bullet. Loading was thus greatly facilitated.

Attracted by these improvements, the United States Army tentatively adopted rifles as early as 1803. (Lewis and Clark took a few army rifles west with them on their great transcontinental trek.) Rifles, indeed, became the favorite weapon with which to experiment. When the Army contracted for its first breech-loading gun in 1819, the weapon was a rifle—but not a very satisfactory one because the complicated breech-loading mechanism, which allowed bullets to be inserted directly into the rear of the barrel, fouled quickly and jammed, and the belch of gas that escaped around the fittings tended to disconcert shooters. Still, when a short-barreled weapon, handy for use on horseback—the carbine—was authorized in 1833, it too was a breech-loading rifle.

More significantly, rifles were the first United States Army guns to employ percussion caps. These caps were the result of a discovery that certain powders called fulminates could be ignited by a blow rather than by sparks. The implications for weaponry were enormous. The insurmountable hazard for the flintlock was rain. The priming pan had to be opened for the powder to receive sparks from the flint, but the least dampness precluded ignition. Fulminates, however, could be wrapped in foil and sealed with varnish. The resultant caps could then be placed over a hollow nipple leading to the powder charge in the barrel and ignited by a blow from the gun hammer, which no longer was equipped with a flint. The steel plate, or frizzen, was thus eliminated, and the simpler mechanism that evolved was of course easier to keep in repair.

Military men at first were dubious about the caps. Careless handling exploded them and caused maimings. They were easily dropped while being fumbled onto the nipple under stress of battle. But their resistance to weather demanded that they be tested thoroughly. The 1833 breech-loading carbine employed them, and when the Army in 1841 authorized a full-length rifle, it too was equipped with percussion caps. Production started slowly, however, and only a few weapons of the new model were available at the outbreak of the war with Mexico. The initial supply went to Jefferson Davis' Mississippi volunteers. Because of that regiment's famous stand at Buena Vista, the 1841 rifle promptly became known as the Mississippi rifle.

Muskets as well as rifles could be adapted to firing by percussion. The conversion was just beginning at the time of the Mexican War, however, and as a consequence only a relatively few percussion-cap muskets saw use in the northern provinces during the first year of the conflict. To Army officers, particularly those who had to work with the short-term militia, the lack was not significant. As far as they were concerned, any musket whatsoever, either flintlock or percussion cap, was preferable to a rifle.

Rifles might be accurate, but rifles were temperamental. For top performance a rifleman had to know perfectly his own gun's whimsies about powder charges and aiming. Frequent cleaning was necessary. Though a hunter would take the requisite pains, a regimental mass of grumbling militiamen would not. For them, it was thought, the simplest sort of mechanism was best.

A musket was just that. The standard bore was .69 inches, slightly smaller than a twelve-gauge shotgun. A ball of .69 caliber weighed one ounce—sixteen to a pound. In actual practice, balls that weighed eighteen to the pound were used for ease in loading. Powder already measured in the proper amount, together with the projectile, came to the soldier in a paper cartridge of standard size. To load, the shooter tore the cartridge open with his teeth, shook a priming charge into the pan, rested the butt of the musket on the ground, poured the rest of the powder down the muzzle, and with his ramrod tamped in the ball, still wrapped in its cartridge paper.

After very little practice a man could load and fire three times a minute. True, he could not aim carefully in that time. But he did not have to, in those days when troops were customarily maneuvered in line of battle in close formation. The idea at Buena Vista, and at other battles of the era, was to pour out a few sweeping volleys at close range, counting on ricochets from the ground (unless it was plowed) to inflict at least ten per cent of the casualties, and then to close with the enemy in hand-to-hand combat utilizing the bayonet. (Rifles, being long-range weapons, were not designed for bayonets, which was another reason for preferring muskets.) Subtleties of marksmanship had little place in such fighting. As one authority expressed the matter as late as 1863, "Considering the difficulties of teaching principles of accurate firing and proper management of the rifle, we can not expect that the weapon in the hand of the masses will ever be more formidable than the old smoothbore musket. . . . At that supreme moment of life or death when passion takes the place of judgment, we can hardly expect the soldier to go through a series of calculations that require coolness and self-possession."*

The best muskets available during the heyday of the weapon were those of French design. This excellence, added to bonds of friendship growing out of the French alliance during the Revolution, led American gunsmiths naturally toward French prototypes. The model that evolved on this side of the Atlantic and that became the Army's chief reliance against the Mexican foot soldier was a gun of .69 caliber, 57.8 inches in over-all length. The barrel was 42 inches long; the blade of the bayonet, 18 inches. Weight without the eleven-ounce bayonet was nine and three-quarter pounds. The powder load was, on the average, 110 grains. The weapon could fire buckshot as well as ball, a versatility that further attracted the Army. On discharge it emitted clouds of white smoke, so that after a few volleys whole battalions were often wreathed in acrid mist and at times could not even see their opponents.

The Mexicans, who had few gunsmiths of their own, purchased weapons wherever they could and as a consequence suffered the usual inconveniences that come from lack of standardization. Their most common weapon was the "Brown Bess," a brass-mounted, twelve-pound, .75 caliber flintlock that had been employed by British troops during the American Revolution and, with the modifications, during the War of 1812. As later models displaced it, the Brown Bess was sold in quantity to the Mexican government. It was by no means an obsolete weapon, and its main drawback was caused by the Mexicans themselves. In trying to compensate for their inferior powder, they persistently overloaded the cartridges passed out to the soldiers. The increased recoil caused shooters to flinch, or even to fire from the hip, and helps explain the notoriously poor marksmanship of the ill-trained Mexican infantrymen.

* J. Roemer, *Cavalry: Its History, Management, and Uses in War* (New York, 1863), pp. 122–130, quoted in Russell, *Guns on the Early Frontiers,* p. 333.

The fieldpieces at Buena Vista were, in effect, overgrown muskets—smoothbores whose barrel lengths varied, according to the type of gun, from fifty-three to seventy-eight inches. The pieces were classified according to the weight of the solid projectile they fired. A 6-pounder gun had a caliber of 3.67 inches. Loaded with one and a quarter pounds of coarse-grained black powder, it threw a solid round iron or brass shot weighing 6.1 pounds a distance of about fifteen hundred yards. A 12-pounder gun, caliber 4.62, used twice as much powder to achieve a range of 1,660 yards (not quite a mile) with a solid shot weighing 12.3 pounds. A 12-pounder *howitzer* (to confuse matters) had the same caliber as a 12-pounder gun but fired a lighter (9-pound) shot a thousand yards at an expenditure of only one pound of powder. The howitzer's main advantage was lightness. Together with its carriage it weighed 1,688 pounds, as compared to 2,930 for a 12-pounder gun and carriage. Even a 6-pounder gun weighed more—1,784 pounds with carriage.

Until the opening decades of the nineteenth century, metal casting was not well understood. Gun barrels had to be heavy to prevent bursting. The gun's iron trail (analogous to a musket's stock, the trail rested on the ground and steadied the piece) was so massive that rapid readjustment after each firing was almost impossible. Carriages for moving so much weight were also heavy and ponderous in movement.

During the Napoleonic wars, better castings were developed, especially of bronze. This allowed lighter guns and more maneuverable carriages. Even so, it took six horses harnessed two abreast, with a driver mounted on each off-wheel animal, to whirl the new guns and their ammunition transport around the battlefields at a smart trot.

Hitched immediately behind the rear two-horse team was the limber, a two-wheeled carriage supporting a single ammunition chest resting above and parallel to the axle. A chest for a

6-pounder carried fifty rounds and weighed, when full, 560 pounds; a chest for a 12-pounder weighed about fifty pounds more when full and held thirty-two rounds. The gun carriage was hooked on behind the limber, its trail attached to the underside of the ammunition carrier and its muzzle pointing to the rear. Detaching the gun for action was called unlimbering.

Additional ammunition was carried into battle by another separable four-wheeled vehicle, one vehicle for each gun. It too was drawn by six horses. The front half of the vehicle was another limber supporting a single ammunition chest. Hooked on behind the limber was a two-wheeled caisson carrying two chests. This ammunition carrier and the fieldpiece it accompanied had to stay close together, for between them they transported the gunner who aimed the piece and his eight cannoneers, called matrosses, who brought ammunition to the piece, sponged it out, loaded it, and fired it. Three of these nine men rode atop the ammunition chest on each limber, and three on the caisson.

In spite of handrails, the ride was dangerous. Matrosses jolted overboard on rough ground often broke limbs or were crunched under the wheels. For their sakes, drivers sometimes were cautious in difficult terrain. To increase safety and speed, Captain Samuel Ringgold, Battery C, Third United States Field Artillery Regiment, decided about 1838 to mount his gunners and matrosses on horseback and train them to ride in close coordination with the teams. Two horse holders went along to manage the animals during firing. Results were good enough that shortly before the conflict with Mexico the War Department authorized one battery of horse artillery—or, more popularly, "flying artillery"—per regiment. The Mexicans, it should be noted, possessed neither such lightweight, highly maneuverable field guns nor powerful horses for pulling the guns they did use. If they had, the outcome at Buena Vista might have been different.

Though the American pieces were mobile, they were not notably accurate. After the weapon had been set up, the powder rammed home in its cloth case, and the shot tamped on top, the gunner simply squinted along the barrel (night firing was considered futile), moved the elevation screw as desired, and ordered his matrosses to shift the trail right or left, as needed. The Number Three matross, who until this time had kept the touchhole covered with a gloved hand, then pierced the cloth powder case with a vent pick. Primer tubes were thrust through the opening. The second gunner blew his slow match to a glow (it was a combustible cord attached, for handling, to a forked stick called a linstock) and with it ignited the primer tubes. The discharge heaved out dense clouds of smoke. The gun recoiled violently and had to be dragged back into position with ropes hooked to the trail and carriage axles.

Solid shot was used, generally, for battering down fortifications. When troops were attacked, the fieldpieces were often turned into oversized shotguns hurling clusters of musket balls. Depending on how these balls were packaged, the projectile was known as grape, canister, or spherical case. Grapeshot was a clump of balls an inch or more in diameter held between plates that flew apart at the moment of discharge. Canister was more sophisticated: a cylindrical tin container nailed to a wooden base, or sabot. An inner charge set off by a fuse that was ignited by the flash of the gun's firing burst the container open during flight. Spherical case, as the name suggests, was round; the balls it held were smaller than those in canister or grape and were embedded in sulphur. It too was burst by an inner charge.

Effective range for canister, the most common antipersonnel case shot, was from 350 to 500 yards. Had good rifles been employed for picking off horses and men, the fieldpieces could not have approached that close to their targets. Muskets, however, had not range enough to harm the gunners, and thus it was possible for Taylor's men at Palo Alto and again at Buena Vista to shift their guns about aggressively, using them not just in artillery's traditional function as support for infantry but as independent units of attack. On those two battlefields, at least, a mere handful of the smart little fieldpieces and the canister they hurled at moments of crisis almost surely spelled the difference between defeat and victory.

NOTES

<hr />

1. For Taylor's career, see the biographies by Dyer, Hamilton, and McKinley and Bent. Full publishing data is in the Bibliography.

2. For background data on Mexico and Texas I have relied on McMaster, *History of the People of the United States*, Vol. VII; Bancroft, *History of Mexico*, Vols. IV and V; Rives, *The United States and Mexico*, Vol. I; Stephenson, *Texas and the Mexican War;* Barker, *Life of Stephen F. Austin.* Two sound and readable popular accounts are Carter, *Doomed Road of Empire* and Horgan, *Great River.* For useful summaries, see Billington, *The Far Western Frontier*, pp. 14–22, 116–142, and Hollon, *The Southwest, Old and New*, pp. 67–151. Since Chapters I, II, and III of my text are, by and large, a highly compressed compendium of all this material, I have, with minor exceptions, omitted footnote citations as not particularly instructive.

3. A vigorous defense of Wilkinson, which runs counter to gen-erally accepted theories about his guilt, is in Francis S. Philbrick, *The Rise of the West, 1776–1830,* (New York, 1965) pp. 175–184, 229–252.

4. For Santa Anna, see biographies by Callcott and Hanighen listed in the Bibliography. For the Guitiérrez rebellion, see Carter, *op. cit.*, pp. 217–238; Horgan, *op. cit.*, pp. 422–430.

5. Dyer, p. 8.

6. *Ibid.*, p. 23.

7. Scott, *Memoirs*, Vol. II, pp. 390–391.

8. *Diary and Letters of Josiah Gregg*, Vol. I, p. 307. Gregg's population figure was for 1846. Presumably it had not changed greatly in the twenty-four years since Austin's ride.

9. Bancroft, *op. cit.*, Vol. V, p. 421 n.

10. For Stephen Austin's own skimpy reports about his first trip into Mexico, see Barker (ed.), *Austin Papers*, pp. 485 ff.

CHAPTER 2

1. J. Smith, *War with Mexico,* Vol. I, p. 42.

2. There is no unanimity about Mexican casualties at the Alamo. See Bancroft, *History of Mexico*, Vol. V, p. 168 n; Billington, *Far*

Western Frontier, p. 128; Horgan, *Great River*, p. 532.

3. Bancroft, *op. cit.*, Vol. V, pp. 169–171. There is some question in Mexican sources (though not in Texan) as to whether or not Urrea actually promised clemency—or, if he did, whether Santa Anna knew it.

4. A synopsis of the treaty terms is *ibid.* pp. 173–174 n.

5. For the French troubles, Rives, *U.S. and Mexico*, Vol. I, pp. 435–444; Bancroft, *op. cit.*, Vol. V, pp. 186–200.

6. Rives, *op. cit.*, Vol. I, p. 460; Hanighen, *Santa Anna*, pp. 179–180.

7. Kendall, *Narrative of the Texan-Santa Fe Expedition.*

8. For the early Rangers: Webb, *Texas Rangers*, pp. 67–116. For the Colt revolver, *ibid.*, pp. 84–86, and Webb, *Great Plains* (Grosset and Dunlap edition), pp. 167–176. Statements that Walker developed the so-called Walker Colt in 1841 are probably erroneous (Edwards, *Story of Colt's Revolver*).

9. Chamberlain, *My Confession*, p. 39.

10. For the Mier adventure, see Green's *Journal of the Texian Expedition Against Mier. . . .* An excellent summary is in Horgan, *op. cit.*, pp. 592–600.

CHAPTER 3

1. Taylor to General Henry Atkinson, June 2, 1832, quoted in Hagan, *The Sac and Fox Indians*, p. 166.

2. Taylor's letters to Wood, collected by William Bixby of St. Louis, were edited by William Samson and published as *The Letters of Zachary Taylor from the Battlefields of the Mexican War*. They will be cited hereafter as *Battlefield Letters*.

3. "I shall never forget how faithfully and ably General Taylor sustained me in Florida. . . ." Jesup to Captain John Sanders, July 5, 1846. *House Executive Document 60, 30th U.S. Congress, 1st Session, 1847–48* (Washington, 1848), cited hereafter as *HED 60*.

4. As usual there is no firm agreement about casualties. I follow the figures in Hamilton's *Zachary Taylor*, Vol. I, pp. 129–133. But see John Tebbel and Keith Jennison, *The American Indian Wars* (New York, 1960), pp. 209–219, who give 28 killed, 111 wounded.

5. McMaster, *History of the People of the U.S.*, Vol. VII, pp. 431–432.

6. Rives, *U.S. and Mexico*, Vol. II, pp. 102–103. J. Smith, *War with Mexico*, Vol. I, pp. 3, 407.

7. Again authorities disagree on figures. J. Smith, *op. cit.*, Vol. I, p. 139, and Ganoe, *History of the United States Army*, p. 196, give 8,613 men as the Army's authorized strength. I follow Ivor D. Spencer, who in his biography of William Marcy, Polk's Secretary of War, *The Victor and the Spoils*, gives 7,833. Estimates for the actual numbers enrolled range from 7,200 (Smith) down to 5,300 (Ganoe). Rives, *op. cit.*, Vol. II, pp. 195 ff, perhaps as dependable as any, suggests 42 men for each company of infantry and artillery and 50 for dragoons, for a total of 5,612 privates, musicians, and noncoms, plus 633 commissioned officers.

8. L. Lewis, *Captain Sam Grant*, pp. 117–118.

9. Grant, *Memoirs*, p. 60; Ganoe, *op. cit.*, p. 190.

10. *HED 60*, p. 232.

11. Ganoe, *op. cit.*, pp. 199–200; J. Smith, *op. cit.*, Vol. I, p. 142; Bill, *Rehearsal For Conflict*, p. 85.

12. Barna Upton, manuscript letter home from Corpus Christi, August 31, 1845 (Yale University Library, Western Americana Collection); hereafter cited as Upton. Other details on Corpus Christi from William S. Henry, Ethan A. Hitchcock, Ulysses S. Grant (see Bibliography). The official correspondence is in *Senate Executive Document 1, 29th U.S. Congress,* *2nd Session*, pp. 220 ff., hereafter cited as *SED 1*.

13. Quoted in J. Smith, *op. cit.*, Vol. I, p. 144.

14. Bancroft, *History of Mexico*, Vol. V, p. 347.

15. Rives, *op. cit.*, Vol. II, pp. 59 ff.; *HED 60*, p. 115.

16. Rives, *op. cit.*, Vol. II, pp. 72 ff.

17. Benton, *Thirty Years' View*, Vol. II, pp. 693–694.

18. J. Smith, *op. cit.*, Vol. I, pp. 207 ff.; Rives, *op. cit.*, Vol. II, pp. 118–119; Spencer, *op. cit.*, p. 148.

CHAPTER 4

1. Participants whose accounts of the march have been utilized here include Hitchcock, Grant, Henry, and French, plus the official correspondence in *HED 60*. See also Horgan, *Great River*, Vol. II, pp. 609–612; Lewis, *Grant*, pp. 134–137.

2. Quoted in J. Smith, *War with Mexico*, Vol. I, p. 141.

3. Upton, manuscript letter from Matamoros, July 9, 1846.

4. For the deserters: articles by Finke and Wallace (see Bibliography); also Rives, *U.S. and Mexico*, Vol. II, p. 228; Kenly, *Memoirs*, pp. 39–41. Copies of the Mexican proclamations are in *House Executive Document 119, 29th U.S. Congress, 2nd Session* (hereafter *HED 119*). Taylor's counterproclamations, *HED 60*, p. 284.

5. Horgan, *op. cit.*, p. 670.

6. As usual, figures of deaths vary, from 11 (Horgan, p. 671) to 16 (L. Lewis, pp. 140–141). See also *HED 60*, pp. 291–292.

7. Again there are discrepancies in the figures. Webb, *Rangers*, says 15 were killed. Taylor's preliminary report of May 3, 1846, to the Adjutant General (*HED 60*) lists 5 killed, 5 missing.

8. Upton, *op. cit.*

9. Hamilton, *Zachary Taylor*, p. 288; L. Lewis, *op. cit.*, p. 141; J. Smith, *op. cit.*, Vol. I, p. 162; Bancroft, *Mexico*, Vol. V, p. 352; Horgan, *op. cit.*, pp. 670–672.

10. *HED 60*, p. 299.

11. The smaller figure is Rives's (Vol. II, p. 146), quoting Mexican sources. The larger is Taylor's estimate. (His reports for this period are in *HED 60*, pp. 293–296.) J. Smith (Vol. I, p. 164) says Arista had 4,000 or so men. By now it should be evident that authorities do not agree on figures, and sources of the discrepant statistics will no longer be cited in detail, for the matter is hardly edifying.

12. A Mexican surmise that the Americans deliberately set the fires is probably incorrect (Bancroft, Vol. V, p. 355).

13. For the battle of Palo Alto: *Senate Document 388, 29th U. S. Congress, 1st Session*, pp. 2–23 (hereafter cited as *SD 388*); *HED 60*, pp. 293 ff, 1102–1104; J. Smith, *op. cit.*, pp. 166–167; Bill, *op. cit.*,

pp. 94–96; Rives, *op. cit.*, Vol. II, pp. 144–151; Bancroft, *op. cit.*, Vol. V, pp. 353–356; Horgan, *op. cit.*, pp. 682–685.

14. As just cited, *SD 388; HED 60*, pp. 296, 1104–1106; J. Smith, pp. 170–176; Rives, Vol. II, pp. 152–156; Bancroft, Vol. V, pp. 357–360; Bill, pp. 96–99; Horgan, pp. 685–689.

15. Lewis, *op. cit.*, p. 149. Grant, *Memoirs*, pp. 60–61.

16. *HED 60*, pp. 297–298.

17. *HED 60*, pp. 298–300; J. Smith, pp. 177–178; Bancroft, Vol. V, pp. 360–367; Horgan, pp. 696–700; Upton, letters of May 24, July 9, July 29.

18. Scribner, *Campaign In Mexico*, p. 29.

19. Taylor to Adjutant General, May 21, 1846, *HED 60*, p. 300.

CHAPTER 5

1. Billington, *Westward Expansion*, pp. 578–579; DeVoto, *Year of Decision*, pp. 185–186; Rives, *U.S. and Mexico*, Vol. II, pp. 157–161.

2. Spencer, *Victor and the Spoils*, p. 154.

3. J. Smith, *War with Mexico*, Vol. I, p. 196.

4. *Ibid.*, p. 198.

5. Spencer, *op. cit.*, pp. 153 ff.

6. Horgan, *Great River*, pp. 693–694.

7. Hanighen, *Santa Anna*, p. 197. Rives, *op. cit.*, Vol. II, pp. 119–123. DeVoto, *op. cit.*, pp. 69–70.

8. McMaster, *History of the People of the U.S.*, Vol. VII, pp. 447–448.

9. The Polk-Scott-Marcy correspondence concerning command is in *Senate Executive Document 378, 29th U.S. Congress, 1st Session*, pp. 4–17, hereafter cited as *SED 378*. See also Spencer, *op. cit.*, pp. 154–156; Rives, *op. cit.*, Vol. II, pp. 204–207; J. Smith, *op. cit.*, Vol. I, pp. 196–200.

10. Marcy to Taylor, June 8, 1846, *HED 60*, pp. 324–326.

11. Marcy to Taylor, July 9, 1846, *Ibid.*, pp. 335–336.

12. For McCulloch's activities during the summer of 1846, see Reid, *Scouting Expeditions*, which covers events only through the battle of Monterrey.

13. Taylor began planning an advance on Monterrey on May 21, three days after occupying Matamoros (*HED 60*, p. 300). Charges by Justin Smith, and by DeVoto, who followed Smith's lead, that Taylor sank into sloth on the Rio Grande are unjustifiably severe.

14. For the volunteer problems, *SED 378*, pp. 19–61 *passim; HED 60*, pp. 307–323.

15. *Battlefield Letters*, pp. 13–35 *passim*; Hamilton, *Zachary Taylor*, Vol. I, pp. 197 ff.

16. *Battlefield Letters*, pp. 9–10.

17. *Ibid.*, pp. 13–14, 17–19.

18. L. Lewis, *Grant*, pp. 159–160, 163.

19. Rives, *op. cit.*, Vol. II, pp. 232–236.

20. McCormac, *Polk*, p. 440.

21. Taylor to Adjutant General, July 2, *HED 60*, p. 331; Taylor to Polk, August 1, *ibid.*, pp. 336–338.

22. Quaife (ed.), Polk's *Diary*, Vol. II, pp. 118–119.

23. Upton, manuscript letter, August 28, 1846, tells of four troopers being killed when they dropped behind to look for a strayed mule.

24. Nichols, *Zach Taylor's Little Army*, p. 128.

25. *Ibid.*, p. 133.

26. Bancroft, *History of Mexico*, Vol. V, pp. 377.

27. Quoted in L. Lewis, *op. cit.*, p. 165.

28. *HED 60*, pp. 557–558.

29. Quaife (ed.), Polk's *Diary*, Vol. II, pp. 118–119.

30. *HED 60*, pp. 588–559.

31. For Santa Anna, Havana to Mexico City, see Hanighen, *op. cit.*, pp. 198–200; J. Smith, *op. cit.*, Vol. I, pp. 213–222; Rives, *op. cit.*, Vol. II, pp. 241–246. See also J. Smith, *Letters of Santa Anna*, p. 358.

32. Rives, *op. cit.*, Vol. II, pp. 230–231, 245–246; McCormac, *op. cit.*, pp. 441–453.

33. Bancroft, *op. cit.*, Vol. V, pp. 399 ff.

CHAPTER 6

1. For the fortifying of Monterrey, see J. Smith, *War with Mexico*, Vol. I, pp. 226–233.

2. *Ibid.*, p. 494.

3. *Ibid.*, pp. 494–495.

4. Gregg, *Diary*, Vol. I, p. 356.

5. *Ibid.*, p. 351.

6. *Terry's Guide to Mexico*, revised by James Norman (New York, 1963), p. 136.

7. Gregg, *op. cit.*, Vol. I, p. 351.

8. J. Smith, *op. cit.*, Vol. I, p. 249, says the tannery mounted two guns. Most accounts agree on four: Rives (Vol. II, p. 262), McMaster (Vol. VII, p. 453), Gregg (*loc. cit.*), etc.

9. More discrepancies on numbers: J. Smith (p. 232–233), says eight guns; Rives (Vol. II, p. 262) says eight or ten. I follow Gregg (Vol. I, p. 351), who examined the field shortly after the battle and says twelve.

10. Official reports on Monterrey are in *House Executive Document 4, 29th U.S. Congress, 2nd session*, pp. 76–109, hereafter cited as *HED 4*. Accounts of participants include those of S. G. French (pp. 64–66), U. S. Grant (Vol. I, pp. 110–118), W. S. Henry (pp. 192–212), J. R. Kenly (pp. 97–120), and Samuel Reid (pp. 153 ff.). Later histories include Bancroft (Vol. V, pp. 392–401), Nichols (pp. 142–162), Rives (Vol. II, pp. 263–273), and J. Smith (pp. 239–259).

11. J. Smith, *op. cit.*, Vol. I, pp. 239, 244.

12. J. Smith, who is violently critical of Taylor, credits the plan to Worth (Vol. I, p. 497). Other commentators generally credit Taylor.

13. Webb, *Texas Rangers*, p. 104.

14. For instance, DeVoto, *Year of Decision*, p. 283.

15. J. Smith, *op. cit.*, Vol. I, p. 244.

16. For Worth's report, see *HED 4*, pp. 103 ff.

17. Irreconcilable differences exist in the accounts that touch on Backus' activities. By and large I follow Smith (Vol. I, p. 252 f.).

18. Bancroft, *History of Mexico*, Vol. V, pp. 383–385, quoting Mexican sources.

19. Upton, manuscript letter to his brother, November 29.

20. Rives, *U.S. and Mexico*, Vol. II, p. 269.

21. Upton, *op. cit.* Other sources (for instance, Rives, Vol. II, p. 269) say the lancers were ineffective.

22. French, *Two Wars*, p. 66.

23. Upton, *op. cit.*

24. Worth's report, *loc. cit.*, p. 105; J. Smith, *op. cit.*, Vol. I, pp.

256–257; Bancroft, *op. cit.*, Vol. V, p. 395.

25. Taylor in *HED 4*, p. 86 ff.; J. Smith and Bancroft as before.

26. *Ibid.*, plus S. C. Smith, *Chile Con Carne*, pp. 94–95.

27. The terms are in *HED 4*, pp. 80–81.

28. Bancroft, *op. cit.*, Vol. V, pp. 399–401.

29. Jefferson Davis vigorously defended the armistice in a letter published in the Washington *Un-ion*. The letter is reprinted in Reid, *Scouting Expeditions*, pp. 205–209.

30. *HED 60*, pp. 359–360. See also Taylor's letter of November 5 to Edmund P. Gaines, published first in the New York *Morning Express*, January 22, 1847, and reprinted extensively. It is most readily available today in *Niles Register*, LXXI: 342–343.

31. *HED 60*, p. 341.

32. J. Smith, *op. cit.*. Vol. I, p. 223.

CHAPTER 7

1. Rives, *U.S. and Mexico*, Vol. II, p. 279.

2. J. Smith (ed.), *Letters of Santa Anna*, p. 368; *HED 60*, pp. 339–340.

3. *HED 60*, p. 372.

4. *Battlefield Letters*, pp. 17–20.

5. *HED 60*, p. 373.

6. *Ibid.*, p. 344.

7. *Ibid.*, pp. 341–343.

8. Quaife (ed.), Polk's *Diary*, Vol. II, p. 181.

9. *Ibid.*, pp. 183–186.

10. Marcy to Taylor, October 13, 1846, *HED 60*, pp. 355–357; McCormac, *Polk*, p. 449.

11. Webb, *Texas Rangers*, p. 110.

12. Gunn, "Ben McCulloch," *Southwest Historical Quarterly*, LVIII: 8.

13. Edwards, *Colt's Revolver*, pp. 215–227. Cf. Webb's *Texas Rangers*, pp. 84–86, and *Great Plains* (Grosset and Dunlap edition), pp. 167–176, where a different account of the Walker Colt is given.

14. *HED 60*, pp. 350–354.

15. For Taylor's suspicions, see his letter of November 10 to Wood (*Battlefield Letters*, pp. 66–67). Polk's doubts about Taylor are in his *Diary*, Vol. II, pp. 229–230. A good summary of the antagonism between the two men is in Singletary, *Mexican War*, pp. 102–116.

16. *HED 60*, p. 354.

17. As in preceding Note 10.

18. Nichols, *Zach Taylor's Little Army*, p. 177.

19. *Battlefield Letters*, p. 67.

20. *HED 119*, p. 152.

21. *Niles Register*, LXXI, 342–343; Singletary, *op. cit.*, p. 112: *HED 60*, pp. 359–360.

22. *HED 119*, p. 156.

23. The official report of Wool's advance is in *Senate Document 32, 31st U.S. Congress, 1st Session*. Other firsthand accounts are Gregg's *Diary*, Vol. I, pp. 233–300; Isabel Wallace (ed.), *Life and Letters of General W. H. L. Wallace*, pp. 21 ff. Chamberlain's purported description in *My Confession* is not reliable. Secondary accounts include Baylies, *Narrative of General Wool's Campaign*, pp. 1–20; Carter, *Doomed Road of Empire*, pp. 349–357; Freeman, *Lee*, Vol. I, pp. 203–217.

24. Baylies, *op. cit.*, p. 17.

25. Taylor to Gaines, November 5, 1846; reprinted in *Niles Register*, LXXI, 342.

26. *HED 60*, p. 361.
27. *Ibid.*, pp. 363–367.
28. *Ibid.*
29. *Ibid.*, pp. 374–376.
30. J. Smith (ed.), *Letters of Santa Anna*, pp. 368–370.
31. Gregg, *Diary*, Vol. I, p. 274.
32. Wallace *Letters*, p. 25.
33. Gregg, *Diary*, Vol. I, pp. 275, 297.
34. Baylies, *op. cit.*, p. 19.
35. Gregg, *Diary*, Vol. I, pp. 293–294.
36. Wallace *Letters*, pp. 27, 28.
37. Chamberlain, *My Confession*, p. 68; Duncan, "A Morgan County Volunteer," *Journal of the Illinois Historical Society XLI*, 392.

38. Baylies, *op. cit.*, p. 20; Wallace *Letters*, p. 28.
39. *HED 60*, 379–381.
40. *Battlefield Letters*, p. 78.
41. Polk's high opinion of Patterson is indicated by his suggesting that the Philadelphian be elevated over both Taylor and Scott to the supreme command of the Army in Mexico. Elliott, *Winfield Scott*, pp. 439–440.
42. For the Taylor-Patterson troubles, see *HED 119*, pp. 100 ff; also W. S. Henry, *Campaign Sketches*, pp. 240–248.
43. *Battlefield Letters*, p. 76.

CHAPTER 8

1. Quaife (ed.), Polk's *Diary*, Vol. II, p. 231; Chambers, *Old Bullion Benton*, pp. 308–309.
2. *Diary*, Vol. II, pp. 236, 240–241.
3. *Ibid.*, p. 230.
4. As in Note 1.
5. Scott's various memoranda on Veracruz and Mexico City are in *HED 60*, pp. 1268–1273.
6. Elliott, *Winfield Scott*, p. 434.
7. *Diary*, Vol. II, p. 243; J. Smith, *War with Mexico*, Vol. I, p. 351.
8. *Diary*, Vol. II, pp. 249–250.
9. *Ibid.*, pp. 244–245; Elliott, *op. cit.*, pp. 438–440; Singletary, *Mexican War*, p. 111.
10. J. Smith, *op. cit.*, Vol. I, pp. 354, 356; Elliott, *op. cit.*, p. 442.
11. Quoted in Rives, *U.S. and Mexico*, Vol. I, p. 300.
12. *HED 60*, pp. 1274–1275.
13. *Ibid.*, pp. 373–374.
14. *Battlefield Letters*, p. 75.
15. Buley, "Indiana in the Mexican War," p. 288.

16. Quoted in Perry, *Indiana in the Mexican War*, pp. 127–128.
17. Withers to Boyd, manuscript letter of December 29, 1846; *Encarnación Prisoners*, pp. 24 ff.
18. As usual cynics found this admirable explanations for the haste. Gregg, traveling with Wool and disliking him intensely, said the General fled to Worth for shelter, not to help him, and would have abandoned the wounded if his staff had not protested (*Diary*, Vol. I, p. 325). Views more flattering than Gregg's are in Carleton, *Buena Vista*, pp. 176 ff.; Baylies, *General Wool's Campaign*, pp. 20–22; Wallace *Letters*, pp. 29 ff.; and Freeman, *Lee*, Vol. I, p. 211.
19. Baylies, *op. cit.*, p. 22; Duncan, "A Morgan County Volunteer," p. 395.
20. As in Note 15. See also *HED 119*, pp. 104–105.
21. Wallace *Letters*, pp. 29 f.
22. Carleton, *Buena Vista*, pp. 177–186, plus the official maps of the area as surveyed by Captain

T. B. Linnard of the Corps of Topographical Engineers. Carleton checked his memory about the selection of the site by submitting his account to Wool, who okayed it and later vouched for its correctness in a private letter to John Abert, January 3, 1848.

23. Wallace *Letters*, pp. 55–56.

24. The exact sequence of the alarms and Putler's orders about Wool's camp cannot be determined with certainty; see Baylies (pp. 23–24), Carleton (pp. 180–181), Freeman (Vol. I, pp. 213–216), Gregg (Vol. I, 323 ff.).

25. *HED 60*, p. 848.

26. Nichols, *Zach Taylor's Little Army*, p. 192.

27. May's account, *HED 60*, pp. 1095–1097. See also Gregg, *Diary*, Vol. I, p. 340.

28. Scott's biographers still assume a deliberate avoidance (Elliott, p. 447; also J. Smith, Vol. I, p. 358). Taylor's biographers retort that his presence in Victoria was necessary (Hamilton, Vol. I, p. 228).

29. J. Smith, *op. cit.*, Vol. I, p. 362.

30. Rives, *op. cit.*, Vol. II, pp. 340–342.

31. For the interception, *HED 60*, pp. 849–850; Gregg, *Diary*, Vol. I, p. 340; Webb, *Texas Rangers*, p. 111.

32. *HED 60*, pp. 862–863.

33. Gregg, *Diary*, Vol. I, pp. 329–333, 344, 349; *Encarnación*

Prisoners, p. 32; Scribner, *Campaign in Mexico*, p. 57.

34. Wallace *Letters*, p. 33.

35. Baylies, *op. cit.*, p. 25.

36. Chamberlain, *My Confession*, p. 95 n.

37. Quotation from Withers to Boyd, manuscript letter of January 31, 1847. The fullest account of the capture of the patrols is the pamphlet, *Encarnación Prisoners*, written by one of the prisoners. Somewhat discrepant details are in Wool's report, *HED 60*, pp. 1106–1108; Gregg, *Diary*, Vol. I, pp. 346, 349; Wallace *Letters*, pp. 35–37.

38. Garnett to "My Dear L.," March 2, 1847.

39. Gregg, *Diary*, Vol. I, pp. 330–366 *passim*.

40. *Battlefield Letters*, *passim*; J. Smith, Vol. I, pp. 352–353.

41. J. Smith, Vol. I, p. 368.

42. *HED 60*, pp. 1100–1102.

43. *Battlefield Letters*, pp. 83–84.

44. Carleton, *op. cit.*, pp. 2–4; Rives, *op. cit.*, Vol. I, p. 347.

45. Smith, Vol. I, p. 373.

46. Polk's *Diary*, Vol. II, p. 307; *HED 60*, p. 389.

47. *HED 60*, p. 864.

48. *Battlefield Letters*, p. 85.

49. *Ibid.*, p. 86.

50. Polk's *Diary*, Vol. II, pp. 353–356; Nichols, *op. cit.*, pp. 198–200; Singletary, *Mexican War*, pp. 112–113.

51. *HED 60*, p. 1162.

52. *Battlefield Letters*, p. 87.

53. *HED 60*, p. 1110.

CHAPTER 9

1. Rives, *U.S. and Mexico*, Vol. II, pp. 308–316.

2. *Ibid.*, pp. 419–422. Quaife, Polk's *Diary*, Vol. II, pp. 325–326.

3. J. Smith, *War With Mexico*, Vol. I, pp. 378–380.

4. Rives, *op. cit.*, Vol. II, pp. 340–342; Bancroft, *History of Mexico*, Vol. V, pp. 415–416.

5. Finke, "San Patricio Units," *Military Collector and Historian*, X: 36–37.

6. Rives, *op. cit.*, Vol. II, p. 362.

7. Translated in *SED 1*, pp. 153–154. This publication also contains Taylor's official report and the subreports of his officers about the battle of Buena Vista.

8. Webb, *Texas Rangers*, p. 122; *Encarnación Prisoners*, pp. 44-45.

9. Carleton, *Buena Vista*, pp. 229–232; *SED 1*, pp. 154 ff.; Rives, *op. cit.*, Vol. II, p. 362; Bancroft, *op. cit.*, Vol. V, pp. 415-417. (Bancroft's statement, p. 417 n, that 4,000 of Santa Anna's men deserted during the march seems too high.)

10. *SED 1*, p. 132; Reid, *Scouting Expeditions*, p. 235; Webb, *op. cit.*, p. 112.

11. J. Smith, *Letters of Santa Anna*, p. 383.

12. Carleton, *op. cit.*, p. 2; Gregg, *Diary*, Vol. II, p. 34.

13. Carleton, *op. cit.*, p. 26; Garnett to "My Dear L.," March 2, 1847.

14. Baylies, *General Wool's Campaign*, p. 26; Wallace *Letters*, p. 39; Rives, *op. cit.*, Vol. II, p. 347.

15. Garnett, *op. cit.*

16. Gregg, *Diary*, Vol. II, pp. 37-39.

17. Duncan, "A Morgan County Volunteer," p. 395.

18. Perry, *Indiana in the Mexican War*, pp. 133–134; Buley, "The Buena Vista Controversy," in *Indiana Magazine of History*, XVI, pp. 66-67.

19. For May's reconnaissance, see Carleton, *op. cit.*, pp. 12–18, 144-145.

20. *SED 1*, p. 132; Webb, *op. cit.*, p. 113.

21. Scribner, *Campaign in Mexico*, p. 58.

22. For the evacuation of Agua Nueva and the first night at Buena Vista, see Wool (*SED 1*, pp. 144-145); Carleton (p. 24), and Duncan (p. 397).

23. For the burning of Agua Nueva, see Carleton (pp. 25–26), Gregg (Vol. II, p. 24), and Wool (*SED 1*, p. 145).

24. Gibson, *Letter*.

25. For the deployment: Taylor (*SED 1*, pp. 132-135), Wool (*ibid.*, p. 145), Carleton (p. 32–35), Rives (Vol. II, pp. 351–352), and Nichols (pp. 214–215).

26. The description in the text is deduced from *SED 1* (pp. 133, 215) and Baylies (p. 29). It is tentative, awaiting further evidence.

27. Taylor, *SED 1*, pp. 132-133; French, *Two Wars*, p. 77.

CHAPTER 10

1. Translated in Carleton, *Buena Vista*, pp. 232-235.

2. *Ibid.*

3. Rives, *U.S. and Mexico*, Vol. II, p. 360.

4. Carleton, *op. cit.*, pp. 27–29; Garnett, manuscript letter of March 2, 1847; Taylor to Butler, March 4, 1847, quoted in Baylies, *General Wool's Campaign*, p. 27.

5. The reports of the American commanders consistently speak of Santa Anna as having 20,000 men. The figure is based on McCulloch's estimate and on Santa Anna's own statement in the letter demanding Taylor's surrender (see text). The same sources set Miñon's strength at 2,500. Santa Anna, however, was exaggerating to impress his foe. He had, perhaps, 15,000 to 16,000 men. Miñon had no more than 1,500. Taylor's force at Buena Vista numbered 334 officers and 4,425 men. There were 800 more at Saltillo during the battle. Another 300 or so were called up from Monterrey and the Rinconada (*SED 1*, pp. 127,

142–143; Rives, *op. cit.*, Vol. II, p. 362).

6. The weakness was also recognized by the Americans: see Gibson, *Letter*, p. 1, and Wallace *Letters*, pp. 53, 55–56.

7. Bancroft, *History of Mexico*, Vol. V, p. 425 n.

8. J. Smith, *War with Mexico*, Vol. I, p. 385.

9. *SED 1*, pp. 97–98; Wallace *Letters*, p. 41.

10. Carleton, *op. cit.*, pp. 40–41.

11. Marshall's report, *SED 1*, pp. 163–165; Gorman, *ibid.*, pp. 189 f.

12. Wallace *Letters*, p. 43.

13. As in Note 11.

14. Carleton, *op. cit.*, p. 47.

15. Gibson, *Letter*, p. 3.

16. Carleton, *op. cit.*, p. 49.

17. The tale about Bowles is reconstructed chiefly from the reminescences of Lt. Col. W. R. Haddon of the Second Indiana, in Perry, *Indiana in the Mexican War*, pp. 293–294. See also Scribner, *Campaign in Mexico*, p. 62. A somewhat different account is in Buley, "The Buena Vista Controversy," *Indiana Magazine of History*, XVI: 50 ff.

18. Bancroft, *op. cit.*, Vol. V, pp. 424–425; Carleton, *op. cit.*, pp. 53 ff.

19. Wool, *SED 1*, pp. 146–147; Trail's report, *ibid.*, p. 178.

20. Buley, *op. cit.*, pp. 54 ff.

21. As in Note 18.

22. Wallace *Letters*, p. 43; Chamberlain, *My Confession*, pp. 114 f.

23. Baylies, *op. cit.*, p. 32; Gibson, *op. cit.*, pp. 2–3.

24. Wool, *SED 1*, p. 147; Bragg,

ibid., p. 200; Carleton, *op. cit.*, p. 58; Wallace *Letters*, p. 44.

25. Joseph Lane, *SED 1*, p. 181; John P. J. O'Brien, *ibid.*, p. 160; Carleton, *op. cit.*, pp. 50, 58.

26. Duncan, "A Morgan County Volunteer," p. 398; Gibson, *op. cit.*, pp. 3–4; Wallace *Letters*, p. 43.

27. Buley, *op. cit.*, p. 57.

28. The retreat of the Indiana Regiment is in Wool, Gen. Lane, and O'Brien, *SED 1*, pp. 147, 182, and 160. These official reports are relatively restrained, especially concerning Bowles. For franker views by participants, see Carleton (pp. 59–62) and Scribner (pp. 60–62). Charges and countercharges concerning the affair, the most controversial happening of the battle, are reproduced in Perry; see especially Joseph Lane's statement, pp. 300–311. The various arguments are reviewed by Buley (*Indiana Magazine of History*, XV: 299–310; XVI: 46 ff.).

29. Bissell, *SED 1*, pp. 176–177; Carleton, *op. cit.*, pp. 64–65.

30. Marshall, Roane (for the Arkansas cavalry), Trail and Gorman reports are in *SED 1*, pp. 148, 166–167, 172, 179, 190. See also *West Point Atlas of American Wars*, Vol. I, map 14.

31. Wool letter to Joseph W. Moulton, May 20, 1847.

32. Baylies, *op. cit.*, p. 33; Nichols, *Zach Taylor's Little Army*, pp. 220–221.

33. Bancroft, *op. cit.*, Vol. V, p. 427.

34. Gibson, *op. cit.*, p. 10; Hamilton, *Taylor*, Vol. I, p. 241.

CHAPTER 11

1. For affairs in Saltillo: Taylor, *SED 1*, pp. 133, 136; W. S. Shover, *ibid.*, pp. 203–209; Carleton, *Buena Vista*, pp. 119–222; Baylies, *General*

Wool's Campaign, pp. 37–38.

2. Taylor, *SED 1*, p. 135; Jefferson Davis, *ibid.*, p. 191; Carleton, *op. cit.*, p. 75.

3. Baylies, *op. cit.*, p. 33.

4. Bancroft, *History of Mexico*, Vol. V, p. 429; Carleton, *op. cit.*, pp. 83–84.

5. Wallace *Letters*, pp. 44–45.

6. Taylor, *SED 1*, p. 139; Carleton, *op. cit.*, pp. 84–90.

7. Buley, in *Indiana Magazine of History*, *XV*: 301.

8. Davis, *SED 1*, p. 192.

9. Buley, *loc. cit.*, pp. 301–302; Carleton, *op. cit.*, pp. 81, 187–189.

10. Marshall, Roane, Trail, Gorman: *SED 1*, pp. 167, 172–175, 178–180, 191; Also Scribner, *Campaign in Mexico*, p. 65; Carleton, *op. cit.*, p. 99.

11. Jefferson Davis, from the hospital in Saltillo, to W. W. S. Bliss, written on narrow strips of brown paper two feet long and reproduced in *SED 1*, pp. 191–193; Strode, *Jefferson Davis*, pp. 179–180.

12. Davis, *SED 1*, p. 193. Captain Thomas Gibson, frontispiece map and p. 5 of *Letter*, suggests a long oblique line squared at one end by one company—his. Col. Lane (*SED 1*, p. 187) says two companies were squared against the column and that the rest of the line was oblique; this would produce a V-like angle of sorts, its right arm much stubbier than the left. Lt. Col. Haddon (Perry, *Indiana in the Mexican War*, pp. 293–294) seems to agree with Davis. The reader can take his choice.

13. Quoted in DeVoto, *Year of Decision*, p. 471.

14. Gregg, *Diary*, Vol. II, pp. 49–50 (he was watching from across the stream); G. W. Trahern, "Cowboy Soldier from Mier to Buena Vista," in *Southwest Historical Quarterly*, *LXIII*: 77.

15. As in Note 10, plus Carleton, *op. cit.*, pp. 90–94 (he was there), and Taylor, *SED 1*, p. 135.

16. Carleton, *op. cit.*, pp. 100–103.

17. Taylor, *SED 1*, p. 135; May, *ibid.*, pp. 197–200.

18. Carleton, *op. cit.*, pp. 101–102; Rives, *U.S. and Mexico*, Vol. II, p. 357.

19. Taylor, *SED 1*, p. 136.

20. Taylor, Wool, Bragg, *SED 1*, pp. 136, 148–149, 203; Carleton, *op. cit.*, pp. 103–106; Wallace *Letters*, p. 46.

21. Bancroft, *op. cit.*, Vol. V, pp. 429–430.

22. Carleton, *op. cit.*, pp. 107 f.; Wallace *Letters*, p. 47.

23. Bragg, *SED 1*, p. 202.

24. Wallace *Letters*, p. 47.

25. Accounts differ about which of the ravines. Wallace (p. 47) says the southernmost of the short gullies. Carleton (pp. 108–109) says the center gully. Bissell (*SED 1*, p. 177) says simply "ravine." Unable to reconcile these discrepancies by persons actually on the field at the time, I conclude that both gullies were used, which seems logical in view of the number of men spread across the plateau.

26. O'Brien, *SED 1*, p. 161.

27. Taylor, Bissell, *SED 1*, pp. 136, 177; Carleton, *op. cit.*, pp. 109 ff.; Wallace *Letters*, pp. 47–49.

28. *SED 1*, p. 136.

29. Gregg, *Diary*, Vol. II, p. 51.

30. Wool, *SED 1*, p. 149; Carleton, *op. cit.*, pp. 110–117; Bancroft, *op. cit.*, Vol. V, pp. 430–431.

31. Finke, "San Patricio Units," p. 37.

32. Davis, *SED 1*, p. 195; May, *ibid.*, p. 200; Gibson, *Letter*.

33. Carleton, *op. cit.*, p. 119.

34. Taylor, *SED 1*, p. 137. Many of the wounds were so slight that Inspector General Churchill later revised the total to 272 killed (five of the wounded had died), 388 wounded, 6 missing.

35. For one instance, Gregg, *Diary*, Vol. II, p. 52.

36. Wool to Joseph W. Moulton, May 20, 1847.

37. Duncan, "A Morgan County Volunteer," p. 398.

38. *SED 1*, p. 150.

39. Rives, *op. cit.*, Vol. II, p. 359.

40. Taylor, *SED 1*, p. 99; Carleton, *op. cit.*, pp. 131–150; Gregg, *Diary*, Vol. II, pp. 54–72.

41. Bancroft, *op. cit.*, Vol. V, pp. 432–433.

42. Gregg, *Diary*, Vol. II, p. 72; Carleton, *op. cit.*, p. 152; Wallace *Letters*, p. 52; Baylies, *op. cit.*, p. 39.

CHAPTER 12

1. Carleton, *Buena Vista*, pp. 131–150; Gregg, *Diary*, Vol. II, p. 57.

2. For Urrea's attacks, *SED 1*, pp. 210–214; S. C. Smith, *Chile Con Carne*, pp. 153–162; J. Smith, *War with Mexico*, Vol. II, p. 169; Baylies, *General Wool's Campaign*, p. 49.

3. Quaife (ed.), Polk's *Diary*, Vol. II, pp. 433–435 (March 20–23, 1847).

4. *Battlefield Letters*, pp. 90–94.

5. Polk's *Diary*, Vol. II, entries of April 1, 7, 16, pp. 451–452, 462, 480.

6. Mexican dispatches translated in Carleton, *op. cit.*, pp. 215–217.

BIBLIOGRAPHY

PRIMARY SOURCES

Manuscripts

The manuscript material used in the preparation of this account came from the Western Americana Collection at the Yale University Library—in which connection I wish to express my appreciation to the Library, to Mr. Archibald Hanna, Curator, and to Mr. William Goetzmann, now at the University of Texas.

The principal documents concerned are the letters of Barna Upton to his family, ending with the battle of Monterrey; five letters from William T. Withers to Dr. Montgomery Boyd, September 7, 1846, to January 31, 1847; a sixteen-page letter from Taylor's aide, Robert Selden Garnett, written at Agua Nueva on March 2, 1847 (a week after the battle of Buena Vista), to "My Dear L."; two letters of General John E. Wool, one of May 20, 1847, to Joseph W. Moulton and the other, dated January 3, 1848, to Colonel John J. Abert.

Government Documents

1. *Senate Executive Document 378, 29th U.S. Congress, 1st Session.* Contains correspondence concerning command of the Army in Mexico at the outbreak of the war, the early volunteer problems, etc.

2. *Senate Document 388, 29th U.S. Congress, 1st Session.* Useful to this book primarily for its official reports on the battles of Palo Alto and Resaca de la Palma.

3. *House Executive Document 119, 29th U.S. Congress, 2nd Session.* Contains the administration's correspondence with Gen. Taylor concerning operations in northeastern Mexico.

4. *House Executive Document 4, 29th U.S. Congress, 2nd Session.* Contains the official reports on the battle of Monterrey.

5. *House Executive Document 60, 30th U.S. Congress, 1st Session.* An enormous catchall of letters and reports concerning the campaigns and problems encountered by the Army in northeastern Mexico.

6. *Senate Executive Document 1, 30th U.S. Congress, 1st Session.* Official reports and subreports on the battle of Buena Vista and its aftermath.

7. *Senate Document 32, 31st U.S. Congress, 1st Session.* Contains George W. Hughes's official "Memoir" of Wool's march from San Antonio.

Books

Barker, Eugene (ed.). *The Austin Papers. Annual Report of the American Historical Association for 1919* (Washington, 1924).

Benton, Thomas Hart. *Thirty Years' View* (2 vols., New York, 1854–56).

Carleton, James H. *The Battle of Buena Vista* (New York, 1848).

Chamberlain, Samuel. *My Confession* (New York, 1956).

French, Samuel G. *Two Wars* (Nashville, 1901).

Grant, Ulysses Simpson. *Personal Memoirs* (vol. I, New York, 1895).

Green, General Thomas J. *Journal of the Texian Expedition Against Mier* (New York, 1845).

Gregg, Josiah. *The Diary and Letters of Josiah Gregg,* edited by Maurice G. Fulton (2 vols., Norman, Okla., 1941, 1944).

Henry, William S. *Campaign Sketches of the War with Mexico* (New York, 1847).

Hitchcock, Ethan Allen. *Fifty Years in Camp and Field,* edited by W. A. Croffut (New York, 1909).

Kendall, George W. *Narrative of the Texan-Santa Fe Expedition* (New York, 1847).

Kenly, John R. *Memoirs of a Maryland Volunteer* (Philadelphia, 1873).

Perry, Oran. *Indiana in the Mexican War* (A compilation of letters, reminiscences, newspaper accounts, etc., Indianapolis, 1908).

Quaife, Milo M. (ed.). *The Diary of James K. Polk during His Presidency, 1845–49* (Vol. II, Chicago, 1910).

Reid, Samuel. *The Scouting Expeditions of McCulloch's Texas Rangers* (Philadelphia, 1848).

Samson, William (ed.). *The Letters of Zachary Taylor from the Battlefields of the Mexican War* (Rochester, N.Y., 1908).

Scribner, B. F. *A Campaign in Mexico* (Philadelphia, 1850).

Smith, Justin (ed.). *Letters of General Antonio López de Santa Anna Relating to the War. Annual Report of the American Historical Association for 1917* (Washington, 1920).

Smith, S. Compton. *Chile Con Carne, or The Camp and the Field* (New York, 1857).

Wallace, Isabel. *Life and Letters of General W. H. L. Wallace* (Chicago, 1908).

Pamphlets and Magazine Articles

Niles Register, Vol. LXXI (January 30, 1847).

Duncan, John. "A Morgan County Volunteer" (edited by A. J. Henderson), *Journal of the Illinois Historical Society,* XLI: 383–399 (1948).

Encarnación Prisoners (Louisville, Ky., 1948). (Anonymous.)

Gibson, Thomas W. *Letter Descriptive of the Battle of Buena Vista,*

Written Upon the Ground (Lawrenceburgh, Ind., 1847). (Courtesy Yale University Library.)

Trahern, G. W. "Cowboy Soldier from Mier to Buena Vista" (edited by A. R. Buchanan), in *Southwest Historical Quarterly*, Vol. LXIII (July, 1954).

Secondary Sources

Books

Bancroft, Hubert Howe. *History of Mexico*, Vols. IV, V (San Francisco, 1885).

Barker, Eugene C. *Life of Stephen F. Austin* (Nashville, 1925).

Baylies, Francis. *A Narrative of General Wool's Campaign in Mexico in the Years 1846, 1847, 1848* (Albany, 1851).

Bill, Alfred Hoyt. *Rehearsal for Conflict* (New York, 1947).

Billington, Ray A. *The Far Western Frontier* (New York, 1956).

——. *Westward Expansion: History of the American Frontier* (2nd ed., New York, 1960).

Calcott, Wilfred H. *Santa Anna: The Story of an Enigma Who Once Was Mexico* (Norman, Okla., 1936).

Carter, Hodding. *Doomed Road of Empire* (New York, 1963).

Chambers, William N. *Old Bullion Benton, Senator from the New West* (Boston, 1956).

Coggins, Jack C. *Arms and Equipment of the Civil War* (New York, 1962).

Craige, Capt. John Houston. *The Practical Book of American Guns* (Cleveland and New York, 1950).

DeVoto, Bernard. *The Year of Decision, 1846* (Boston, 1943).

Downey, Fairfax. *Sound of the Guns* (New York, 1955).

Dyer, Brainerd. *Zachary Taylor* (Baton Rouge, La., 1946).

Edwards, William B. *The Story of Colt's Revolver* (Harrisburg, Pa., 1953).

Elliott, Charles W. *Winfield Scott, The Soldier and the Man* (New York, 1937).

Freeman, Douglas Southall. *Robert E. Lee* (Vol. I, New York, 1949).

Ganoe, William A. *The History of the United States Army* (New York, 1942).

Hagan, Walter T. *The Sac and Fox Indians* (Norman, Okla., 1958).

Hamilton, Holman. *Zachary Taylor* (2 vols., New York, 1941).

Hanighen, Frank C. *Santa Anna, the Napoleon of the West* (New York, 1934).

Haskins, William L. *The History of the First Regiment of Artillery* (Portland, Me., 1879).

Hollon, W. Eugene. *The Southwest, Old and New* (New York, 1961).

Horgan, Paul. *Great River: The Rio Grande in North American History* (2 vols., New York, 1954).

Lewis, Berkeley. *Small Arms and Ammunition in the United States Service* (Washington, D.C., 1956).

Lewis, Lloyd. *Captain Sam Grant* (Boston, 1950).

McCormac, Eugene I. *James K. Polk, a Political Biography* (Berkeley, Calif., 1922).

McKinley, Silas B., and Silas Bent. *Old Rough and Ready: The Life and Times of Zachary Taylor* (New York, 1946).

McMaster, John B. *History of the People of the United States*, Vol. VII (New York, 1914).

Millis, Walter. *Arms and Men* (New York, 1956).

Nichols, Edward J. *Zach Taylor's Little Army* (New York, 1963).

Peterson, Harold A. *The Treasury of the Gun* (New York, 1962).

Rives, George L. *The United States and Mexico, 1821–1848* (2 vols., New York, 1913).

Russell, Carl P. *Guns on the Early Frontiers* (Berkeley and Los Angeles, 1962).

Singletary, Otis A. *The Mexican War* (Chicago, 1960).

Smith, Justin. *The War with Mexico* (2 vols., New York, 1919).

Spaulding, Oliver O. *The United States Army in Peace and War* (New York, 1937).

Spencer, Ivor D. *The Victor and the Spoils, a Life of William L. Marcy* (Providence, R.I., 1959).

Stephenson, Nathaniel W. *Texas and the Mexican War* (New Haven, 1921).

Strode, Hudson. *Jefferson Davis: American Patriot* (New York, 1955).

Webb, Walter P. *The Great Plains* (New York, 1957).

———. *The Texas Rangers, A Century of Frontier Defense* (New York, 1935).

West Point Atlas of American Wars (edited by Col. Vincent J. Esposito), Vol. I (New York, 1959).

Magazine Articles

Buley, R. C. "Indiana in the Mexican War," *Indiana Magazine of History*, Vols. XV (September–December, 1919) and "The Buena Vista Controversy," *ibid.*, XVI (March, 1920).

Finke, Detmore H. "The Organization and Uniforms of the San Patricio Units of the Mexican Army, 1846–48," *Military Collector and Historian*, Vol. X (Summer, 1957).

Gunn, Jack W. "Ben McCulloch: A Big Captain," in *Southwest Historical Quarterly*, Vol. LVIII (July, 1954).

Wallace, Edward S. "The Battalion of Saint Patrick in the Mexican War," in *Military Affairs*, Vol. XIV, No. 2.

INDEX